HISTORY AND MYTH IN AMERICAN
FICTION, 1823–52

HISTORY AND MYTH IN AMERICAN FICTION, 1823–52

Robert Clark

St. Martin's Press   New York

St. Martin's Press, Inc., 175 Fifth Avenue, New York, NY 10010
Printed in Hong Kong
Published in the United Kingdom by The Macmillan Press Ltd.
First published in the United States of America in 1984

ISBN 0–312–37407–0

Library of Congress Cataloging in Publication Data

Clark, Robert.
  History and myth in American fiction, 1823–52.

  Includes index.
  1. American fiction – 19th century – History and
criticism.   2. Historical fiction, American.   3. Myth
in literature.   4. United States in literature.   I. Title.
PS374.H5C55   1984   813′.3′09   83–40161
ISBN 0–312–37407–0

Contents

Acknowledgements

I would like to thank my students and colleagues at the Universities of Essex and East Anglia, who have assisted this work in many ways. In particular I would like to thank Malcolm Bradbury, John Broadbent, Ellman Crasnow and Eric Homberger, who encouraged the work and suggested improvements. My greatest debts are to John Ashworth, Gordon Brotherston, George Dekker and Peter Hulme, without whose friendship and assistance the work would not have been what it is.

Chapter 4.2 first appeared in *Poetics Today*, vol. 3 no. 4, and is reprinted by kind permission of the editors.

R. C.

Introduction

Most studies of pre-Civil War fiction in the United States assume that because the American novel is a romance, constructed according to archetype and myth, it has little to do with the political or economic conditions of the society in which it was produced. The novelists themselves fostered this idea by saying that their works aspired to the '*beau idéal*' or existed 'somewhere between the real world and fairy-land', and by producing texts which did not appear to be pictures of reality or political statements. In this study I suggest that when Cooper and Hawthorne described their works as romances they were reluctantly conceding to critical demands that their works be mere entertainments and therefore politically irrelevant. Behind these concessions their works were so acutely addressed to the political life of the nation that a failure to understand their politics becomes a failure to understand their central literary significance.

In the first chapter of this study I therefore set out the main aspects of political belief and economic history in the years leading up to the Civil War and offer a theory of how and why classic American fiction expressed the dominant ideology of American regeneration. In this chapter, as throughout, I am guided by the belief that a text's literary significance consists in its articulation of the dominant ideological contradictions of its historical moment. I develop this materialist premise to show how the narrative representation of America as a virgin land inhabited by an innocent hero is a mythologizing transformation of Jacksonian political belief. In order to discover how individual texts perform this transformation I offer two chapters which discuss the relationship of literary activity to the general linguistic, philosophical and aesthetic culture. I thus hope to provide a model of literary production which will allow particular texts to be read in terms of their determining conditions and as articulations of the general cultural dilemmas.

After so many decades of New Criticism it will undoubtedly seem heterodox to some to begin a literary study with a discussion of contextual factors. According to the dominant critical tendency, the value of a literary text consists in its a-historical literariness. Its relationship to the culture in which it was produced is thought to be no more relevant to our understanding than the biography of its author. My own view is that our contemporary response to a literary text only seems a-historical in the measure of our incomprehension of the history that is being made around us: we are rarely able to see the connections between the distant war, the deodorant advertisement, the soap opera and our preference for Verdi or Wagner. Nonetheless such phenomena are interrelated and I believe it is the task of the critic not to yield to apparent fragmentation but to discover the logic of the totality which determines our aesthetic response. In other words, our task is to reconstruct materially and theoretically reconstruct the unities and contradictions which structure apparently disparate phenomena. To do this for litera- ture of the past has the same value as to do it for the literature of today for when on has understood how historical experience is expressed in the works of Cooper, Hawthorne and Melville, one draws closer to understanding how the modern world is construc- ted and expressed. One can also begin to understand the basis of past literature's contemporary appeal: the stories produced in the heyday of United States continental expansion articulated the founding ideals of the newly independent nation and the historical contradictions of the enterprise. They thus provide a site where the nation's sense of itself can be reinvented or deconstructed, a place where the individual reader can reaffirm his or her imaginary relationship to the past or press beyond that to a more demanding truth. This will continue to be the case until we find different ways of relating to the world.

1 The National Task: Narrative, Ideology and Myth

We Americans are driven to a rejection of the maxims of the Past, seeing that, ere long, the van of the nations must, of right, belong to ourselves. . . . We Americans are the peculiar, chosen people – the Israel of our time; we bear the ark of the liberties of the world. Seventy years ago we escaped from thrall; and . . . God has given us, for a future inheritance, the broad domains of the political pagans, that shall yet come and lie down under the shade of our ark, without bloody hands being lifted. God has predestinated, mankind expects, great things of our race; and great things we feel in our souls.

(Melville, *White Jacket*[1])

1.1 POLITICAL BELIEFS AND ECONOMIC ACTIONS

One of the first ideological tasks to which American intellectuals gave their attention in the years following independence was the creation of a unifying national culture. Like their European contemporaries, similarly engaged in forging the nineteenth-century nation state, they understood that a sense of nationhood depended upon there being a body of national characteristics and ideas which would differentiate their citizens from those of other countries. Whilst European nations struggled to create such an identity against the resistance of distinctive regions and hostile social classes, the United States was confronted with the more ambiguous task of distinguishing the 'American' in America from the heritage of British American institutions.[2] Since the American language was English, and the culture of the United States evidently derived from the British colonial past, the governing metaphor in the struggle for

1

independent nationality became that of purging the culture of the legacies of the colonial past. In the early years Noah Webster, the founding editor of *An American Dictionary of the English Language*, argued that

> a *national language* is a bond of *national union*. Every engine should be employed to render the people of this country national; . . . However they may boast of independence, . . . yet their *opinions* are not sufficiently independent; an astonishing respect for the arts and literature of their parent country, and a blind imitation of its manners, are still prevalent among the Americans.[3]

A little later, James Fenimore Cooper railed against the difficulties of writing fiction in such an underdeveloped culture and announced that it was the intention of his novels to foster 'the mental independence of America'. Edgar Allan Poe, for his part, urged the American author to 'snap asunder the leading strings of the British Grandmamma', and expostulated that:

> First, we have the injury to our national literature by repressing the efforts of our men of genius; for genius as a general rule, is poor in worldly goods and cannot write for nothing. Our genius being thus repressed, we are written at only by our "gentlemen of elegant leisure," and mere gentlemen of elegant leisure have been noted, time out of mind, for the insipidity of their productions. In general, too, they are obstinately conservative, and this feeling leads them into imitation of foreign, more especially of British models. This is one main source of the imitativeness with which, as a people, we have been justly charged, although the first cause is to be found in our position as a colony. Colonies have always naturally aped the mother land.
>
>   In the second place, irreparable ill is wrought by the almost exclusive dissemination among us of foreign – that is to say, of monarchical or aristocratic sentiment in foreign books; nor is this sentiment less fatal to democracy because it reaches the people themselves directly in the gilded pill of the poem or the novel.[4]

The fact that Poe's complaint echoes almost thought for thought the manifesto of Democratic belief with which John L. O'Sullivan prefaced the first issue of *The United States Magazine and Democratic*

Review in 1838 is but one indication of the degree to which literary nationalism was involved in the wider campaign for a unifying national identity.[5] British books, like British manufactured goods, sold more cheaply in the United States than indigenous productions. The writer therefore had the unenviable choice of 'aping' the dominant European forms and selling badly because his work was more expensive, or trying to foster mental independence and putting his relationship with the readers in jeopardy. Given such a choice many writers opted for imitation of European novels and some made a handsome living. The writers whom we now consider important, however, took the more difficult route of literary nationalism and struggled to find native materials and themes. This biased them towards the Democratic party for it was the Democrats rather than the Whigs who succeeded in creating the ideology of a unique American identity. The central element of this identity was the belief that the independence of the United States had been a 'dividing point in the history of mankind . . . the moment of the political regeneration of the world'.[6] Because the United States was a democracy, unique in its constitutional perfection, and because it had vast natural resources, it was destined to be, in Melville's words, 'the van of nations'.

As the growth of the nation consisted in territorial expansion and the destruction of the Indians, so the most significant fictions of the period are those which articulate the ambiguities of land conquest, settlement and ownership. This concern is not limited to the representation of life in the wilderness but often takes the form of a meditation on men's spiritual relationship to nature. Making the problem spiritual, however, is but one way of displacing the fundamental contradiction of the new Republic: that only by expropriating the original inhabitants could America fulfil its promise of being a superior form of society. Neither of the two dominant political persuasions opposed territorial expansion on ethical grounds, rather the reverse. Both Whigs and Democrats believed that because the United States was white, civilised, democratic and technologically advanced, it had a self-evident right to dispossess the Indians. There were differing opinions about strategy and timing. The Whigs, traditionally the party of the commercial and banking 'aristocracy', wanted the United States to follow the British path of industrial growth, and therefore proposed moderating the pace of settlement. Too rapid an expansion drained capital from commercial activity, raised the price of labour and threatened to shift the political centre of gravity away from the eastern seaboard. To the Democrats, on the other hand, continental expansion was necessary if Democracy was to defeat Whig élitism and save America from the horrors of industrialisation and urbanisation. The Democratic party had a strong Southern faction which needed to replace the cotton-exhausted lands of the South, and so it argued that expansion was necessary to furnish cheap lands to America's sturdy yeomen farmers whose ownership of land would provide the basis of an independent, self-respecting and prosperous community. Living in daily contact with regenerating nature, consuming only what they produced, the yeomen farmers would naturally work together to maintain the democratic independence of the people.[7]

The domestic and international aspects of this ideology were inseparable. The Declaration of Independence was said to have liberated the United States from the corruptions of the Old World and to have allowed the new nation to become an 'asylum' where the poor and oppressed could regenerate themselves. Europe was frequently described as being 'despotic', 'feudal', 'aristocratic'; its historical destiny was to struggle to realise in itself the constitutional perfection that the United States had already achieved.[8] Even before the term 'Manifest Destiny' was coined, the idea of the United States as the most perfect form of society yet to appear on earth, indeed as the end point of human history, was providing the nation with a sanctified mission to extend what Jackson called 'the area of freedom' into lands occupied by supposedly backward peoples.[9]

As has been noted by many historians of ideas, the representation of the United States as a potentially perfect society had its antecedents in the colonial past, and had been especially vigorous in the Puritan vision of New England.[10] From the first description of the New World by Christopher Columbus, down through the writings of the Pilgrim Fathers and such eighteenth-century works as Crèvecoeur's *Letters from an American Farmer*, writers had been inclined to see the American continent as the site where man could construct a 'City upon a Hill' or discover an earthly paradise. These concepts differ in that the earthly paradise presupposes achievement without toil, whereas the Puritan conception of the city emphasised the need to labour in its construction, but they agree in the image of an earthly perfection that the New World holds out to the Old. Democratic political rhetoric can be seen as fusing the agrarian idyll and the Puritan idea of labour as morally beneficial into a newly invigorating ideology that explained and motivated land settlement: when one believed that the United States was an inherently perfect republic of yeomen farmers, and yet had to work to augment its perfection, then one had every justification for extending the national domain.

To understand how literary texts express these beliefs, it is necessary to understand firstly the manner in which settlement was achieved, and then the way in which ideology represents it. In contrast to the popular image the process of settlement did not consist in a spontaneous and gradual advance of yeomen farmers across the continent. It consisted in diplomatic purchases or military conquest to obtain title to the land, and then in local military campaigns to drive off the Indians. Nor was the process of bringing the soil into cultivation an easy matter: it required an investment of capital and labour far beyond the scope of the ordinary working man and was therefore undertaken predominantly by middle-class entrepreneurs. Often the land was bought from the government by speculative land companies, operated on behalf of eastern stockholders, and mortgaged to small farmers. In the South, a few large plantations were rapidly established by the tiny élite of rich planters moving to more fertile lands. The more usual process, however, was for an entrepreneur to borrow capital, often at an extortionate rate of interest, and then pay off the debt by selling cash crops. When the ground had been brought into cultivation and communications had been improved, one could sell the farm at a profit and begin again further west. Staying put and contributing to the life of a growing community was less frequent than we have been led to believe, especially since pioneering was a high risk enterprise in which abrupt changes in market prices, land fertility, communication routes and climate could often result in bankruptcy. In the 1830s, for example, as Emerson prepared to extol the joys of communing with nature, a rise in British consumer spending sent up the price of cotton and touched off a bout of land speculation in the United States. When the price of cotton fell, there was panic selling of lands, widespread bankruptcy, and a sharp fall in commodity prices. The speculative mechanisms were little different from those operating in commodity markets today, but in this case land was the basis of the national economy. The increase or decrease in its value affected the entire nation.

The scale of land settlement did precisely what the Whigs feared it would do; it prevented the growth of manufactures and produced an economy that sold agricultural exports and imported manufactured goods. Apart from some industrial growth in the northeast during the 1840s and 1850s, the nation remained predominantly rural and agricultural, expanding its surface area by more than two million square miles within fifty years, and augmenting the value of its cotton exports alone from 17 million dollars in 1815 to 191 millions in 1860. The growth rate was phenomenal, as were the material benefits it conferred on some of the white peoples of the globe. However, given the inability of the slave economy to grow by changing its relations of production, increased output was achieved mainly by extension of the area under cultivation. By 1854 the South had ensured that nearly two-thirds of the nation's territory would be open to slavery, but in the North merchant capitalists had been realising the advantages of specialising production and achieving economies of scale. Those industries supplying agricultural equipment and processing agricultural products were beginning to constitute a nascent industrial formation which aimed to reproduce itself by constant reinvestment in new means of production and by transforming relations between producers. The conflict of interests between the two systems created such tensions as made a revolutionary struggle inevitable.[11]

1.2 ECONOMY, IDEOLOGY AND NARRATIVE

The ideology that motivated and explained the expropriation of Indian land was composed of many quasi-legal and quasi-rational elements. In the main it represented Indians as thinly scattered nomadic hunters who possessed little or no cultural refinement and who of right and necessity should give way to a civilised and agricultural people. There were variants of this belief from simplistic assertions of Indian backwardness to citations from Genesis that God had destined the earth for those 'who increase and multiply, replenish the earth and subdue it'. When the Indians happened not to be nomadic but to be a settled, agricultural people, as were the Iroquois, their crops were burnt in the ground and they were turned into nomads. When they embraced Christianity, built permanent homesteads, took up the plough and began printing their own newspapers, as did the Cherokee, the arguments were turned upside down: in their case it was held that only when wandering in the woods was the Indian truly noble; settled Indians were a violation of natural law, and it was therefore a kindness to drive them off their lands and abandon them in the western deserts. Evidently the white man's desire to turn nature into a marketable commodity brooked no non-white presence.[12]

The representation of the white farmer as innately superior to the red nomad was therefore a central component in the ideology of American expansion. In order to motivate individuals in the hazardous and arduous activity of pioneering, and in order to justify the initial expropriation of land, the rhetoric of the Democratic party represented the 'yeoman' farmer as innocent, moral, independent, happy, virtuous, living a life neither luxurious nor idle because a bounteous nature ensured that if he worked within reason he was unreasonably rewarded.[13] In the words of one contemporary spokesman,

> Thousands of independent and happy yeomen, who have emigrated from New England to Ohio and Indiana, – with their numerous, healthy, and happy families about them, with their ample abundance that fills their granaries, with their young orchards, whose branches must be propped to sustain the weight of their fruit, . . . and with the prospect of settling their dozen children on as many farms about them, – would hardly be willing to exchange the sylvan range of their fee simple empires . . . to contemplate the whirl of innumerable wheels for fourteen hours of six days of every week in the year. . . . While there are uncounted millions of acres of fertile and unoccupied land, where farmers can rear their families in peace, plenty and privacy, under the guardian genius of our laws, we hope, that farms will continue to spread on the bases of the Rocky Mountains. Farmers and their children are strong, and innocent and moral almost of necessity.[14]

Evidently this image is produced by deleting the negative aspects of the farmers' lot (cold and drought, crop failure, exorbitant interest charges, hard labour, bankruptcy, death) and by emphasising natural abundance, physical health and the moral benefit to individual and society. The relationship of this rhetoric to economic conditions may be exemplified in the following ideal-type propositions. In economic reality we know that:

1. Banks finance farmers to augment surplus value of land.

Whereas in Democratic ideology we are told that:

2. Society benefits from yeomen who improve moral worth through work on the soil.

Evidently the ideology does not so much distort real conditions as conceal negative aspects by substituting moral or spiritual processes for the economic. The farmer who, as self-interested entrepreneur, acts as a functionary of the banking system and the state, and who works the land to improve his own financial position, is encouraged to see himself as the morally regenerate origin of society.[15] In times of crisis such as the boom and slump of 1836–7 when the banks started calling in their loans, then a variant proposition could come into play: 'Banks threaten the yeomen who . . . ' a proposition of which Andrew Jackson made good use in his fight against the 'Mother Bank'.

If fictional narratives gave straightforward representation to Democratic ideology we would expect them to tell the story of a young man who leaves his east-coast sweat shop and goes West in search of free or cheap land. He finds his plot, clears the forest, fights off an Indian attack, breaks the sod, and builds a house. He marries the daughter of a neighbour, raises many children who settle neighbouring plots, and dies a peaceful death surrounded by the loving grandchildren who now constitute a small but thriving community of independent yeomen. His last glimpse is of a white clapboard church raising its spire to heaven against a background of rolling green pastures. If the narrative starts to lose momentum, dramatic tension can always be had from the Indians, unscrupulous land speculators, ruthless bankers, or the arrival of agricultural machinery.

Such narratives as these are lost in the margins of literary history. In *Virgin Land*, Henry Nash Smith discusses one, *George Mason, The Young Backwoodsman* (1829), which conforms in certain respects to this pattern, but according to Smith such narratives are invariably poor in literary qualities and serve to show that 'the literary imagination moved very slowly towards the acceptance of the democratic principles so glowingly embodied in agrarian theory'.[16] Smith is obviously correct if we take 'democratic principles' to mean the idea that an independent yeomanry constituted the essence of American democratic perfection. We have no classic fictions which directly express this belief. However, if we take 'democratic principles' in the broadest sense it is evident that, far from being remote from political concerns, the novels of Cooper and Melville are expressions of democratic ideology. Although Natty Bumppo and Ishmael are not farmers, they believe that the rapport between man and nature is morally redemptive, they believe in the fundamental equality of all men, and they believe that the way to safeguard this equality is to let nature take its course with minimal interference from civilisation. All of these are components of Democratic belief. The same principles inspire Hester Prynne's struggle against the Puritan establishment and also inform Holgrave's position in *The House of the Seven Gables*.

Yet, even when we have recognised the importance of political beliefs in these fictions, Smith's remark remains pertinent because there is no work of literary magnitude produced in the United States which extols the virtues of husbandry or of pioneering land. The nearest we come to a direct representation of the dominant national activity is in Cooper's *The Pioneers* where the activity of settlement is contrasted unfavourably with Natty's life in the woods, a life which depends upon hunting rather than agriculture, a life which has no engagement with work on the soil nor with any kind of accumulation of merit through time (whether financial or spiritual). Indeed, it is the contrast between Natty's morally elevated harmony with nature and the determination of the pioneers to bring the land into economic production that generates most tension in the novel.

One can explain the hostility of Natty to husbandry in *The Pioneers* by reference to Cooper's ambiguous status as a land-owning Democrat, torn between the contradictory desires to build up the national economic base by rapid settlement, and to slow the rate of settlement so as to retain the élitist privileges of the gentry.[17] Whilst this explanation opens up many aspects of Cooper's fictions, however, we need a more general explanation for the hostility of the American hero to the activities of pioneering and settling if we are to embrace other significant fictions within the same theory. Melville and Hawthorne did not share Cooper's relationship to land ownership, yet in their works we notice the same fundamental oppositions. The hero or heroine appears as the protagonist of natural innocence, striving to live in harmony with the natural world, yet this effort is contradicted by the forces of civilisation – in Cooper, the settlers, the towns and the law; in Melville, industry, conquest, tyrannical power and abstract systems of belief; in Hawthorne, the Puritan tendency to repress all forms of natural and democratic sentiment in favour of the artificial and hierarchical.

Viewed in isolation, this opposition would seem to have little to do with the propositions of Democratic ideology. But if we cast the oppositions in the form of a simple statement we begin to perceive that the narrative structure of classic fictions is not as divorced from Democratic beliefs as Smith suggests, nor is it as divorced from contemporary social phenomena as post-war literary criticism has tended to maintain. In classic literary narratives we have the following:

$$
\left.\begin{matrix} \text{Settlers/towns/law} \\ \text{Industry/intellect} \\ \text{Puritans/history} \end{matrix}\right\} \text{against} \left\{\begin{matrix} \text{Natty} \\ \text{Ishmael} \\ \text{Hester} \end{matrix}\right\} \begin{matrix} \text{in} \\ \text{harmony} \\ \text{with} \end{matrix} \left\{\begin{matrix} \text{woods/lakes} \\ \text{whale/ocean} \\ \text{body/heart} \end{matrix}\right.
$$

Reducing these towards their common elements we find the basic structure:

$$
\text{Civilisation threatens} \begin{matrix} \text{Adamic} \\ \text{Innocent} \end{matrix} \text{living in harmony with} \begin{matrix} \text{Edenic} \\ \text{Nature} \end{matrix}
$$

When this last proposition is compared with the basic proposition of Democratic ideology we perceive that there is a structural homology between the literary text, dominant political belief and primary economic activities. However, where the ideological proposition expresses economic processes in morally redemptive terms, the central proposition of the literary narrative has been divorced from economic actions. The literary proposition in effect effaces all notion of work, improvement and growth, and leaves us with only some of the moral aspects advanced in the ideology of American perfection. These moral aspects now exist in a state of threat from precisely those agencies which had a problematic existence in democratic ideology: the social institutions which enabled the 'yeoman' to work on the land (banks, communication systems, markets, cities), and which profited and expanded as a result of his labours, are here encapsulated by the anathematic term 'civilisation'. What has evidently occurred is that the literary text has found a way of separating out the contradictions of Democratic ideology and of temporarily resolving them by placing them in dramatic opposition.

1.3 THE INNOCENT IN THE GARDEN

The way the texts deal with the contradictions of Democratic ideology evidently owes something to the Edenic myth, although the condition of regeneration is optative rather than achieved, the hero desiring to escape from history and abstract knowledge into the blissful immediacy of natural life. Since the myth of Eden had been used since 1492 to explain the Christian presence in America it is possible to assume, along with Northrop Frye and R. W. B. Lewis, that the literary text derives its shape from myth, and not from material life or from its ideological representation. As Lewis suggests, to a Bible-reading generation, what would have been more natural than to see one's relationship to America in terms of Eden regained, especially since such an interpretation had been advanced by propagandists of many previous generations.[18] Such an explanation, however, insulates literature from the material experience of its writers and readers, and scants the question of why the myth should dominate literary production at this moment in United States history when it had been marginal at others. Rather than myth existing just because myth has existed, myth seems to be reproduced, stored, refashioned and re-used, as the briefest inspection of anti-Semitic myth or other polity-defining myths will show. The production and reproduction of myth is a function of social needs, so the question posed by the dominance of myth in *antebellum* literature is why the transformation from ideology was necessary, and how it was performed.[19]

The transformations we have already noticed, and the general indebtedness to Freud of modern commentators on myth, indicate that a theory of mythogenesis might best draw example from Freud's method of dream interpretation.[20] As Freud himself observed in *Totem and Taboo*, both myths and dream feature characters whose significance is archetypal rather than 'natural', both rely on a limited and predetermined set of narrative operations, and in both, implausibility is either apparent or scarcely kept at bay. Both forms also leave us with the impression that they are radically condensed expressions of a plenitude to which they cannot admit. In Freud's words they are 'brief, meagre and laconic in comparison with the range and wealth of the dream thoughts'. What Freud means is that the dream text – and, he will argue elsewhere, the mythic text – indirectly represents a complex, unconscious network of desires and significations. Materials from this unconscious network are condensed and displaced into a set of symbols that allow partial recognition of what remains hidden, one of the chief features of the translation being to fulfil the wish 'If only it had been the other way around'.[21] The transformation of the wish 'If only . . .' into the affirmative 'It is . . .' frequently involves the inversion of cause into effect and of object into agent; it also involves the removal of subtle syntactic relations and the abolition of all signs of a contradiction or negation so that the eventual text consists of simple, concrete signs standing in a displaced and radically reductive relationship to their originals. In order that the problematic nature of this set of signs should not be apparent, it undergoes a secondary revision which restores the appearance of intelligibility.[22] One is finally offered a text which has succeeded in apparently resolving those contradictions of material life which prevent the satisfaction of what is deeply desired.

Applying this understanding to the myth of the innocent in the garden one immediately notices that the myth represents real conditions 'the other way around' in order to provide a wish-fulfilling image of man's relationship with nature. Where we know that in historical reality individuals and state institutions were bent on the conquest of the continent for material gain, in the mythic representation we are shown a solitary individual living in spiritual harmony with nature and threatened by society. Where in historical reality we know that blacks and Indians were exploited and expropriated by the whites, in the mythic representation we are offered the famous couples – Natty and Chingachgook, Ishmael and Queequeg, Huck and Nigger Jim – in which the innocent white man is symbolically allied with his victim in opposition to the advance of white civilisation. Evidently the figure of the white innocent has been produced by condensation and displacement of both material and ideological elements and can be interpreted as acting either as a denial of real conditions (implying 'I wasn't one of the colonisers, I was one of the victims'), or as a recuperation of them (implying 'it wasn't a conquest at all – we were entering spiritual communion with nature'). Whichever interpretation one adopts, it seems probable that the figure of innocence has originated in the contradiction between the ideological representation of the United States as the morally superior form of civilisation, and the fact that its wealth derives from the violent expropriation of the original American inhabitants. The myth thus presents us with an inversion of real conditions and a wish-fulfilment of the values contained in

Democratic ideology: in place of the agents of the state (soldiers, cartographers, land speculators, bankers, farmers, canal builders) it puts an individual who almost succeeds in living the morally regenerate life which the ideology offers as the justification and goal of the conquest. This individual is in effect the signifier of the values which were originally signified in the ideological sign, but these values have now been severed from the bearer to which they were initially attached and are serving to generate a narrative whose relationship to real conditions is even more distant than that of the original ideology. Although myth resembles ideology in that it represents the relationship between the individual, the society, and the material world, like a dream the myth inverts cause and effect, removes contradictions, and leaves us with a timeless image of concord where there was once work, economy, history, politics, and struggle.[23]

In making a general distinction between mythic and ideological discourse we should not assume that they are alternative and mutually exclusive processes of signification. Mythic speech has evident ideological functions in that it contributes to the imaginary relationship which subjects have with the world, but it is probable that mythic speech influences this relationship only in an ancillary manner since when mythic speech is pure its depoliticisation must weaken its ability to influence material life directly. The mythologising lectures of Ralph Waldo Emerson, for example, doubtless helped his hearers recast their economic relationship to the land in the imaginary terms of a morally redemptive relationship with nature, but, because the lectures deliberately avoided engagement with material practice, they did not allow immediate recognition of their social purpose. As mythic speech, they could mask the key ideological contradictions (between individual and social need, between material exploitation and spiritual satisfaction, between democracy and hierarchy) but they could not become a total signifying system. Were they to have done so all social relations would have become imaginary and material production would have ceased.

If this is accepted then it follows that what one would expect to see at any historical moment is a range of discourses that could be ranked according to their relative degrees of mystification. In such a range, ideological speech would normally constitute the middle and quantitatively dominant ground, combining real conditions with varying amounts of the imaginary but always retaining a basis of material address. Purely mythic discourse would be reserved for areas of acute contradiction between beliefs and practices of different parts of the social formation, and in ideological speech itself one would expect to find mythic signs maintaining the appearance of order at those points where the belief system threatens to reveal its arbitrary and paradoxical nature. In the period with which we are concerned terms such as 'natural right to the land', 'freedom', 'civilisation', 'savagery', 'providence', 'manifest destiny', appear in political rhetoric at those points where the contradictions of social experience are too acute to allow further ideological elaboration. The reason why United States fictions tended to myth in the years before the Civil War may well be a consequence of the prominence of mythic signs in ideological discourse, a prominence which in turn derives from the difficulty of otherwise maintaining the ideological justifications for geographical expansion.

If we narrow our focus for a moment and look at the specific transformations which have occurred in the movement from ideology to myth we can perhaps gain some insights which will be valuable both for literary analysis, and for a general psychological understanding of mythic discourse. Although we must remember that we are still dealing with artificial 'ideal-type' propositions, the examples quoted above show that in moving from ideology to myth 'society' has been converted into 'civilisation', 'yeoman' into 'innocent', 'work' into 'harmony', 'earth' into 'nature'. All these changes have followed the path suggested by Roland Barthes: the moral connotations signified by the ideological sign (notably the idea of spiritual goodness) have been separated off from the material signifieds to which they were joined (farmers, work) and become hypostatised essence.[24] As mythic signs they then *allude* to their ideological origin by a kind of metonymy: an essence which was in the first place attached to a material bearer for ideological purposes (as 'goodness' was attached to 'farmer' to produce 'yeoman') has subsequently been removed from the bearer and now only points back to it as a reliquary part to the original whole. Thus:

Myth: Innocence
                                      ↑
Ideology: Yeoman plus moral goodness
                              ↑
Reality: Farmer

The allusion is of course difficult to recognise since knowledge of its origins has been repressed. All one has in the structure of a myth is a series of abstract signs masquerading as natural substances; their origins and effective interconnections have been obscured.[25]

We may clarify the route of mythogenesis with the help of Saussure's description of the relationship between signifier, S, and signified, s, $\frac{S}{s}$, where the bar between the signifier and the signified was introduced to indicate that concepts and words exist in a fluid relationship one to the other.[26] If we express the word 'yeoman' in terms of this notation we have:

$$\frac{S}{s} \quad \frac{\text{yeoman}}{\text{farmer, moral goodness, antiquity, independence}}$$

Saussure's notation allows us to see that one signifier may signify an entire sequence of signifieds (and vice-versa), and that there is indeed a flexible relationship between terms in the upper chain of signifiers and terms in the lower chain of signifieds.

The place occupied by yeoman in the ideological proposition is filled in the mythic proposition by the innocent hero. If we put the entire chain of characterising discourse in the place of the signifier we produce:

$$\frac{S}{s} \quad \frac{\text{(the American Hero)}}{\text{innocence, harmony with nature, independence}}$$

One could elaborate the chain of signifieds more fully than I have done here but a comparison of the two notations should suffice to make graphically apparent that in moving from ideology to myth we have lost the referent 'farmer', along with other traces of economy, labour, and historicity, and that the moral value which was originally attached to 'farmer' by the signifier 'yeoman' has been displaced to generate a new chain of significations. Its final resting place has been determined by other elements in the matrix of ideological and real materials which constitute the latent content of the myth. Since the word 'innocence' implies its contrary, guilt, and since we generally find the figure of innocence associated with a representative of the white man's victims (black or red), we can deduce that foremost among these elements must be a knowledge of the facts of conquest that contradicts the dominant ideology. Enriching our model we can then see the genesis of the concept of 'innocence' at the point of intersection between contradictory thoughts in the latent content.

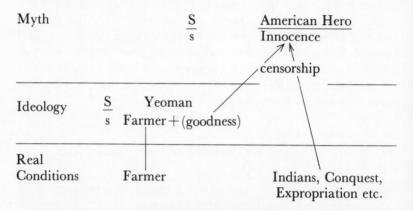

This model is highly simplified for the sake of graphic representation.[27] To be comprehensive it should include the central propositions about the status of the Indians, the arguments for and against conquest, and, not least, the Bill of Rights, all of which will be implicated in the network of contradictions that is resolved by the myth of innocence. Such a multi-faceted representation would require three-dimensional display but the simplified model should serve to suggest the kind of transformation that has served in the movement from ideological to mythic discourse.

We can clarify these differences by examining two sentences, one written by James Fenimore Cooper and the other by Walter Scott, both of which describe the fate of a group of people who have become nearly extinct as a consequence of historical progress. Scott's sentence ends a lengthy paragraph in the Postscript to *Waverley* where he describes the destruction of the Highland clans in the rebellion of 1745. He concludes with the remark:

> This race has now almost entirely vanished from the land, and with it, doubtless, much absurd political prejudice; but also, many living examples of singular and disinterested attachment to the principles of loyalty which they received from their fathers, and of old Scottish faith, hospitality, worth, and honour.[28]

According to the analysis being developed here, Scott's discourse is an ideological interpretation of historical change. One of the chief values in this ideology is objectivity so Scott is anxious to present an apparently balanced view of the positive and negative features of the clan system. He asserts their political absurdity, praises their sense of honour, and implies that historical change has produced gains in political rationalism and losses in noble virtues. As Scott is well aware, this is no more than an interpretative attitude towards historical experience. The word 'doubtless' indicates that Scott knows that some might argue that the modern political constitution is no less absurd than the preceding one, and that there has been no significant change in the quantity of noble virtues.

There is then in this sentence an explicit sense of particular values being applied to real experience, a sense of an ideological representation being made. The one point where this is less than clear is the word 'race' which, like the word 'yeoman', approaches the status of a mythic sign but does not quite reach it. 'Race' implies that the Highland clans had genetic features in common, which is probably true. But the word is used to imply that race was the cause of their feudal political system because now that the race has vanished from the land so has the catholic-absolutist political tendency. The word 'race' thus naturalises many pejorative values by fusing them with the social group to which Scott has decided they belong. However, it is important to note that as we knew that 'yeoman' referred to 'farmer' plus 'moral goodness', so here we know that 'race' refers to 'clans' plus 'various typical features'. In the ideological sign, referent and values are potentially separable, potentially distinct.

If we now look at a sentence taken from Cooper's 1826 Preface to *The Last of the Mohicans* we will be able to exemplify the difference between ideological and mythic discourse. Writing about the Lenni Lenape or Delaware, Cooper says:

Robbed by the whites, murdered and oppressed by the savages, they lingered for a time around their council fire, but finally broke-off in bands, and sought refuge in the western wilds.[29]

The most immediate difference between this sentence and Scott's is that where Scott *argues* a political view of history, Cooper presents us with an apparently value-free description of an organic process. The passivity of the subject of the sentence, the verbs 'lingered' and 'broke-off', contribute a sense of fatal inevitability to the destruction of an organic wholeness. The agencies of this destructive process are represented by signs which signify essential groups rather than political ones: 'whites' actually refers in the full context of the paragraph to 'Dutch', and 'savages' refers to 'Mengwe', Cooper's version of history being that the noble Lenape were trapped in a conspiratorial pincer-movement by the hostile Iroquois (or Mengwe) and the Dutch. In fact this is erroneous history, and the lack of material support for Cooper's sentence has much to do with its mode of construction, but rather than compare Cooper's view to the historical facts, what I want to do here is emphasise its strictly discursive features.[30] The function of the words 'whites' and 'savages' is firstly to attribute presumed characteristics to races, and then to play these attributes back into the world as causes. 'Whites' signifies a moral essence which has been returned to the world to act as the single and material property of a group; 'savages' has followed a similar path and stands in opposition to 'whites' because it signifies all that 'whites' are incapable of.[31]

With this in mind we can begin to understand the complex play of significations in Cooper's sentence. Its primary complexity derives from Cooper's desire to admit that the 'whites' did not behave entirely as they should have behaved if their name was to be worthy of its signifieds. Accordingly, one has the semantic solecism 'robbed by the whites' which admits part of the truth – the expropriation of Indian lands by whites – in order to conceal the profounder part, extermination. The 'whites', it is implied, may have committed a felony against the Lenape, but the savage act of murder was performed by the Iroquois, the very antithesis of the noble white man. The conjuring trick worked in this sentence gives the 'whites' an alibi for the 'savagery' they shared with the Indians by means of metonymic leaps from part to whole (Dutch to all 'whites'; Iroquois to all 'savages', Lenape excepted in this instance) and from whole groups to abstracted essences (Dutch to essence of whiteness, Iroquois to essence of savagery) that are entirely typical of mythical speech. The processes of condensation and displacement have evidently been at work so that an historical experience which involved a triangular pattern of violence between the Lenape, the Iroquois and the English, and in which it would be arbitrary to decide who behaved with greater or lesser morality, can be represented as a process involving one robber, one murderer, and one victim. The consequence of this representation is to leave us with the idea that the Lenape were not 'savages', were militarily inactive, accepted their fate with due humility, and went forth into the wilderness to seek refuge. Not only does this image contradict history (the Lenape having fought against the English), but it bears the signs of this contradiction in the last verb: the oxymoron of seeking refuge in the wilderness may resound with biblical overtones but in its deeper meanings it speaks the truth: the Lenape went looking for shelter where there was no habitation and nothing to eat. One does not 'seek' such a destiny.

From this gloss on one sentence it is evident that the process of reading a mythic text must involve as much deviousness and complexity as was used by the original processes of condensation and displacement. In Chapter 4.2 on *The Last of the Mohicans* I will show how such a technique of reading can be used to illuminate an entire literary text, but since such a reading requires the exhaustive reconstruction of the latent content it is only possible where the determining factors are relatively accessible. However, even where such a specific reading is not possible, the analytic techniques suggested here may help us to understand the general formation of mythic representations, more especially as they invite us to see that the mythic text has reduced the complexity of historical experience to a schematic play of positive and negative essences which actually express the mythologist's own values, but which appear to us under the guise of real constituents of material life. We should also expect that since these essences have been produced in order to resolve a repressed network of contradictions, a large amount of secondary revision will have been required to restore the appearance of intelligibility. In the process of trying to make the essences intelligible, secondary revision will have tried to embed them within apparently logical relations, but it will always have been forced to operate in a circular and self-constituting realm of signifieds – 'a world elsewhere' – that has a highly mediated signifying relationship with social life.

If most myth criticism has begun at this point and proceeded to ignore the materiality of myth, we may excuse the critics for being blinded by the mirror that myth itself holds out. Since myth has been formed by repressing real conditions and de-politicising ideology, it presents us with a surface which rational analysis cannot easily grasp. Even when we bring to it the facts in which it originated, it cannot be exhaustively analysed precisely because it was in order to recuperate these problematical facts that the myth was initially conceived. Once made, the myth is proof against the most sceptical critic. When asked, for example, why it is that the citizens of the New World are not actually behaving in the manner expected of innocents, the mythologist has always been able to reply, as did the Transcendentalists, because they are denying their own nature. Since the American is naturally innocent, so the argument goes, any abhorrent behaviour on his part consists of an unnatural and un-American denial of his own nature. In the curious logic of this thought we see displayed all the virtue of the mythic sign: 'nature' is being used as if it really were an objective essence which characterises the American soul, but this 'nature' is actually only a *word*, a word whose significations can be transformed at the speaker's will so that they embrace or exclude whatever categories are desired. Since in any myth there is more than one of these rapidly mobile signs, each of which masquerades as a natural essence, the mythic code becomes endless and indefatigable. It is with good reason that Roland Barthes has said, 'it does not matter if one is later allowed to see through myth, its action is assumed to be stronger than the rational explanations which may later belie it'.[32]

What Barthes did not perceive, however, was the extent to which the irrational strength of myth consists in the defences it has incorporated 'against reason'. It is to Hayden White that we owe the suggestion that in any myth there appears an agency which prohibits absolute satisfaction of the desire the myth appears to satisfy.[33] In the myth of the innocent in the garden this prohibitory agency is encapsulated in the 'civilisation which threatens', an agency which might seem irrelevant to the image of the garden but which in effect provides its necessary boundary. Standing in the place of 'If only' in the phrase 'If only things were the other way around', the prohibiting 'civilisation' is in effect the reservoir for the contradictory pressures which the myth has neutralised in coming into being. It stands for history, for politics, for economy, for labour; for reality itself; or for any aspect of reality which threatens to constrain, to penetrate, or to expose the mythic imagination.[34] Like all mythic signs 'civilisation' is flexible enough to embrace anything, even any aspect of the nature to which it is supposedly opposed but which the mythologist chooses to make an anathema.[35]

Paradoxically, because the myth has been produced by the repression of most of material life, the prohibitory agency becomes the element most capable of elaboration. Giving veiled access to the excluded origins of the myth, the area denoted by 'civilisation' yields a richer discourse than the paradisiacal harmony it seems exterior to. Analysing the Edenic myth in *Paradise Lost*, John Armstrong made the pertinent observation that Satan and the Fall provided

Milton with a richer ground for language than did the state of bliss.[36]
This perception can be extended to United States literature where
one notes the pallidness of the heroic innocent in comparison with
his or her satanic anti-type. What is Hester compared to
Chillingworth, Ishmael compared to Ahab, Uncas compared to
Magua, Judith compared to Hetty Hutter? Although our moral
sympathies are biased towards the good character, it is the diabolic
that generates most of the discourse. The innocent remains almost
an absence, an unwritten space, a transparent eyeball. As an alibi for
the conquest of the continent the innocent hero is capable of
soliloquising about his moral regeneration through nature only until
the vacuity of his discourse becomes apparent; evil 'civilisation' must
then be brought back on stage to rescue him from bathos. And if this
'civilisation' can be associated with 'European' then foreign origins
can be imputed to those American institutions which are controlling
the conquest of continental space.

Having demonstrated the relationship between the myth of the
innocent in the garden, contemporary political beliefs, and contemporary social actions, there remains the task of describing the
conditions which motivate the resort to myth. It is axiomatic in the
foregoing commentary that myth is neither a private phenomenon
nor the product of a-historical mythopoeic imagination. It is better
understood as a methodical translation of the dominant social codes
which can occur whenever their political and ideological features
are repressed. The main cause of this repression would seem to be the
discovery that dominant ideology is inadequate. However, the
discovery of ideology's inadequacy is not infrequent, and the usual
response is either to revise the ideology or to transfer political
allegiance to an alternative social group. Why then was myth such a
dominant feature of United States literary production in the
antebellum period?

One explanation which will be more fully developed in the next
chapter is that social criticism at this time was received with great
hostility. Although the Democrats and the Whigs had different ideas
about how national prosperity was to be achieved, there seems to
have been almost universal support for the idea that America was
morally superior to the Old World and endowed with a regenerative
mission in world history. When writers such as Cooper and Melville,
who generally subscribed to these ideals, pointed out some of the
lapses, they provoked critical hostility and found themselves
alienated from their readers. As a long tradition of United States

writers observed, the complexity of ideological situations in the class-stratified societies of contemporary Europe provided the author with possibilities which were lacking to the writer in the United States.[37] Baudelaire and Charlotte Brontë, for example, were both able to oppose the dominant progressive rationalism of French and British society, and yet were still able to find marginal support in groups not entirely in agreement with dominant beliefs. Furthermore, in France and Britain social criticism occupied an ideologically privileged situation since it was through criticism of the aristocracy in the eighteenth century that the bourgeoisie had justified its claims to social power. Even when the bourgeoisie had succeeded in becoming dominant, it retained a place for criticism since industrial capitalism progresses through constant improvement of its intellectual and material instruments of production. However, if, for the British and French, historical progress was dependent upon critical understanding, in the United States the belief that America was the *telos* of world history engendered a restrictive attitude towards the critical intellect. If one believed that America was already perfect, what function could the mind have other than affirmation?[38]

In producing fiction, then, the writer in the United States could only try to affirm the nation's moral superiority and give expression to an ideology which was scarcely capable of explaining the contradictory facts of territorial expansion. When the writer remarked these contradictions he was not able to find an alternative system of belief and could only repress his awareness of historical experience and move to myth, or openly declare his hostility and alienate himself from the readership. As will be seen in the following commentaries, the traditional product of this dilemma is a text structured by myth and yet breaking away from myth into ideological affirmation, radical denunciation, or allegorical communication of heterodox perceptions. The uneven nature of literary productions in the years before the Civil War may be explained by the transformation of a contradictory latent content into a mythic text which has required considerable secondary revision to provide it with a logical appearance. When the secondary revision is successful the text achieves a fragile aesthetic harmony; when it fails the text is seen to be contradictory and discontinuous.[39]

2 Writer to Reader: Conditions of Literary Production

After the temporary animosity generated by the struggle for independence had subsided the affection of the people for England revived in nearly all its former force. England was still the mother country. She was still in our estimation, if not in fact, our moral and intellectual superior. She continued to manufacture our cottons and woollens, our knives and forks, our fashions, our literature, our sentiments and opinions.[1]

2.1 PUBLISHING AND CRITICISM

A description of the general cultural formation in which a text has been produced does not provide direct insights into its meanings: the relationship of the author to the culture is a complex mediation determined by the author's ideology (a function of his/her relation to his/her social class), and by his/her relationship to the prevailing conditions of literary production. The writer lives as a worker in words and since the language the writer reproduces comes informed with the values of society, the writer's attitude to those values is crucially determinant of the eventual form of his work. Thus, the fact that the citizens of the United States gave credence to certain beliefs in the years before the Civil War is an insufficient explanation of the form these ideas take in a literary fiction. For an explanation of their literary formulation we must consider how the special domain of literary production is related to the general economic formation, and how this relationship conditions the form of the literary text.

We are fortunate in that the basis of this relationship has already been charted by William Charvat from whose research we know that in the early nineteenth century, publishing experienced the same underdevelopment as other aspects of the manufacturing economy. Publishing was initially centred in Philadelphia which had access to south and west along roads to Savannah and Pittsburgh, and by coastal traffic. In the 1820s New York also became important as it gained access to the Ohio and Mississippi markets via the Erie Canal, an advantage which was to become crucial when population density in the North surpassed that of the South in the 1840s. The centralisation of publishing in these cities indicates that from the beginning of the century publishers were aiming at the economies of scale of a national market, and that accordingly, writers were under encouragement to address a widely scattered and sectionally diverse readership.[2]

The exploitation of this growing national market, however, was hampered by the lack of commercial expertise and finance capital which afflicted all areas of domestic manufacturing. Publishers were vulnerable to any downturn in the market and bankruptcies were common. It is therefore hardly surprising that publishers were reluctant to accept the works of untried native authors and preferred instead to reprint the works of established Europeans, to whom, in the absence of any international copyright agreement, they had no legal obligation to pay royalties. The basic division of the retail price of a book was one third for manufacturing costs, one third for the retailer, and one third for the author and publisher. Given that the publisher paid no royalty on imported works he could afford to offer them to booksellers at attractive discounts, and since European works had been pre-selected by their own national markets and arrived in the New World with the cachet of cultural esteem, everything encouraged their sale in large numbers. Conversely the risks involved in publishing an American fiction were as high as the potential for profits was low. As Fenimore Cooper bitterly remarked, 'no man will pay a writer for an epic, a tragedy, a sonnet, a history, or a romance, when he can get a work of equal merit for nothing'.[3]

The interest in native authored works increased in later decades as the culture became more self-assuredly nationalist. After a cut-throat war in the reprint market in the early 1840s which resulted in novels selling at between ten and fifty cents – thus leaving magazines as the only outlet for Poe and Hawthorne – prices improved and brought prosperity to some native writers. Most of the works which were successful, however, were sentimental and moralistic tales produced by what Hawthorne described as 'a d—d mob of

scribbling women'. At the same time, the reprinting of European
works continued unabated, rival companies offering complete
editions of Scott, Dickens, Eugène Sue and Bulwer Lytton at prices
with which no native work could compete. The American author
was thus placed in a situation of extremely disadvantageous
competition with European texts, a situation which was rendered
yet more problematic by the fact that few American works of note
had yet been written and the author therefore had to turn for
inspiration to those very European works which were preventing
him from achieving a living wage from his own literary production.
The best interests of the United States writer were thus served by
support for any campaign which fostered United States nationalism,
both because this raised the prestige of native works, and more
distantly, because the growth of the national economy could only
augment the national self-consciousness of the reading public. These
factors may help to explain why so many of the writers of this period
who are now famous were nominally Democrats. To support the
Whigs was to support the idea that literature should be judged by
the highest universal standards – which meant, in effect, by existing
European standards – rather than be judged by their contribution to
American cultural independence. In this situation it is hardly
surprising that many authors fulminated against the importation of
European texts and saw in the supervaluation of the European
heritage the corruption of American Democratic ideals of Old
World feudalism.[4]

A further consequence of the underdevelopment of publishing
was that it made the writer extremely vulnerable to hostile reviews.
There was no system of national advertising, and recommendation
by word of mouth, so important in Europe, could not function in the
less densely populated United States. The only way to broadcast
news of books was the periodical or newspaper review, usually
authored on the east coast and reprinted across the nation. Hostile
reviews tended to have a fatal effect and the critical establishment
wielded enormous power. Since the chief periodicals and newspapers were in Whig hands, the majority of the reviewers were
conservative lawyers and clergymen who, in Charvat's words,
considered it their duty to 'repress any writer who tended to disrupt
the political, economic, and moral *status quo*'. Published anonym-
ously, the reviews of this watchdog class savaged any departure from
an affirmation of existing institutions and could generally be
expected to approve only of 'factual' narratives and openly didactic

fictions. History, biography and travels were the approved genres and writers were successful so long as their work appeared to conform to these conventions. When, like Melville, writers departed from the norms of autobiographical adventure, they met with hostile reviews and economic failure.[5]

The predisposition of the critical establishment towards reliable fact resulted from the dominance of Common Sense philosophy in educational institutions. At Bowdoin, Hawthorne was taught by Thomas Upham, a keen exponent of Common Sense, so his work bears its mark particularly deeply, but since Common Sense was the official epistemology of the age no writer could escape its influence. As the name implies, Common Sense was a derivative school of Lockian empiricism and maintained that only what is known through the five senses offers reliable knowledge. Any knowledge that depends upon logical inference, such as the idea that there must be a reverse side to the moon, was considered speculative rather than reliable, possible rather than probable. Obviously such a philosophy considered imaginative works as likely to produce confusion about what could be reliably known, and therefore counselled that they should be treated with great caution. Whilst the imagination was allowed by some to be an undeniably important human faculty, it was thought to be useful only when being applied to practical ends and when proceeding by disciplined and reasonable patterns of association. Disorderly associations and over-indulgence in imaginative musing were proscribed because they threatened to make man doubt the orthodox and conventional view of the world.

Hawthorne's short story 'Young Goodman Brown' provides a dramatic representation of what Common Sense meant in practice, and it also implies a critique of its ideological purposes. The narrator of the tale is called a 'Goodman' to indicate that he is fit to act as a juror, but when he leaves his wife Faith for the night he perceives that the Puritan elect might not be the saints they appear to be in daylight but might be frolicking in satanic revels in the forest. At the moment of revelation Brown calls on his Faith, banishes the satanists, and restores himself to the probable knowledge of his own senses, but he is then left in the perpetual doubt whether what he saw in the forest was a dream conjured from his own wicked imagination or a truth concealed by everyday appearances. His inability to decide whether to trust himself and doubt orthodox conventions, or to doubt himself and have faith in the orthodox, blights the rest of his days. In either case Brown's conclusion is that 'evil is the nature of mankind', a reversion to Calvinistic belief in man's fallen nature that contradicts the sunny reformism of the 1830s as surely as it undermines Puritan protestations of American moral regeneration. Brown's epiphany thus inverts contemporary and historical political pieties at the same time as it questions the behaviour of the social elect of all ages, revealing social beliefs to be ideological masks which are held in place by the naive *faith* of the citizens. By the very fact of leaving security behind and going for a walk in the forest at night Brown is made aware of 'state secrets' which the Puritans have carefully repressed: he discovers that these august men of God began the building of a New World by burning Indian villages and scourging heterodox religionists. The collapse of Common Sense and acceptance of the imagination are clearly revealed to have radical political and historical significance.

Hawthorne's awareness of the recognitions that lay beyond the limits of Common Sense is shared by Melville, as is his fundamental ambiguity about how to respond once one has acknowledged that the self-evident truth is no more than a refusal to inspect how and why meaning is constructed. The idea that all men are created free and equal, for example, was a self-evident truth that Melville observed in *Mardi* self-evidently excluded blacks from the category of being human.[6] In his later tale 'Benito Cereno', Melville represented the naivety of Common Sense in his narrator-captain, Amasa Delano, a man whose benign sense of superiority to blacks allows him to deduce from seeing a naked negress suckling her child that blacks are 'loving as doves'. This unquestioning association of ideas is ultimately exposed when we learn that the negresses have just butchered their owner in a particularly barbarous manner. At the end of the story the captain of the slave ship, Benito Cereno, is driven to his grave by the discovery that behind the signifier, 'the negro', lies no simple signified. Delano, however, retains untouched his confidence in a simple and natural relationship of signifier to signified, proving perhaps that Common Sense is too entrenched in its own naivety ever to be taught by experience. In 'Billy Budd' Melville's representation of Common Sense is yet more knowing and sophisticated. Vere, the devotee of the approved genres of history and biography, is a man who 'in the spirit of common sense [philosophises] upon realities', and 'whose settled convictions were as a dike against . . . invading waters of novel opinion, social, political and otherwise'. In considering the case brought against Billy this captain-judge decides that speculation about Billy's motives can only lead to a questioning of conventional authority; what matters is only the self-evident fact that Billy killed a superior officer. He must hang in order to keep signs in orthodox relations.[7]

The Common Sense tendency to repress imaginative and speculative thinking represented in these stories is the nineteenth-century manifestation of a tradition which descends from the Puritans. They too had a preference for 'facts', a distrust of the imagination, and a contradictory tendency to move from direct observation of material details to an abstract revelation of their concealed providential significance.[8] Larzer Ziff and Sacvan Bercovitch have noted how Puritan journals move from a scrupulous record of the mundane events to allegorical explanations of their significance in the terms of the holy mission. Critics of nineteenth-century literature have presumed from this continuity a direct transmission of ideas and forms from the Puritans to Melville and Hawthorne, but while this continuity is undeniable, the model of inheritance seems a poor explanation for the persistence of such a radical (and uncomfortable) separation of fact from idea.[9] Continuity presupposes discontinuity and therefore indicates that the determinant conditions had remained constant when they could have changed. It therefore seems that if we are to understand the continuity of forms of thought we should ask what it is that confers preferential value on factual discourse throughout the seventeenth, eighteenth and nineteenth centuries.

It is evident from colonial history that the Puritans' hostility towards the imagination and their preference for factual records derived from fears that the unfettered mind might produce unorthodox ideas about social organisation and the Puritan task. The Puritan repression of the unorthodox was necessary because, given the Puritan desire to found an exemplary earthly society, the colony could not be allowed to dissolve into factions which maintained different views of how the society was to be constructed. The survival of the colony depended upon rational organisation, upon mutual action against indigenous tribes, and upon a devotion of mental and physical energies to the exploitation of the material environment. Orthodoxy was thus a material and ideological necessity.

The limitations placed upon imaginative creativity, and the demand that people should either pay attention to immediate facts or read the Bible, was also necessitated by the divorce between what the Puritans were actually doing and the elaborate justifications produced to explain their actions: essentially the Puritans were involved in converting nature into property and yet explained this activity in remote theological terms, so it was only possible to maintain the credibility of their explanations by proscribing certain kinds of questioning.[10] In the nineteenth century much had changed but this basic divorce between material practice and mental explanation remained constant. As we have seen, the colonisation of new territories was justified in terms of a 'manifest destiny', the expropriation of the Indians was explained in terms of enlarging 'the area of freedom', the military means which were used were called 'civilised' whilst the tactics of resistance were termed 'savage'. Given the vulnerability of such ideas to even minimally sceptical consideration, it was evidently necessary to curtail imaginative and speculative freedom so that people would not recognise the incongruity of fact and idea. By confining the realm of reliable knowledge to immediate sense experience, conservative intellectuals were able to condemn any imaginative grasp of United States activity as being in direct contradiction with the supposed moral regeneration of the nation. The widespread adherence among reviewers and readers to such a conformist, pragmatic world view explains in part the marginal status of the great imaginative works of the period. It also explains the adoption of aesthetic strategies intended to satirise or bypass the attitudes of the reading public, or which were the consequence of the social isolation visited upon writers who explored the inadequacies of prevailing beliefs. Cooper, Poe, Hawthorne and Melville were all in their various ways to experience the venom of the reviewers and find the readership refusing to buy their works.[11]

Of these writers Cooper was both the most successful and the best protected. Private financial resources allowed him to dictate contractual terms to his first publishers and, especially in the early years, to receive reasonable proceeds from his work. Nonetheless he was constantly vexed to see his own work selling more expensively and less well than reprints of Scott, and then to find himself praised as the 'American Scott', an epithet that confirmed the insult to his pocket with an insult to national pride. Such double-edged praise was, however, not the worst that was in store. Returning from Paris in 1833, Cooper began to criticise the manners of his countrymen, remarking that 'the American nation . . . is lamentably in arrears as to its own avowed principles'.[12] The Whig press sharpened its critical quill, Cooper's sales collapsed, and a libellous fight began which was to tax Cooper's energy for nearly a decade. Poe,

Hawthorne and Melville were not even this fortunate. Poe eked out a precarious existence by moving from one editorial position to another and expressed his discordant view of American society in stories which offer the reader the apparent security of a common sensical narrator who records only things said and done and the deductions which may legitimately derive therefrom. (The 'madness' of some of his narrators is heightened rather than reduced by their scrupulous factuality.) The reception of Poe's 'Balloon Hoax' as a true account of a balloon journey from New York to London, like the acceptance of 'Facts in the Case of M. Valdemar' as a true scientific account, is as revealing of the common sense naivety of the readership as it is of Poe's satirical pleasure in exploiting it. When his stories are eloquently sober disquisitions on the arts of mystification they parody the central unspoken belief that language is a reliable namer of meanings. When they are more than this they are dark allegories of the genocide, slavery and madness that lies beyond the conventional world of 'facts'. Although the literary establishment could not fail to recognise the intelligence of Poe's work, it is scarcely surprising that he could not sell in volume form: too consistent an exposure to his commentaries on gulling, diddling and all the arts of fooling people into accepting the arbitrary as the true has the effect of making one sceptical, and scepticism is the enemy of conforming acquiescence.

Hawthorne and Melville were similarly disadvantaged by their failure to find a readership and were forced to make a living as government officials because their writing would not pay. After writing esteemed but little-known short stories for twenty-one years, Hawthorne experienced only a brief and qualified period of financial success with *The Scarlet Letter* and *The House of the Seven Gables*, his second novel, selling seven thousand copies in 1852 largely as a sequel to the first. These sales, however, compared poorly with such works as Maria Cummins' *The Lamplighter* which sold one hundred thousand copies in 1854. Whilst 'scribbling women' might make ten thousand dollars a year out of hearth and home sentiment, Hawthorne at his best made fifteen hundred. After *The House of the Seven Gables* he spent eight years futilely trying to recover his public.[13] Melville knew a similar ascent and decline. His first works, *Typee* and *Omoo*, were successful because they could be assimilated into the 'factual' genre of true-life narratives, even though some of his more perceptive critics were quick to anathematise the elements of romance and social criticism in these works.

Irritated by such criticisms Melville then embarked on *Mardi*, 'a *real* romance', writing to his publisher that it began as 'a narrative of facts' but that as it progressed he 'began to feel an incurable distaste for the same; & a longing to plume [his] pinions for flight . . . cramped & fettered by plodding along with dull common places'. *Mardi*, the fruit of this impulse to break with the conventions of factual discourse, bewildered Melville's readers and may even have escaped the understanding of the author himself. 'Time', he wrote, 'which is the solver of all riddles, will solve *Mardi*'.[14] To regain his readership Melville then produced *White Jacket* and *Redburn*, 'two jobs . . . done for money', straightforward narratives of seagoing life which restored him to the readers' favour. But in *Moby-Dick* Melville returned to his more allegorical style and was again greeted with incomprehension and hostility. Melville's struggle to find a fictional form which would allow him to express his heterodox views continued through *Pierre* and *The Confidence Man*, works which finally signalled the impossibility of publishing a saleable yet critical representation of his society and left him still in debt to his publishers for their cash advances. Acutely conscious of the effective censorship which Common Sense imposed on the American writer, Melville wrote to Hawthorne, 'what I feel most moved to write, that is banned – it will not pay', and elsewhere protested that 'in this world of lies truth is forced to fly like a white doe in the woodlands'.[15]

The writers whom we now consider to be important were thus in an embattled situation, struggling unsuccessfully, as Hawthorne put it, 'to open an intercourse with the world'.[16] Although their fictions articulated the most pressing contradictions of contemporary belief, unlike their European contemporaries they could not orchestrate traditional forms and new social attitudes into deliberate commentaries on the dominant world-view. Their work is rather the expression of a more capacious and critical view than contemporary opinion was prepared to admit and often needs to be read as an attempt to communicate unpalatable perceptions across the censorship imposed by readers who, in Cooper's words, were not only extraordinarily 'like each other', but who were also 'remarkably like that which common sense tells them they ought to resemble'.[17]

2.2. THE LANGUAGE OF COMMON SENSE

It is typical of the American writers' ambiguity that in the same year in which Cooper disclaimed the common sensical uniformity of his readers, he also wrote that 'the true Augustan age of Literature can never exist until works shall be as accurate in their typography as a "log book," and as sententious in their matter as a "watch-bill"'.[18] The desired literature should evidently present itself as a common sensical description of what could be reliably known, a 'log-book' discourse of fact and event in which the word is wedded to the thing.

Cooper was scarcely successful in inaugurating his Augustan age but there are moments when he showed us what it might be like. Consider, for example, the description of Tom Hutter's house in *The Deerslayer:*

> A good deal of art had also been manifested in the disposition of the timber of which the building was constructed, and which afforded a protection much greater than was usual to the ordinary log cabins of the frontier. The sides and ends were composed of the trunks of large pines, cut about nine feet long and placed upright, instead of being laid horizontally as was the practice of the country. These logs were squared on three sides and had large tenons on each end. Massive sills were secured on the heads of the piles, with suitable grooves dug out of their upper surfaces, which had been squared for the purpose, and the lower tenons of the upright pieces were placed in these grooves, giving them a secure fastening below. Plates had been laid on the upper ends of the upright logs, and were kept in their places by a similar contrivance, the several corners of the structure being well fastened by scarfing and pinning the sills and plates. The floors were made of smaller logs, similarly squared, and the roof was composed of light poles, firmly united and well covered with bark. The effect of this ingenious arrangement was to give its owner a house that could be approached only by water, the sides of which were composed of logs closely wedged together, which were two feet thick in their thinner parts, and which could be separated only by a deliberate and laborious use of hands, or by the slow operation of time.[19]

We can also find this kind of writing in the works of Melville, Thoreau and Poe when they are writing about practical activities or describing material objects. Here, the discourse resembles a manual of pioneer architecture, but it is just as adept at relating how to clear a forest, how to sail a boat, how to hunt a whale, the whale's interior anatomy or the customs of Marquesan islanders. It is the language of the handbook, or of the scientific account; a language of practical technique and expertise. It tells how things are done, and it tells in a language in which the word appears entirely adequate to the thing. The author of the discourse is implied rather than apparent and his consciousness is an absence: he is present merely as a recorder of what is perceived.

There are three respects in which this discourse is the desired writing of the age: firstly, it is obedient to the Common Sense precept that only that which is immediately perceived constitutes reliable knowledge; secondly, it is a discourse which appears to have no relation with ideas or with the imagination; thirdly, it relates practical activity or material objects in a manner that can be understood by all.[20]

The sheer length for which such passages retain their interest – the description of Hutter's house runs to nearly five hundred words of which I quote only half – is an indication of the ideological power they put in harness. They are written in a language that appeals to what Perry Miller called 'the common auditory', and not least because in them the language engages with the conditions of production: it expresses efficiently the activities of conquest (hunting, fishing, pathfinding, killing, pioneering, constructing) and echoes the mental techniques that transform raw materials into cultural products.[21] As the language has been reproduced in becoming literature, so it has elevated these activities to the status of art and conferred upon them an iconic value which furthers the activities it describes. At the level of language, this is to say, Cooper's novels of the forest and the sea, like Melville's epic of whaling and Thoreau's *Walden Pond*, join into high culture the basic activity of dominating the continent that provides the wealth of their society. Whatever else these novels do, they critically reinscribe the mentality of subjugation and settlement that was fundamental to nineteenth-century imperialism.[22]

It is for this reason that when producing the factualist style the writer is most at ease. It allows him to narrate in a manner acceptable to Common Sense critics and accessible to a generality of readers for whom practical, material activity is the common interest. However, the difficulty with this style is that it can only operate by restricting thought to immediate observation, elementary deduction, and sensible response. At its extremity it allows for romantic descriptions of nature and fight scenes such as Natty's famous first kill (*The Deerslayer*, Ch. 7) where the sequence of event and gesture offers the elementary message that Natty is honest, loyal and accurate whilst the Indian is treacherous and a poor shot, but it does not allow even an ironic reflection that its positivist theory of signs might be only one theory among others.

With such restrictions inherent to the factualist style it can only provide a partial element in a work concerned to be more than a first person account. When the writer fails to recognise this he runs the risk of producing a text of endless banality, a text which refuses to speak any coherent intellectual message and reduces towards fragmented descriptions. We can observe such an effect in Poe's *The Narrative of Arthur Gordon Pym* where the range of meaning is ruthlessly held down to that permitted in the conventions of Common Sense philosophy. Consider the following description in Chapter Fourteen:

> Captain Guy was a gentleman of great urbanity of manner and of considerable experience in the southern traffic, to which he had devoted the greater portion of his life. He was deficient, however, in energy, and consequently, in that spirit of enterprise which is here so absolutely requisite. He was part owner of the vessel in which he sailed, and was invested with discretionary powers to cruise in the South Seas for any cargo which might come most readily to hand. He had on board, as usual in such voyages, beads, looking-glasses, tinder-works, axes, hatchets, saws, adzes, planes, chisels, gouges, gimlets, files, spoke-shaves, rasps, hammers, nails, knives, scissors, razors, needles, thread, crockery-ware, calico, trinkets, and other similar articles.
>
> The schooner sailed from Liverpool on the tenth of July, crossed the tropic of Cancer on the twenty-fifth . . . [23]

I could have chosen a passage more easily suited to the present argument, one of those passages when Pym is stowed-away in the hold of the *Grampus* and trying to deduce his prospects for escape from all manner of discrete facts, or one of those passages that details techniques of survival in order to pass the narrative time. To select such a passage, however, might be too obviously germane. It is more interesting to note that even in the passage quoted above where opportunity exists for the development of the signified, the opportunity is refused. Captain Guy is sketched with a few phrases common enough in Poe's repertoire – his urbanity of manner, his want of energy – but no attempt is made to connect this proto-characterisation to a plenitude of significations provided by the body of the text. Captain Guy remains remote from his ship, linked to it only eponymously (it is called the *Jane Guy*), confined to an isolated moment of the discourse. Reading such a passage with the hindsight provided by having read Melville, one can see how it could have been different. The collection of trade-goods, their presence in the sealer-trader, the use to which they are put (tricking the savages into harvesting enormous surplus value in the form of *bêche de mer*), these could provide the beginning of rich significations. But Poe makes none of them. Throughout *The Narrative of Arthur Gordon Pym* isolated puns, veiled allusions, and bits of 'sober mystification' apart, Poe's intelligence remains slave to the elementary problem of narrative advance, so much so that the text, for all its appearance of factuality, endlessly violates the verisimilistic code upon which it relies. Meticulously logical, always deducing from the perceptually self-evident, it becomes absurdly illogical: briefly one might mention Chapter Nine where Pym realises that the *Grampus* cannot sink because laden with empty oil tanks (therefore why all the panic up to this point?); Pym's being strong enough to fight fully grown piratical sailors after weeks spent deprived of light, food, water and air in the ship's hold; and, in Chapter Twenty-Five, the discovery that the savages of Tsalal have black teeth, a fact not once remarked during many days in their company. Many of Poe's short stories and sketches take pleasure in showing that any semiological system is arbitrary but usually constructed to appear natural and self-evident, but such implausibilities as there are in *The Narrative of Arthur Gordon Pym* confirm the inability of factualist prose to develop rich thematic significance. When rigorously obeyed, the precepts of Common Sense deny a meaning to events deeper than that which appears on the surface. The eye (or the pen that describes its experience) is trapped in one instant of time, succeeded by another instant, in a series which has only chronology as its guide. Contingency stands in the place of historical relations.[24]

It follows that the development of character presents the writer with difficulties, firstly, because the effect of character is created by the aggregation of features in time and the articulation of different textual codes; secondly, because human character is not a self-evident fact but entails evaluative interpretation by the writer. Thus in order to move from factualist description of material objects and events, the writer must leave a safely restricted domain of signification and encounter the problem of the Other, of social relations, and of the act of signifying in itself.[25] This movement is therefore reluctantly made, the preference being to restrict personality to emblematic caricature, to the simple embroidery of abstract terms such as nobility, honesty, coquetry, or any other quality which will suffice as a controlling centre of thought. When working within the limits of the short story, Poe and Hawthorne in particular are able to confine character to allegorical meaning and produce some of the masterpieces of the genre. In longer fictional forms, however, the character tends to expand, leading the author into more problematic meanings, and must then be brought back to type or dropped from the story. The more achieved novels of the period are therefore those which present transactions between relatively fixed types (Ishmael/Hester versus Ahab/Chillingworth; nature versus knowledge – but even here it is remarkable how infrequently the protagonists actually meet), whereas when the writer is not able to restrict character to emblem (as Hawthorne is not in *The House of the Seven Gables* and *The Blithedale Romance*, and Melville is not in *Pierre*) the characters quickly become contradictory, enigmatic, evident projections of unresolved personal dilemmas.

The authors' success with types and their failure with realistic characterisation are obviously related to the dominance of myth. As we have seen, in myth the hero stands as a condensed symbol for the contradictory materials of a latent content which has been reductively represented as a play of essential oppositions. Because realist characterisation is to a degree rationalised, it can be shown as animated by codes which are at times in conflict; the mythic hero is, however, absolute; his discourse is a monologue. Between the contradictions of realism and the absoluteness of myth, allegory and symbolism offer ways of compromise: in them, language is neither represented as arbitrary nor as natural but is seen as cultural convention. The slippage of the sign away from what Common Sense terms as licit into the illicit, unfathomable, diabolic and comic (a slippage which animates *Moby-Dick*) is prevented by allowing the word to be a symbol signifying a finite range of signifieds within the author's control. Poe, with his love of mathematics, was efficient at limiting the meaning of the symbol by placing it in multiple equations that defined its range. Thus, the red death in 'The

Masque of the Red Death' could symbolise the plague, the spiritual revenge of the Red Indians, or the generalised guilt that Prince Prospero wants to banish from his consciousness. Prospero, equally, can be taken as the spirit of prosperity, as the commercial intention to thrive, as aristocracy, or as a generalised representative of the ruling class. Each signification, however, is sufficiently proximate to the others for a bounded domain of meaning to be established.

Poe is on record as having disliked Hawthorne's use of allegory, but whilst Hawthorne was capable of using restricted symbols which are easily interpreted, he was also capable of working with symbols which have an indeterminate domain of signification. The most notable example is his scarlet letter which Hawthorne presents to the reader with the words, 'Certainly there was some deep meaning in it, most worthy of interpretation, and which, as it were, streamed forth from the mystic symbol, subtly communicating itself to my sensibilities, but evading the analysis of my mind'.[26] When we associate Hawthorne's admission that his central symbol evades the analysis of his mind, with Melville's admission that the meaning of *Mardi* had escaped him, we can begin to perceive one of the more profound consequences of Common Sense factualism.[27] In restricting the range of meaning to a narrow utilitarianism the Common Sense school was trying to repress much of human mental capability. When the mind escaped the bounds of Common Sense it therefore found that there were few conventions or regulations to assist it.[28] There was neither a viable alternative philosophy of worldly knowledge, nor were there the social institutions to support such an alternative. Once released, then, the imagination was completely unfettered but also potentially trapped in a prison of its own fantasies, prone to narcissistic doubts about the viability of its beliefs, and estranged from a readership which had been taught to suspect what it had to offer. Liberated into the recognition that the relationship between signifier and signified was arbitrary, it could make of language a lexical playfield of puns, symbols, and allusions, of intuited rather than comprehended meanings, but the writer could not always be sure of his own intentions, nor of the way his meanings affected the world.

Writing in this period thus moves between the approved but limiting style of self-evident factualist narration in which the word appears wedded to the thing, to a discomforting recognition that language assigns ideological meanings and that writing involves the writer in representing the world according to a culturally determined set of beliefs. Given that the dominant ideology emphasises American regeneration, and that American experience provides no evidence that it has been achieved, factualist writing cannot produce the desired self-evident truth. If the writer is to avoid the financially disastrous course of pointing out the discrepancy between fact and idea he can repress the political and resort to myth, conceal the political in allegories that can only be deciphered by a coterie, or surrender meaning to the numinous play of the signified in indefinite symbols.[29] The last solution is in a sense the most desperate of all for there the writer loses control over his materials and can only stab randomly towards meaning. The route of allegory is the most daunting for there is always the possibility that one's meaning will be detected and one will be pilloried for one's pains. And the route of myth is the most damaging because it involves surrender to the unconscious where the voice of common desire is most insistent.

Myth, quite paradoxically, has its own form of enticement in that whilst it is furthest from factualist discourse it is also closest to it. This paradox is made possible because whilst mythic speech makes the signified into a natural substance, factualist speech makes the *sign* natural and conceals the signified.[30] Both mythic and factualist speech thus give us the impression of a completely impartial world of signs: on the one hand, through myth, we see essences that are material, and on the other hand, through factualism, we see material that appears to be in itself an essence. In neither world is there anyone to accept responsibility for the attribution of values, and in neither can humanity be represented as the responsible agent in its own history.

3 The Aesthetic Ideology: History, the Novel and Romance

3.1 HISTORY AND ROMANCE

The dominance of Common Sense attitudes towards the imagination placed the nationalist author in a difficult position. The novelist of domestic sentiment could claim to have observed at first hand the experiences represented in his or her fictions, but the pioneering experiences which formed America's unique identity could rarely be offered as the personal experience of the writer. More usually they had to be offered as products of the imagination, and the author's works were then considered improbable and scarcely worth serious attention. The publishing history of Melville's *Typee* illustrates the point: at first refused publication because it was thought fictitious and so without real value, its later acceptance as an autobiographical account amounted to a denial of Melville's authorial responsibility for its construction.[1] Melville's subsequent attempts to escape being reduced to 'the man who lived with the cannibals' can be seen as a struggle against the literalism of readers who could only see books as either factual and true or imaginative and false. If Melville succeeded as an imaginative author his work was inferior, but if his work was accepted as a true-life report, then he was no author at all.

The absoluteness of distinctions between fact and imagination is evident in an early essay on romance which Charles Brockden Brown wrote for the *Monthly Magazine* in 1800. Brown begins by setting up the conventional distinction between history as a true representation of what happened, and romance as a 'tissue of untruths . . . which never had existence'.[2] He then rigorously applies Common Sense logic to demolish the proposition that history reports the truth of events and shows that history is also romance:

> The observer or experimentalist . . . who carefully watches, and faithfully enumerates the appearances which occur, may claim the appelation of historian. He who adorns these appearances with cause and effect, and traces resemblances between the past . . . [and] the present . . . is a dealer, not in certainties, but probabilities, and is therefore a romancer.[3]

Because anything which is not a datum in immediate sense perception is a matter' of speculation, of possible rather than probable knowledge, Brown argues that the historian and the scientist are strictly limited to recording only what can be immediately known through sense perception. When it comes to knowing what motivates historical individuals, he remarks that 'motives cannot be certainly known. They are merely topics of conjecture'. It follows that when we try to produce accounts which explain the underlying meaning of events we are not 'historians but romancers'.

Brown's argument is designed to show that his own gothic novels have as much right to be considered true as the works of any historian, but his essay nonetheless indicates the key oppositions which will dominate United States aesthetics until the end of the century. History is true, and anything that is not history is romance, but since all prose representations involve some degree of interpretation, even history tends to dissolve into romance. To avoid slipping into the unreliable and subjective world of romance thus becomes as important as it is to maintain a degree of imaginative freedom from the narrow demands of the historical.

Hawthorne neatly outlines the dilemma in his biographical sketch of Sir William Phipps, the Governor of Massachusetts from 1692 to 94:

> The knowledge communicated by the historian and biographer is analogous to that which we acquire of a country by the map, – minute, perhaps, and accurate, and available for all necessary purposes, but cold and naked, and wholly destitute of the mimic charm produced by landscape-painting. These defects are partly remediable, and even without an absolute violation of literal truth, although by methods rightfully interdicted to professors of

biographical exactness. A licence must be assumed in brightening the materials which time has rusted, and in tracing out half-obliterated inscriptions on the columns of antiquity: Fancy must throw her reviving light on the faded incidents that indicate character, whence a ray will be reflected, more or less vividly, on the person to be described.[4]

In his sketch, Hawthorne sets Sir William about his daily business and imagines the kinds of intercourse he had with his fellow men, providing in the process a small example of the prerogatives of the historical novelist. The author takes pains to work within what is known about the period, and yet allows himself to go further than would be permitted to an historian by imagining scenes for which there is no documentary support. In strict epistemological terms, however, the extent of his licence is not much wider than that of the historian. Hawthorne invents scenes which dramatise the spirit of the age as he perceives it, much as an historian interpolates motives and general principles into the factual account. Both the novelist and the historian, then, exercise a degree of imagination in reconstructing the past; the question is how much.

In the early nineteenth century, history writing was such an important genre that the question of the historian's relationship to his materials was not a scholastic quibble. The production of histories flourished in the developing nations of Europe and North America because histories could encourage a sense of national identity and serve to explain the rapid changes which were occurring in the contemporary world.[5] Official history writing was paralleled by the invention of the historical novel which provided a more dramatic representation of events than was permitted in history proper. Since it was fiction, the historical novel had to be self-conscious about its claim to be a faithful representation of the past. Sir Walter Scott, whose *Waverley Novels* established the genre as a respectable literary form, approached historical fiction determined to produce works which would represent human experience as it had actually been lived. He resolved the problem of the status of his historical knowledge by asserting that 'it is that extensive neutral ground of manners and sentiments . . . common to us and our ancestors . . . arising out of the principles of common nature' that allows the historian to have access to individual and institutional motivations in distant periods of time. For Scott, in effect, the idea of a 'common nature' overcame Brockden Brown's reduction of history to a merely romantic activity by providing a metahistorical system of values which he believed were not subject to historical change and which therefore allowed him to observe the objective principles of historical development. It was because of this 'neutral ground', because there are 'passions common to all men in all stages of society . . . which alike agitate the human heart', that Scott believed himself capable of writing credible and authentic historical fictions about events he knew of only through hearsay or documentary evidence.[6]

If we accepted Brockden Brown's argument that any interpolation of motives involves the historian in romancing, then it would follow that Scott's 'neutral ground' does not provide a secure basis for historical knowledge but is an attempt to represent as true the unreliable speculations of the author. History would then dissolve into romance and there would be no grounds for discriminating the one from the other. However, such an approach to historical knowledge would be naively reductive since the admission that history is partisan only devalues its knowledge if one believes pure knowledge is possible. Brown does not admit that the observations of even the most self-consciously objective scientists are always influenced by their preconceptions so in effect he reinscribes the myth of pure historical objectivity in the very act of pointing up the subjectivity of human knowledge. By maintaining the distinction between history-as-fact and romance-as-imaginative-art, his parodic repetition of Common Sense oppositions occludes the more exacting philosophical task of distinguishing between different kinds of linguistic representations, none of which is in the end either totally true or totally false.

There are two areas where such discrimination may begin, the factual and the interpretative. We may decide that an historian has omitted important information and see this as an error, or as a prerogative of the historian's focus, depending on our own idea of what is important to the subject. Or we may disagree with the way the historian has interpreted events, with the kind of motivations he believes operated in the past, or with his view of the general causes of social behaviour. Issues at the factual level are easy to resolve; but at the level of interpretation any significant disagreement will take the form of presenting an alternative account, derived from an alternative view of human nature and historical experience. Differences of interpretation thus have to be settled by accepting Scott's premise that there is some kind of common nature, and then by proceeding to discuss what constitutes the common nature of man. In the human sciences today this is the ground where most significant intellectual engagement occurs. We tend to agree with Scott that we can understand human experience because humans are fundamentally the same whether living in a tribal society or in an industrial one. Discussion consists in trying to define this 'sameness', but we do not doubt that humanity is the object of study and that the goal is to reach generally verifiable statements about ourselves.

Scott's novels were instrumental in disseminating this theory of historical knowledge throughout the nineteenth century and provided writers in the United States with both textual models and critical anchorage points. Indeed, in so far as Scott's commentaries on the history, novel and romance are concerned, the framework he offered is still being employed today. Scott, in fact, was changing but slightly the position Johnson had developed in the middle of the eighteenth century, especially his discrimination between the 'comedy of romance' being written by Fielding and Smollett in his own day, and the 'heroick romance' of the seventeenth century. The heroick romance, Johnson tells us, was essentially aristocratic, dependent upon marvellous incidents and adventures, idealistic and improbable. The comedy of romance, which some were already calling the novel, was not 'remote from all that passes among men' but arises 'from general converse and accurate observation of the living world'. Johnson appreciated that because the novel represents common experiences the reader can detect 'any deviation from exactness of resemblance'. Novels therefore convince by mimesis rather than rhetoric, and serve as 'lectures of conduct, and introductions to life'. Since the young are easily misled by such a genre, Johnson argued that it was essential they represent the world from a morally sound point of view.[7]

With the benefit of hindsight we can see that Johnson discerned the dominant social function of the novel for the next two hundred years: it would teach its readers to understand a world that the middle class was constantly remaking in its own image. By achieving a judicious balance between mimesis and didacticism it would appear rational and democratic and its world-view would be open to criticism, disputation, proof and agreement. Reading it, even to disagree, would become a primary education in bourgeois ideology. By the beginning of the nineteenth century, Johnson's terms had become basic to commentary on the novel and when

Scott reviewed Jane Austen's work in 1814 he praised her for 'neither alarming our credulity nor amusing our imagination by vivid variety of incident, or by those pictures of romantic affection and sensibility, which were formerly as certain attributes of fictitious characters as they are of rare occurrence among those who actually live and die'. Rather, Scott says, she copies from nature 'as she really exists in the common walks of life' and presents readers with 'a correct and striking representation of what is daily taking place around them'. Using a phrase that will later be taken up by Cooper, Scott allows that the 'romancer paints from the *beau idéal* . . . and is in great measure exempted from the difficult task of reconciling them with the ordinary probabilities of life', whereas the novelist 'places his composition within that extensive range of criticism which general experience offers to every reader'.[8] The same opinion is repeated in his 'Essay on Romance' for the *Encyclopaedia Britannica* of 1824: 'the romance turns upon marvellous or uncommon incidents' and is therefore opposed to the novel 'in which events are accommodated to the ordinary train of human events and the modern state of society'.[9] Even when Scott was writing about medieval England for the most part he eschewed the 'marvellous' and represented social phenomena and individual motivations as rationally intelligible. In the terms of Noah Webster's definitions in *An American Dictionary of the English Language*, which were themselves Common Sense revisions of Johnson's, Scott's works might then be said to be nearer to novels than to romances because whilst they conformed to romance by being 'entertaining stories of adventure' they remained, like novels, within 'the limits of fact and real life'; indeed, they made the understanding of real life into a central didactic purpose.[10] For Scott the accurate comprehension of the past was not merely possible, it was morally necessary. Only through knowing what humanity had been, and through knowing its potentiality in various forms of society, could humanity progress towards an improved form of society. Equally, it was through a clear-sighted understanding of one's place in the present that one could develop one's moral and economic possibilities.

When one compares Scott's opinions and methods with those of his American followers one becomes aware that Scott operates between history and romance in a way that was disallowed by Common Sense criteria. His work was to a degree historically true, to a degree imaginatively developed. Explicitly ideological, it provided a mode of appropriating the world, past and present, in the name of the rationalist values of the middle class. Its effectivity as propaganda was dependent upon its credibility as a mirror of actual states of affairs. However, whilst Scott's European contemporaries saw him as a great historian, his readers in the United States tended to overlook his intention to be objective and categorise him as a romancer. In a survey of 'The Epochs and Events of American History, as Suited to the Purposes of Art in Fiction', the Southern historical novelist William Gilmore Simms praised Scott's fictions for having been instrumental in sweeping away 'the stale outcry of a class . . . by which it was supposed that romance was a disparagement to history, or led only to a perversion of the truth in history'.[11] Like Scott, Simms was conscious of the need to distinguish the respective merits and prerogatives of history and romance, but unlike Scott, and more like Brockden Brown, Simms tended to see the borderline between the two in very factualist terms. In a passage redolent with transcendentalism and imperialism, Simms remarks that:

> The appetite which calls into existence the artist of history, is not satisfied with what he achieves. He provokes a passion which he cannot gratify, and another genius is summoned to continue the progress into those dominions of the obscure and the impalpable which he fears to penetrate. The one is no less legitimate than the other, and the province of the romancer, if its boundaries be not yet generally recognised, at least leaves him large liberties of conquest . . . the liberties of conjecture which are accorded to the historian, become, in his case, the liberties of creation. So far as the moral is concerned, the difference of privilege is no ways important. Their privileges differ only in degree. We permit the historian to look down from his Pisgah into the land of equal doubt and promise; but the other is allowed to enter upon its exploration and take formal possession of its fruits. Both, however, are required to recognise a law in common – that, namely, which rules that the survey and the conquest shall be made for the benefit and blessing of the races which they severally represent.[12]

Were it not for its awful enthusiasm for conquest this passage would provide a percipient critique of Scott's novels as an ideological conquest of the Highland past (and by extension of many 'backward' places like British India) for the benefit of bourgeois democracy.[13] But Simms does not intend such a critique; he intends rather to legitimise the imaginative activity of the romancer as an essential agency in the expansion of the American empire. As a result he has none of Scott's reticence about romance, and little of his desire to place strictures around imaginative activity. For Simms, historical objectivity and romantic creativity are morally equal, provided that they both take possession in the name of the conquering people.

Simms offers a rarely explicit admission of the central function of the romance in this period. Objective history requires that the writer work within what is known, and therefore entails a dialectical struggle between the author's own ideology and the facts of human experience. As we have seen above, the society that Simms addressed was in the process of colonising the continent in the name of ideals which the means of colonisation belied. Unlike British society which was transforming the material world through science and reason, and transforming aristocratic institutions into democratic ones, the United States was appropriating land beyond its political frontier and bringing it into agricultural production within the national domain. Its vision of itself was therefore in large measure the projection of an ideal and about-to-be-realised condition, rather than an appropriation of the past in the name of reason. The accurate historical representation of the events of colonisation could scarcely assist in its fulfilment since the principles of objective historiography would have revealed it for what it was. It is therefore scarcely surprising to find a tradition of thought in the United States which would rather dispense with objective history. In a passage to which that quoted above stands as a recuperation, Simms gives an eloquent dispensation from all factual constraints on the historical imagination.

Sitting among the dismembered fragments which made the citadel of Carthage, – each man becomes his own historian. Thought, taking the form of conjecture, ascends by natural stages into the obscure and the infinite. Reasoning of what should have been from what is before us, we gather the true from the probable. Dates and names, which, with the mere chronologist are every thing, with us are nothing. For, what matters it to us, while tracing hopes and fears, feelings and performances, the greatness which was, and the glories which exist no longer, to be arrested by some cold and impertinent querist who, because we cannot tell him whether these things took place . . . forbids our inquiry as idle.

Hence, it is the artist who is the true historian. It is he who gives shape to the unhewn fact, – who yields relation to the scattered fragments, who unites the parts in coherent dependency, and endows, with life and action, the otherwise motionless automata of history.[14]

Such a view seems in direct descent from Brockden Brown's argument that the historian is a romancer, but where it differs from Brown's argument is in its abolition of all material constraint on the individual imagination: 'Dates and names, which, with the mere chronologist are every thing, with us are nothing'. The constraints of the factual are dissolved so that the mind can rise into a transcendental zone of the 'obscure and infinite', a reference which would seem to indicate that if Simms had not read Emerson's *Essays* he was at least a fellow traveller. In 'Self-Reliance' Emerson had proclaimed that:

. . . the centuries are conspirators against the sanity and authority of the soul. Time and space are but physiological colours which the eye makes, but the soul is light: where it is, is day; where it was is night; and history is but an impertinence and an injury if it be anything more than a cheerful apologue of my being and becoming.[15]

Emerson's rhetorical aim is to encourage self-reliance and demolish the awe of the European past in which he believed his contemporaries were trapped, but in the process of liberating his hearers from their overestimation of institutionalised and historical learning, Emerson goes so far as to make the historical sense entirely subjective: 'time' is a 'physiological colour . . . which the eye makes'; it has no objectivity but proceeds outward from human perception, a form of consciousness at the total disposition of the individual will. (The reversal of causative agency and received effect here is a fine example of the mythic imagination.) History can thus be no more than the servant of desire.

The fact that Simms and Emerson should have felt impelled to make these rhetorical claims indicates that they were well aware of the alternative attitude which confined history to chronological fact, and that they wished to dispense with the threat of historical objectivity by asserting the rights of a speculative imagination. For both of them, however, this speculative imagination was not to be left entirely free to produce whatever vision it fancied; its duty was to provide an affirmative vision which assisted the becoming of the American individual and of the American nation.[16]

3.2 COOPER

One of the principal reasons for offering a novel as historical is to remove from fiction the taint of the lie. The tendency to collapse history into romance deprived the author of the ability to claim that his fiction was above reproach because true to the known record, and, whilst giving him greater freedom in his treatment of the past, also meant he could be held totally responsible for his romancing imagination if it failed to affirm the correct image of American experience. As a result, the American novelist was not eager to call himself a romancer, the more so since 'to romance' carried all the pejorative significations of falseness and deceit which the word has conveyed from Johnson's day to this. The present critical tendency to assume that James Fenimore Cooper was an unabashed romancer is thus poor literary history.[17] In fact, Cooper began his career imitating Austen and Scott, generally disdained the word 'romance' and consistently tried to maintain that his work was factually based and therefore true. Given a readership generally disinclined to accept that a novel could be anything other than imaginary, the way in which his claims are made becomes significant testimony to the difference of opinion between writer and reader. In the 1832 Preface to *The Pioneers*, for example, Cooper describes Leatherstocking as 'a creation, rendered probable by such auxiliaries as were necessary to produce that effect'. He then adds that 'had he drawn still more upon fancy, lovers of fiction would not have so much cause for their objections to his work'. In other words, readers had found Leatherstocking improbable and Cooper wishes to imply that had he been less concerned with the historical truth he would have been able to produce a more credible character. Similar gymnastics may be found in other early prefaces. In the 1827 Preface to *The Prairie*, the reader is informed that 'the portions of the tale, for which no authorities are given, are quite as true as those which are not destitute of this peculiar advantage, and . . . all may be believed alike'. In the 1826 Preface to *The Last of the Mohicans* the female reader who 'expects an imaginary and romantic picture of things which never had an existence' is warned that she 'will probably lay it aside disappointed'.[18]

Although there are differences in their practices, Cooper's understanding of the distinctions between genres is clearly very close to Scott's. In Cooper's terms, 'the romancer is permitted to garnish a probable fiction, while he is sternly prohibited from dwelling on improbable truths'. The historian, on the other hand, has a duty 'to record facts as they have occurred, without a reference to the consequences, resting his reputation on a firm foundation of realities, and vindicating his integrity by his authorities'.[19] The way in which the distinction is put, however, reveals the embattled situation created by Common Sense: historians who must publish 'without reference to the consequences' are historians who must expect critical hostility; romancers who are 'sternly prohibited from dwelling on improbable truths' must know truths which have been banished from what can be thought of as probable.

One such truth, as Cooper's writing was to show, was that Indians could be good human beings, an idea which did not accord with their mythologisation as 'savages'. Although, as I shall explore in the next chapter, Cooper's representation of the Indians is generally malign and misleading, the fact that he represented the Last of the Mohicans as a man of noble sentiments enraged some of his critics, Lewis Cass in particular. The campaign that Cass waged against Cooper was in the end responsible for Cooper abandoning his claim to be considered an historian and his acceptance of the romance as a defensive shield. In the General Preface to the Leatherstocking Tales he is forced to admit that Indians are actually creatures of 'evil passions' and adds, 'especially when treating for the sale of their lands' (the latter a dig at Cass who as Indian agent had been party to many Indian treaties). Having conceded the general point, Cooper then goes on to defend his right as a romancer 'to represent the *beau idéal* of his characters to the reader'.[20] When read in full historical context this much quoted remark can be understood as a concession wrung from Cooper by the dominance of Common Sense attitudes: Indians were as self-evidently savage as blacks were self-evidently subhuman. Any representation that showed even one contrary to the rule exposed as arbitrary a system of identities which was held to be unquestionable.[21] Cooper therefore had to be harried until he had admitted that even his exceptional noble Indians were figments of the romancing imagination.

The first sentence of *The Deerslayer* is further evidence of Cooper's retreat from the claims of objective historiography. He begins his novel with the words, 'On the human imagination events produce the effects of time', thereby coming into agreement with Emerson's Kantian belief that 'time and space are but physiological colours which the eye makes'. The narrative, however, as in the majority of Cooper's novels, negotiates the contradiction between the desire to admit the historical truth of the conquest and the desire to produce an apologia for national expansion. The way to survive this contradiction, as we shall see more fully in the next chapter, is to suspend the rational, objective and critical faculties and to write as if from the position of someone like Natty Bumppo who is proud not to have wasted his time in schools; or perhaps, as Emerson would prefer it, to write like an Indian, an idiot, or a farmer's boy:

> Broader and deeper we must write our annals – from an ethical reformation, from an influx of the ever-new, ever-sanative conscience – if we would trulier express our wide-related nature, instead of this old chronology of selfishness and pride to which we have too long lent our eyes. Already that day exists for us, shines in on us at unawares; but the path of science and of letters is not the way into nature, but from it rather. The idiot, the Indian, the child and the unschooled farmer's boy, come much nearer to these – understand them better than the dissector or the antiquary.[22]

3.3 HAWTHORNE

Hawthorne's practice as an historical writer came closer to Scott's blend of historical research and imaginative development than that of any of his contemporaries. By temperament and education he was sceptical of Emerson's 'ethical reformation' (although he shared the preference for intuition over science), and much of his work is concerned to represent the 'old chronology of selfishness and pride' that may be found at the base of American history. He was not, however, any happier than was Cooper to define his novels as romances; as F. O. Mathiessen pointed out long ago, he produced his most explicit commentary on the romance only as a defence against the hostility shown towards 'The Custom-House'.[23] Although his introductory sketch for *The Scarlet Letter* was generally well-received by contemporary critics, Hawthorne's remarks on his eviction from the post of Surveyor of Customs by the incoming Taylor administration broke the bounds of what was thought permissible comment. The result of the hostile criticism which Hawthorne thus brought on his head was the defensive Preface he attached to the second edition of *The Scarlet Letter*, and the elaborate disclaimer with which he began *The House of the Seven Gables*:

> When a writer calls his work a Romance, it need hardly be observed that he wishes to claim a certain latitude, both as to its fashion and material, which he would not have felt himself entitled to assume had he professed to be writing a Novel. The latter form of composition is presumed to aim at a very minute fidelity, not merely to the possible, but to the probable and ordinary course of a man's experience. The former – while, as a work of art, it must rigidly subject itself to laws, and while it sins unpardonably so far as it may swerve aside from the truth of the human heart – has fairly a right to present that truth under circumstances, to a great extent, of the writer's own choosing or creation.[24]

As we observed in the case of Cooper, the author is forced to disclaim mimetic intentions and to declare his work a romance in order to avoid critical hostility. Hawthorne's case is, however, more complex and more illuminating than Cooper's because until this time his work had been well received by the critics. Hawthorne's defensiveness would therefore seem hyperbolic if we did not understand how hostile comment could crucially damage an already meagre sales revenue. Add to this that *The Scarlet Letter* had been Hawthorne's first try at a novel, and at reaching a national readership, and one can begin to understand his sensitivity. If the mildest satire on customary behaviour resulted in adverse criticism, how could one write a novel which passed wider comment upon contemporary society? How could one write as a Surveyor of Customs? Since, when Hawthorne sent 'The Custom-House' to his publisher he expressed the belief that the introductory sketch might prove, like his previously published prose sketches, 'more widely attractive than the main narrative', it seems reasonable to assume that if Hawthorne hoped to become financially secure as a writer it was with this kind of humorous representation. Criticism of 'The Custom-House' was therefore tantamount to confining his writing to the relatively safe discourse he used in his tales and romances, a discourse which had often been praised for its 'mildness' and 'spirituality' but which because of its very lack of factuality could never establish an 'intercourse' with the broad mass of the reading public.[25]

Once one has restored Hawthorne's statements on the romance to the critical situation in which they were produced one can improve upon the modern critical perspective which tends to emphasise the third sentence of the Preface to *The House of the Seven Gables* over the first two, thereby suggesting that Hawthorne was not inclined to mimetic representation because he was concerned more with the eternal 'truth of the human heart' than he was with the local and mundane. Through this emphasis Hawthorne's statements on the romance have been situated in the tradition which descends from Aristotle's belief that poetry is superior to history because poetry deals with eternal truth whilst history restricts itself to passing events, and have then been said to reveal Hawthorne's romantic belief that the imagination and intuition are more effective instruments of knowledge than is sensory experience.[26] As we have seen above, this inversion of the postulates of Common Sense was being put forward by Transcendentalist philosophers at the time Hawthorne was writing.

To place Hawthorne's aesthetic in such a perspective has some pertinence. In 'The Custom-House' one finds an almost typical expression of the romantic belief in the value of the imagination as the agency which permits dull fact to be transformed into illuminated truth. Dragged down by the workaday atmosphere of the custom house Hawthorne's imagination becomes a 'tarnished mirror' which cannot reflect, 'or only with miserable dimness, the figures with which . . . [he does his best] to people it'. Hawthorne accordingly resorts to night, 'to the glimmering coal fire and the moon' and tries with the aid of these domestic, alchemical and romantic agencies to kindle 'imaginary scenes'.

> Moonlight, in a familiar room, falling so white upon the carpet, and showing all its figures so distinctly, . . . is a medium the most suitable for a romance-writer to get acquainted with his guests. . . . [Things] are so completely seen, are so spiritualized by the unusual light, that they seem to lose their substance, and

become things of the intellect. . . . Thus . . . the floor of our familiar room has become a neutral territory, somewhere between the real world and fairy-land, where the Actual and the Imaginary may meet, and each imbue itself with the nature of the other.[27]

The reference to moonlight, coupled with the state of reverie, locates this scene in the tradition of romantic aesthetics according to which the imagination facilitates the separation of essence from material appearance and opens the way to an exploration of a higher order of reality.[28]

How much weight one should attach to this passage is, however, difficult to decide. There is scant evidence that Hawthorne thought of himself as an heir to the romantic tradition, for, despite an early interest in Rousseau, his literary enthusiasms were more for the neoclassicists and satirists of the eighteenth century and the realists of the nineteenth century than for Wordsworth and Coleridge whom he read in the 1830s. Since Balzac and Scott were favourite authors, and since 'The Custom-House' as a whole seems cast in a vein somewhere between Swiftian satire and realism, it makes more sense to construe this passage as a quotation from an imported literary discourse which provides Hawthorne with the *appearance* of belonging to a tradition, rather than as a firm declaration of identity with the romantic ethos.[29] To qualify further any easy assumption of Hawthorne into the image of the romantic artist one should remember that he did not enthuse about communion with nature but viewed nature with the ambiguity of an incompletely reformed Calvinist who could not decide whether it betokened redemption or damnation. He did not welcome his solitude, but protested that 'thoughts are frozen and utterance benumbed unless the speaker stand in some true relation with his audience'. He did not think of the moment of transcendental connection with the essence of reality as 'sublime', as did Wordsworth, but rather, like a good Scottish realist, saw egotistical understanding as 'an unpardonable sin', a 'Bosom Serpent', and although his writing was evidently informed by the conflict between the optimist and idealist tenets of Transcendentalism and the legacy of Calvinism's more pessimistic view of human nature, the real motivations of this tension deserve to be understood not in the super-structure of abstract ideas that provides only one part of their vocabulary, but in the social conditions which are the main point of Hawthorne's address. His purpose in defining his works as romances seems to have been to establish a 'neutral territory' where his imagination could function without immediately attracting the moral and political inquisition which was visited upon those who did not represent the world in strictly affirmative terms.[30]

Given such conditions of literary production it is easy to understand Hawthorne's sympathy with the Puritans' ambivalence towards the imagination. As we have seen, 'Young Goodman Brown' shows that Hawthorne's interest in the discrepancy between appearance and truth derives more from scepticism about conventional pieties than from romantic theses about the relation of material form to ideal essence. His critique is consistently directed against the egotism and deceit of those in positions of authority. His method, ever cautious about incurring the wrath of such men, is to express himself in allegories which Melville discerned as 'directly calculated to deceive . . . the superficial skimmer of pages'.[31] If Melville, the friend and practitioner of similar arts of deception, could perceive this and praise it, so the less generous mind of the critic could sense it and condemn. Reviewing *The Scarlet Letter* in the *Church Review*, Arthur Cleveland Coxe demanded that Hawthorne come out from behind his mask and say honestly (i.e. *literally*) what he meant:

> We shall entirely mislead our reader if we give him to suppose that *The Scarlet Letter* is coarse in its details, or indecent in its phraseology. This very article of our own, is far less suited to ears polite, than any page of the romance before us; and the reason is, we call things by their right names, while the romance never hints the shocking words that belong to its things, but, like Mephistophiles, insinuates that the arch-fiend himself is a very tolerable sort of person, if nobody would call him Mr. Devil.[32]

A nicer specimen of the integration of moralist criticism with factualist theories of language—'we call things by their right names, while the romance never hints the shocking words that belong to its things' – could not be found. Had Hawthorne accepted Coxe's invitation he would have been more effectively pilloried than he already was. His conviction that the American past contained buried wrongs, that the foundation of the Puritan colonies had involved authoritarian persecution of the heterodox and the expropriation of the poor by the rich (like Matthew Maule by Judge

Pyncheon), and his belief that the crimes of the past were transmitted into the present by the very act of denying their existence; these prevented any simplistic agreement with the prevailing optimism about the regeneration of human nature and the inherent perfection of the United States which dominated social thought in his day. Hawthorne's requirement that the artist should have freedom from a 'minute fidelity . . . to the probable and ordinary course of a man's experience', his cultivation of the rights of the imagination, were neither flights from reality nor avenues which gave access to spiritual essences.[33] They were the means by which he could entertain a wider view than was socially permitted, a view which opened up truths that were being denied.

3.4 NEGATIVE DEFINITION

The demand that representations of America should offer nothing that conflicted with the image of regeneration can be seen to underlie another recurrent theme in the definition of the American novel as a romance: the suggestion that American historical reality was either not dense enough or too familiar to be converted into fiction, that the writer must therefore invent a world in his imagination. In the *Notions of the Americans*, Cooper had written that 'all attempts to blend history with romance in America have been comparatively failures (and perhaps fortunately), since the subjects are too familiar to be treated with the freedom that imagination absolutely requires'. Since Cooper's fictions had been and were to remain blends of history and romance, his parenthetical declaration that the failure had been fortunate must be read as implying that his own works were histories not romances. But his protest that the materials were too familiar for imaginative treatment scarcely makes sense unless one reads in it a reference to those critics who had found fault with his version of American history. Since it is doubtful that his readers would have known much about the French and Indian Wars, the settlement of upper New York State, or about any of his other chosen historical materials, we must read 'familiar' here as yet another reference to the prescribed way of seeing the world. Only if we do so can we then marry the idea of a too familiar reality to the protest Cooper makes earlier in the *Notions* about the 'poverty of materials' that America offers to its authors. 'There are no annals for the historian', he complains, 'no follies for the satirist; no manners for the dramatist; no obscure fictions for the writer of romance'. Since these protested absences are fully present in Cooper's work we are confronted with the paradox of a writer who says that his environment is too well known to be turned into fiction, and that what fiction manages to take from the environment does not exist.[34]

The paradox is not confined to Cooper but is found in other definitions of the American novel as a romance. In his Preface to *The Marble Faun*, Hawthorne declares that:

> Italy, as the site of his Romance, was chiefly valuable to him as affording a sort of poetic or fairy precinct, where actualities would not be so terribly insisted upon as they are, and must needs be, in America. No author, without trial, can conceive of the difficulty of writing a romance about a country where there is no shadow, no antiquity, no mystery, no picturesque and gloomy wrong, nor anything but a commonplace prosperity, in broad and simple daylight, as is happily the case with my dear native land. It will be very long, I trust, before romance-writers may find congenial and easily handled themes, either in the annals of our stalwart republic, or in any characteristic and probable events of our individual lives.[35]

Again the key issues are an enforced idea of the actual, and a fortunate lack of the mystery, antiquity and gloomy wrong that Hawthorne's own writing has proved to exist. Hawthorne's denial of his American materials amounts to literary suicide: the concessive 'must needs be' and his hope that 'it will be very long' before writers discover the very things he has discovered in the American past, indicate a complete submission to the idea that the United States is so regenerate it can need no artistic representation.

Hawthorne's change of his locale from Massachusetts to Italy in *The Marble Faun* becomes literal in Henry James's later emigration to Europe, but James nonetheless continues to represent the United States as an unmarked prosperity which is therefore unusable as a literary subject. In a description of Hawthorne's America which he confesses to be ludicrously hyperbolic, he 'enumerates the items of high civilisation, as it exists in other countries, which are absent from American life'. There is

> No State . . . and indeed barely a specific national name. No

sovereign, no court, no personal loyalty, no aristocracy, no church, no clergy, no army, no diplomatic service, . . . no castles, nor manors, nor old country-houses, . . . no cathedrals, nor abbeys, . . . no great Universities nor public schools . . . no literature, no novels, no museums, no pictures, no political society, no sporting class. . . . Some such list as that might be drawn up of the absent things in American life – especially in the American life of forty years ago, the effect of which, upon an English or French imagination, would probably as a general thing be appalling. The natural remark, in the most lurid light of such an indictment, would be that if these things are left out, everything is left out. The American knows that a good deal remains, what it is that remains – that is his secret, his joke, as one may say.[36]

Some of what James says was absent was indeed absent. But the great universities (like James's *alma mater*), political society, paintings, aristocracy (in the Whig sense), old country houses, diplomatic service, all the institutions of an historically constituted nation state, these were there in plenty, and indeed would make brief appearances in James's novels.

The rhetorical strategy of defining a society by the absence of negative features is characteristic of the utopian vision. When Montaigne idealised the savage life in his famous essay 'Sur les Cannibales', he noted, or it would be better to say imagined, that they had 'no kind of commerce, no science of numbers, no concept of magistrature, . . . no clothes, no agriculture, no metal, no use of wine or wheat. The very words which mean lie, treachery, dissimulation, avarice, . . . are unheard of'.[37] Patently factually untrue, the utopian imagination takes comfort in a vision of paradise defined as a place where the evils of this world have been exorcised. In such bold representations, however, the intention is less escapist than political, for as the versions by Swift, Melville and Thoreau confirm, the aim is to subvert civilisation's self-conceit by indicating that regeneration was both the original condition from which mankind has fallen, and the condition which therefore only awaits rediscovery.[38] Again, as in a dream, the desire for an alternative state of affairs (the 'if only it had been the other way around') is made into the affirmative statement, 'it is'.

When viewed as a variant on this tradition, the American writer's definition of his culture as an absence may be seen as a peculiar affirmation of the Edenic myth. Since art implies knowledge and knowledge implies the Fall, so the flawless United States can have no need of artistic representation, nor can it offer the artist sufficiently differentiated social materials. Evidently the 'absenting' of culture is also as much a response to the uniformity imposed by a pragmatic approach to life, as it is a response to the narrowing of vision imposed by critical taste. James himself admits that after one has enumerated all the absences of American life something is left, but that is the American's 'secret, his joke, as one may say'. The reference to repression might put us in mind of Poe: the obvious has clearly become unspeakable, to such an extent that James tells us:

> History has left in the United States but so thin and impalpable a deposit that we very soon touch the hard substratum of nature and nature herself, in the western world, had the peculiarity of seeming rather crude and immature . . . . A large juvenility is stamped on the face of things, and in the vividness of the present the past, which died so young and had time to produce so little attracts but scanty attention.[39]

In the light of our previous commentary on the economic function of 'nature' one cannot be too surprised that to James 'the past . . . attracts but scanty attention' and that 'nature' seems 'crude'. Any other view would open up the complex world of historical experience to conscious examination. Nor can one be too surprised that James later defined his purpose in romancing as being to deal with experience 'disengaged, disentangled, disencumbered . . . from the inconvenience of a related, a measurable state, a state subject to our vulgar communities'.[40] The vigilance of orthodox critics would seem to have established an enduring climate in which the prose writer was best advised to address social reality 'tangentially', if at all.[41]

3.5 NOVEL AND ROMANCE, IDEOLOGY AND MYTH

As Johnson understood, the novel is both revolutionary and conservative. It represents the new forms that history is bringing into existence and it recuperates their revolutionary potential by colouring the representation according to a morally conservative point of view. In thus making the unfamiliar familiar the novel has to engage with the contradictions between the dominant ideology and the changing economy it seeks to control. Born in the century when ideology and party became for the first time the principal means of social control, the novel seems destined to thrive for as long as there is debate about the constitution of reality.

In proscribing the novel and banishing serious meditation upon social experience to the domain of romance, *antebellum* criticism indicated society's nervousness about the ability of its ideology to account for its behaviour. So much had to be taken as unquestionably self-evident, and so much was far from clear, that the novel's essential procedure of critically representing the world could only seem dangerously subversive. The romance, on the other hand, was produced under a poetic licence which discounted its relevance in advance. Since it was by definition only possible not probable it could not put at risk the prevailing social codes, nor could it represent the gap between ideological image and historical actuality.

Being condemned to the romance, however, had perversely liberating effects. Exiled from the security of social reason and convention, the imagination had little conscious guidance as to how or what to produce but was able to explore the contradictions located in what Frederic Jameson has called 'the political unconscious'.[42] As the name implies, it is there that what the mind is prepared to admit, and what it desires to be the case, play out their subterfuge and reduce the dilemmas of their society to the condensed symbols and schematic oppositions of the dream. If the classic American narratives tend towards the journey motif it may be because flight and pursuit are the narrative manifestations of fear and desire. The movement invariably begins and ends in its opposite, an enclosure that is either sanctuary or prison, and negotiates a space between nature and civilisation, good and evil, regeneration and corruption.

Typically, as I outlined in the first chapter, the key terms of this opposition can be seen as reducing the complexities of historical experience to a contrast of essences, the hero standing in a position of sympathy with the nature that civilisation is about to turn into profits. Whilst the narrative mythologises actual relations in order to prevent recognition of ideological inadequacy, the discourse of the romance is nonetheless inclined to raise the very questions the narrative is trying to avoid. Pursuing the analogy of the dream, this may be likened to secondary revision: the rational mind strives to bring intelligibility to an abstract narrative, strives to embody it in the world. Since the myth is only intensely drawn if the mind that produces it experiences acutely the contradictions of ideology and history, it follows that the same mind will be exacting in its demand for plausibility. The discourse of the romance will thus oscillate between an urgent inscription of myth and an equally urgent attempt to deconstruct it. The latter move, of course, only lends strength to the former, for if deconstruction were to succeed it would manifest the incompatibility of the text and the world.

The resulting works, as I hope the following readings will demonstrate, are radically unstable and endlessly and excitingly difficult to interpret. Heavily over-determined, they require techniques of interpretation as indefatigable and as catholic as their own skill in condensing and relocating the materials of their latent content. The readings that are offered here constitute only a suggestion of how I think we might proceed, but I hope they show that when writers are banished to what might seem like a world elsewhere they discover nothing less than the contradictions they were banished to repress.

4 James Fenimore Cooper's Leatherstocking Tales

The father of an isolated family, destined one day to rise into a tribe, and in farther progress of time to expand into a nation, may, indeed, narrate to his descendants the circumstances which detached him from the society of his brethren, and drove him to form a solitary settlement in the wilderness, with no other deviation from truth, on the part of the narrator, than arises from the infidelity of memory, or the exaggerations of vanity. But when the tale of the patriarch is related by his children, and again by his descendants of the third and fourth generation, the facts it contains are apt to assume a very different aspect. The vanity of the tribe augments the simple annals from one cause; the love of the marvellous, so natural to the human mind, contributes its means of sophistication from another; while, sometimes, from a third cause, the king and the priest find their interest in casting a holy and sacred gloom and mystery over the period in which their power arose.[1]

It was with these words, published in 1824, that Sir Walter Scott described the transformation of history into romance in the medieval period, but the process he described was not confined to the remote past. Vanity, the love of the marvellous, and the mystery which kings and priests like to cast over the origins of their power, were as active in the nineteenth century as they had been in medieval times. Scott's description, beginning as it does with the example of 'the father of an isolated family, destined one day to rise into a tribe, and in farther progress of time to expand into a nation', fits the experience of James Fenimore Cooper so neatly that were it not for the date of Scott's publication, one would think the passage had been written with him in mind. The son of a man who had founded a solitary settlement in the 'wilderness' of upper New York State, Cooper was to retell 'the tale of the patriarch' across a broad

canvas of the actual and imaginary events of settlement, a retelling
which was motivated in part by the desire to furnish the nation with
an historical sense of how it had come into being, and in part by a
personal struggle to come to terms with a family past that had been
typical of the nation's economic activity in the post-revolutionary
period. As the son of a land agent, and as someone brought up in a
pioneer community, Cooper had a more immediate and problematic knowledge of the political economy of United States
expansion than any of his literary contemporaries. It is this
knowledge which furnishes his fictions with their enduring literary
qualities and which by the same token allows us to demonstrate in
them the transformation of history into romance and of ideology into
myth. In order to perform this demonstration we must break
company with those who would like to maintain that Cooper's
fiction constitutes 'a world by itself' which has no relation to
historical actuality, and begin by understanding the basic historical
materials with which Cooper was to work.[2] The intricate details of
Cooper family history will be seen to reappear in displaced
arrangement in Cooper's major fiction.

James Fenimore Cooper was born in Burlington, New Jersey in
1789. In 1793 he moved to Cooperstown in upper New York State, a
town which his father, Judge William Cooper, had founded in 1786
at the foot of the Otsego Lake. The land on which Cooperstown was
built first came into the possession of the whites by the Treaty of Fort
Stanwix of 1768 in which Sir William Johnson, Britain's Indian
agent on the Mohawk River, agreed the cession of Iroquois lands on
the headwaters of the Susquehannah and the Mohawk. The lands
were divided into patents by the colonial authorities and sold to
members of the ruling oligarchy, the lands at the foot of the Otsego
Lake passing to Sir William Johnson's deputy, George Croghan, an
ardent exponent of white expansion. Croghan built a log cabin on
the land in 1769 but there is scant evidence that he ever lived there,
being the patentee of vast tracts of land and much involved in trying
to obtain more. Typical of both colonial and later land operators,
Croghan was a combination of politician, surveyor, Indian agent
and banker, these being the skills needed to map out a suitable piece
of property, negotiate its title with the Indians and the colonial
authorities, and finance its purchase. As economic historians
continue to remind their more fanciful colleagues, it was men cast in
the mould of Croghan who were responsible for opening up the
West, not the lone frontiersman (usually the speculator's employee),
and even less the yeoman farmer.[3]

During the Revolution, Croghan was accused of being a loyalist and charged with treason, and although acquitted of the charge he became a bankrupt and died in poverty. The Otsego patent passed rapidly through the hands of several of Croghan's creditors and was eventually bought by William Cooper and his partner, Andrew Craig. With the benefit of hindsight the purchasers can be seen to have been typical of the class which had favoured rebellion against the British colonial oligarchy. Unlike the well-connected and influential Croghan, William Cooper was the son of poor Pennsylvania Quakers and had made his way up the social scale by eloping with Elizabeth Fenimore, the daughter of a wealthy Quaker family, and by becoming the co-owner of a produce store. William Cooper's upward mobility owed little to formal education and much to the flair for sharp practice which he displayed in obtaining the Croghan patent. In 1785 the patent was in the hands of the Burlington Land Company but William Franklin, the son of Benjamin, retained rights over the patent in bond against a mortgage he had provided to Croghan. Knowing of Franklin's financial rights over the land, William Cooper arranged for the patent to be auctioned at a remote spot in the middle of winter. By this stratagem Cooper was able to buy the land for fifty cents an acre and circumvent the objections both of Franklin and of Croghan's heirs, the Prevosts. The two aggrieved parties therefore hired Aaron Burr to prosecute their case. Cooper hired Alexander Hamilton and a legal battle ensued that dragged on in the Supreme Court until the early years of the nineteenth century. As the Prevosts were the Cooper's neighbours on Otsego Lake this protracted legal action did not escape the attention of Cooper's son, James. It doubtless informed the awareness we find in his work that title to land is a vexed legal issue.[4]

Whilst legal proceedings continued William Cooper lost no time in establishing Cooperstown at the outlet of Otsego Lake and in selling off portions of Croghan's patent. In selling, rather than in leasing, Cooper obviously made restitution difficult. He also broke with the established practice which was for the landowner to lease the land at a fixed rate for a period of years. As Cooper himself explained, leasing discouraged settlement because the settler had no right to the profits which derived from improvements to the land. Cooper therefore sold the freehold on extended credit and by this simple mechanism became one of the most successful land agents in United States history. An unashamed mercantilist, late in his life he recorded that selling lands had been for him 'the principal source . . . of pleasure and recreation'.[5] Having settled the Croghan patent he became the agent for other landowners, always advising his clients to sell rather than lease, and constantly proving that the ownership of a freehold attracted settlers who were willing to work hard at improving their lands. It was this important step towards a more finance-capitalist attitude that allowed William Cooper to settle some seven hundred and fifty thousand acres (over one thousand square miles) of Indian land in his lifetime. In the process he amassed a considerable fortune and rose to a position of influence in Federalist political circles. However, he remained throughout his life the epitome of the *nouveau riche*, liked or disliked for his bluntness and lack of sophistication, inclined to settle disagreements by challenging opponents to a wrestling match, generous and high-handed by turns.

As became the son of a wealthy landowner, James Cooper received the best education that money could buy at a school which introduced him to the sons of New York's power élite. He acquired the polish that his father lacked and in 1811 married Susan De Lancey, daughter of a family that had been one of the most influential in colonial New York. The De Lanceys, although reduced by the losses they sustained as loyalists in the War of Independence, retained some of their former prestige. By marrying Susan, and by adopting his mother's maiden name 'Fenimore', James thus completed the rise in social status inaugurated by his father's acquisition of the Croghan lands. He became a member of the 'established' landed gentry and a spokesman for their privileges and responsibilities.[6]

4.1 *THE PIONEERS:* LEATHERSTOCKING'S GENESIS

It was in transforming his recollections of childhood in Cooperstown into fiction that James Fenimore Cooper discovered Nathaniel Bumppo, the first 'innocent' hero of the American frontier. To judge from the text of *The Pioneers*, and from the critical articles that Cooper published whilst at work on the novel, Cooper began writing with no intention of giving Natty the stature he was finally to achieve. His main purpose seems to have been to imitate Scott and Austen and thus provide a more realistic representation of life in the United States than Washington Irving had recently been able to achieve with *The Sketch Book*. Although the first part of *The Pioneers* is influenced by Irving's episodic technique, the borrowing of many specific devices from Scott, and the overall narrative pattern, seem to point to an imitation of the Waverley Novels which had already inspired Cooper's second novel, *The Spy*, and which had largely contributed to its success.[7] Where in *Waverley* we find a novel structured by the political and geographical opposition of the Highland clans (standing for Catholicism, Feudalism, Idealism, Chivalry and Romance) and the Lowland British (standing for Protestantism, Democracy, Pragmatism and Reason), in *The Spy* we find a novel similarly structured by the opposition of the Continental Rebels and the British Loyalists in the War of Independence. In both novels there is the same wavering hero: in *Waverley*, it is Edmund Waverley who journeys through the Highlands and learns to distrust his own romantic enthusiasm and to appreciate the sober merits of the new democratic order; in *The Spy* it is Harvey Birch, 'the spy of the neutral ground', who explores the relative merits of opposing political systems and tries to enable some kind of synthesis out of the fratricidal strife of historical change.[8]

In *The Pioneers*, Cooper still seems to be working with the structure of *Waverley* in mind. Oliver Edwards, the grandson of the ex-propriated loyalist, Major Effingham, is destined to marry Elizabeth Temple, daughter of a man whom some consider a wartime profiteer and expropriator of the Effinghams, so that the divisions of war will be annulled and the expropriated property can be returned to the rightful heir, without, of course, leaving the hands of the expropri-ators. (As we will see, a similar plot is to be found in Hawthorne's *House of the Seven Gables*.) It is unfortunate, however, that whilst for Scott the opposition between reason and romance, democracy and aristocracy, is still potent, for Cooper the issue of loyalism versus independence has been long decided and cannot provide sufficient motivation for his fiction. As a result Oliver has no real 'neutral ground' to negotiate and performs an ungainly series of movements into and out of the Temple mansion which are more interesting as pointers to Cooper's difficulties with the Scott model of historical progress than as comparisons of different political systems. The significant tension in the novel is in the different attitudes of Judge Temple and Richard Jones towards the land, and in the conflict with Natty Bumppo that emerges in the last twenty chapters, not in the attempt to restore the lands to the Effinghams. As might be expected of a culture engaged in rapid territorial expansion, it is rights of ownership and questions of how best to profit from land use that generate the most interest, not, as with Scott, the relationship of the gentry to their past in an epoch of rapid industrialisation.

The transformation of Scott's historical model to North American conditions can be made clearer by three simple schemas. In *Waverley* we have:

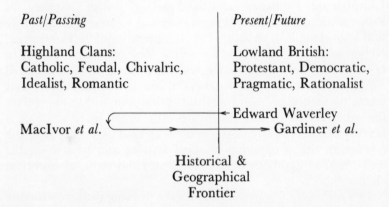

Past/Passing	*Present/Future*
Highland Clans:	Lowland British:
Catholic, Feudal, Chivalric,	Protestant, Democratic,
Idealist, Romantic	Pragmatic, Rationalist

MacIvor *et al.* ← Edward Waverley
→ Gardiner *et al.*

Historical &
Geographical
Frontier

This would seem to have been the model for the Effingham plot in which Edward Waverley's exploration of the relative merits of old and new orders becomes Oliver Edwards' too rapid negotiation of the revolutionary divide:

Past	*Present/Future*
British colonial loyalism	United States
Effingham, Natty, Mohegan	Temple, Jones, Kirby
Edwards ──────→	──────→ Elizabeth

As *The Pioneers* evolves it becomes apparent that this scheme can carry no force, partly because the issue is no longer pertinent, and partly for a complex of biographical and ideological reasons that we shall shortly explore. It is progressively displaced by the following:

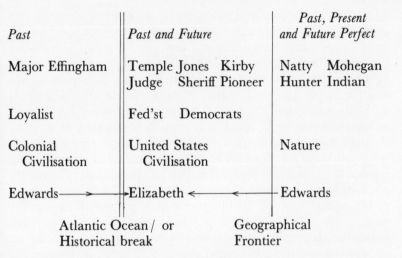

Past	Past and Future	Past, Present and Future Perfect
Major Effingham	Temple Jones Kirby Judge Sheriff Pioneer	Natty Mohegan Hunter Indian
Loyalist	Fed'st Democrats	
Colonial Civilisation	United States Civilisation	Nature
Edwards——→	→Elizabeth ←	←Edwards

Atlantic Ocean / or Historical break   Geographical Frontier

This third schema, which distributes the characters according to their relationship to land and 'civilisation' rather than to the historical past, is the one which emerges through the process of writing, disrupting the Effingham plot, relegating Edwards to a minor role and bringing his loyal bondsman, Natty Bumppo, into heroic relief. In part, this disruption is caused by the recognition that there were two temporal divides in United States experience during the early national period, the divide between the British colonial past and the post-revolutionary United States, and the divide between the United States and the surviving Indian nations to the west. Whilst the former divide is strictly between past and present, the latter divide, 'the frontier', is historically ambivalent since in one sense nature is the continental past, and in another it is its future perfect, the 'will have been' of conquest. It would be naive, however, to think that Cooper's discovery of this geographical frontier arises directly out of his materials. In Cooperstown, as elsewhere in the United States, there was a process of settlement which involved a change in land use but there was no finite line on the one side of which there was culture and on the other side of which there was nature. Only in the mind did this frontier come into existence, a finite opposition between mythical terms (nature/ savagery versus civilisation) which, as has been suggested above, by their very semantic mobility could reduce the contradictions of historical experience to a manageable antithesis.[9]

As *The Pioneers* evolves we can examine the genesis of this opposition. The first picture we have of Templeton is of a half-finished township, built in incongruous architectural styles among the stumps of the surrounding forests. It is only gradually that the cabin of Natty and Indian John begins to symbolise an alternative relationship to the land, standing for a certain kind of natural authenticity against the 'wasty ways' and arbitrary laws of the pioneer community. Indeed, it is only three-quarters of the way through the novel that we learn that the cabin is situated on the other side of the lake from the township and that it then becomes the symbol of a way of life opposed to that of 'civilisation'. The binary opposition is thus not a premise with which Cooper begins, but rather a mythological dichotomy that is produced during the writing in order to resolve problems that the act of writing engenders. Central to these problems is the attempt to combine various characteristics of Cooper's father and father-in-law into the portrait of an ideal founder and patriarch of a pioneer community, a man whose merits will provide an imaginary origin and legitimacy for the colonisation of Indian lands, and a man whose learning and culture will be more in keeping with the social needs of the son than the untutored father who actually established Cooperstown.[10] The project fails because the history that biographical modelling brings along with it consistently ruptures the bounds of the projected ideal, thereby widening the problem it was intended to foreclose. It is therefore necessary to split off the ideal from the character who was supposed to bear it and attach it to a person of no status, virtually an absence, the antiquated faithful servant, Nathaniel Bumppo. By the end of the novel this improbable creature has become the hero of nature and innocence and stands in direct contrast with the Judge who has hypocritically abused the very law that is supposed to mark the white man out as superior to the savage.

The first step in transforming Judge William Cooper into Judge Marmaduke Temple is to give Judge Temple the social position Judge Cooper occupied in real life, but to give him the kind of education that James Fenimore actually received. In becoming Judge Temple, James Fenimore's father is thus transformed from the rough-neck pioneer proprietor who, like Billy Kirby, settled disagreements by wrestling with opponents, into the polished equal of the landed gentry of New York State into which Cooper had married. Cooper's real father, Judge William, has therefore to be moved back one generation to become Marmaduke's father, the man who 'began to reascend the scale of society' and who furnished Marmaduke with a better education 'than had been the practice in the family, for two or three preceeding generations'(18).[11] The second step in transforming Cooper into Temple is to make the Temple dynasty originate in seventeenth-century gentlemanly wealth by attaching it to aspects of De Lancey family history. The first sentence of Chapter Two reads, 'an ancestor of Marmaduke Temple had, about one hundred and twenty years before the commencement of our tale, come to the colony of Pennsylvania, a friend and co-religionist of its great patron' (17). Deducting 120 from 1783 produces 1663 which, as Cooper was well aware, was the year in which the first De Lancey, Stephen, arrived in New York.[12] Thus the Pennsylvania Quaker origins of William Cooper are condensed with the New York origins of the De Lanceys' to begin a Temple family history which will evolve through decline into poverty, the reascent of the social scale by Marmaduke's father, and the complete restoration of proper station through friendship with the Effinghams, an established loyalist family transparently modelled on the De Lanceys. We thus observe that the characterisation of Judge Temple condenses Cooper and De Lancey history in order to provide the Cooper family with imaginary origins in the established ruling class of colonial New York. The effect of this condensation is to cast a mystique of aristocratic inheritance over the real origins of the Cooper family wealth, especially since the aspect of Cooper history most conspicuously de-emphasised by this condensation is William Cooper's activity as a salesman of frontier lands. According to the Effingham plot, Temple bought his friend's lands during the War of Independence and, unbeknownst to the Effinghams' and notwithstanding their suspicion that he is a thief, has merely acted as their trustee in developing them in the intervening years.

Clearly this is a way of admitting William Cooper's underhand purchase of the Croghan patent in 1785 and of providing an entirely imaginary restitution of the lands to his, and to his creditors', heirs.[13] When we recall that Croghan built a log cabin on the Otsego Lake in 1769 and then perceive that in *The Pioneers* this log cabin is occupied by Natty Bumppo, Indian John and Oliver Edwards/Effingham, we can see the extent to which the effacement of Croghan, and thus the denial of history, is the basic activity of the novel. In the novel the place which Croghan actually occupied is filled by Indian John, a ghostly relic of the Indians who once owned the land; by Edwards, the heir of colonial proprietorship; and by

Natty who initially represents a nostalgia for the imaginary honesty of the aristocratic loyalist past.[14]

Each time any of these characters appears in the novel it is to question the rights of Marmaduke Temple to the land, his rights to legislate for its use, or the manner in which the pioneers are wasting its natural abundance. Indian John and Natty frequently point out that the land has been taken from the Indians by force and that any law that Temple promulgates is a morally hypocritical act designed only to protect his own economic interests. Neither of these characters, however, alludes to more than a generalised expropriation of red by white, and Indian John is always rather pathetically remarking that because Temple is just he will one day give the lands back to the Indians. Oliver Edwards presents a more potent threat to the denial of real conditions for he can point to Temple's (William Cooper's) specific activities and he therefore has to be recuperated by being shot, then by being included in the family, after which he must be content to swallow his words and glower angrily at the imaginary father.

The strain of confining Oliver to no more than a token admission of William Cooper's expropriation of Croghan is one of the factors that prevents the Effingham plot from becoming the dominant structure in the novel. Whenever Oliver is being described there is always a risk that the truth will come out, as in the following scene in which the expropriation both of the Indians and of Croghan become so intertwined as to launch the idea of Oliver being half-Delaware into the novel. Indian John is talking to the Reverend Grant and his daughter Louisa:

> "Father, you are not yet past the summer of life; your limbs are young. Go to the highest hill, and look around you. All that you see from the headwaters of the great spring to where the [Susquehannah] is hid by the hills, is [Delaware]. He has Delaware blood, and his right is strong. But the brother of Miquon [Temple, 'brother' of William Penn] is just: he will cut the country in two parts, as the river cuts the lowlands, and will say to the 'Young Eagle,' Child of the Delawares! Take it – keep it – and be a chief in the land of your fathers."
>
> "Never!" exclaimed the young hunter . . . "The wolf of the forest is not more rapacious for his prey, than that man is greedy of gold; and yet his glidings into wealth are subtle as the movements of a serpent."

"Forbear, forbear, my son, forbear," interrupted Mr. Grant. "These angry passions must be subdued. The accidental injury you have received from Judge Temple has heightened the sense of your hereditary wrongs. But remember that the one was unintentional, and that the other is the effect of political changes, which have, in their course, greatly lowered the pride of kings, and swept mighty nations from the face of the earth. . . . The sin of the wrongs which have been done to the natives is shared by Judge Temple only in common with a whole people, and your arm will speedily be restored to its strength."

"This arm!" repeated the youth, pacing the floor in violent agitation. "Think you, sir, that I believe the man a murderer? Oh, no! He is too wily, too cowardly for such a crime. But let him and his daughter riot in their wealth – a day of retribution will come. No, no, no," he continued, as he trod the floor more calmly – "it is for Mohegan to suspect him of an intent to injure me, but the trifle is not worth a second thought."

He seated himself and hid his face between his hands, as they rested on his knees.

"It is the hereditary violence of a native's passion my child," said Mr. Grant in a low tone, to his affrighted daughter, who was clinging in terror to his arm. "He is mixed with the blood of the Indians, you have heard . . ." (138–9)

Up to this point in the narrative no mention has been made of Oliver Edwards' being in fact Oliver Effingham (and we will have to wait another twenty-eight chapters for the relationship to be explained) so this sudden outburst against Judge Temple is contextually incomprehensible. Far from expressing surprise or questioning the young man, however, Reverend Grant acknowledges that Oliver's grievance comes as much from 'hereditary wrongs' as from his recent injury. He then quickly goes on to limit the meaning of 'hereditary wrongs' by presuming Oliver was speaking on behalf of the Indians. In the ensuing paragraphs Grant deduces from Oliver's sympathy that he has Indian blood in his veins, a suggestion which again breaks verisimilitude since until this point Oliver has been characterised as obviously high born. These ruptures in verisimilitude indicate that throughout the exchange Cooper is struggling to find a way of dealing with the claims of both Indian John and Oliver Edwards. His answer to the problem is to launch a theme of miscegenation which will thereafter undermine any attempt by Oliver (Croghan's ghost) to point out that frontier experience really entailed the expropriation of whites by whites, as much as it entailed expropriation of the Indians.

The logic of this attempted containment, and the denial of historical experience which is its motive, is repeated throughout the Leatherstocking Tales because of the ideological need to maintain that there is something intrinsically superior in white civilisation and that this 'something' justifies the destruction of the Indians. As several scholars have shown, the mythological opposition of savagery to civilisation was essential to all explanations of United States progress in the nineteenth century, and even to the concept of the American character.[15] The abstract opposition of savagery and civilisation easily supports the idea of an ineluctable and divinely ordained mission to expand the 'area of freedom' across the continent, but it can hardly be maintained with confidence when the 'area of freedom' is seen to be created by men like Temple, 'greedy of gold' and ready to steal from their friends with the same equanimity as they expropriate the Indian. Much of the action of the *The Pioneers*, and many of the moral debates between its characters, can be seen as conditioned by Cooper's contradictory impulse to admit and yet obscure such facts whilst promulgating a concept of 'civilisation' which will provide sufficient justification for continental conquest.

It is towards the end of the first volume that Cooper completes the logically incredible move of Edwards into the household of his arch-enemy and thus contains the problematic knowledge of the Croghan expropriation behind the figure of the imaginary father who has been invented for the purposes of this denial. The field is then cleared for the scenes and debates for which the novel is usually remembered – the arguments about the rights to the land and the proper use thereof, the night fishing scene and the pigeon shoot. It is in Chapter Nineteen that Edwards takes off his leather-stockings and resumes station as a gentleman. It is in the next chapter that the Temples, Edwards and Richard Jones go for a forest ride and encounter Billy Kirby making sugar from the sap of the maple trees. With the distracting Edwards/Effingham theme contained for the moment in the glowering youth at Temple's side, the growing anxiety about the wasteful abuse of natural resources can be brought to much stronger focus than has so far been possible. The sub-textual rationale of all these manoeuvres is, as we shall come to see, the growth of Cooper's own anxiety about the legitimacy of his own social position and the credibility of ideological justifications for the existence of the United States.[16]

In characteristic vein Marmaduke Temple says to Billy Kirby:

"It grieves me to witness the extravagance that pervades this country," said the Judge, "where the settlers trifle with the blessings they might enjoy, with the prodigality of successful adventurers. You are not exempt from the censure yourself, Kirby, for you make dreadful wounds in these trees where a small incision would effect the same object. I earnestly beg you will remember, that they are the growth of centuries, and when once gone, none living will see their loss remedied."

"Why, I don't know, Judge," returned the man he addressed: "it seems to me, if there's plenty of anything in this mountainous country, it's the trees. If there's any sin in chopping them, I've a pretty heavy account to settle; for I've chopped over the best of half a thousand acres, with my own hands, counting both Varmont and New York states; and I hope to live to finish the whull, before I lay up my ax. Chopping comes quite natural to me, and I wish no other employment; but Jared Ransom said that he thought the sugar was likely to be scurce this season, seeing that so many folks was coming into the settlement, and so I concluded to take the 'bush' on sheares, for this one spring. What's the best news, Judge, consarning ashes? Do pots hold so that a man can live by them still? I s'pose they will, if they keep on fighting across the water."

"Thou reasonest with judgement, William," returned Marmaduke. "So long as the old world is to be convulsed with wars, so long will the harvest of America continue." (232)

Temple's appeal to Kirby to have a greater sense of his historical responsibility towards nature reveals the economic basis of many of Cooper's ambiguous attitudes towards historical consciousness. Cooper devoted his life to the production of historical fiction partly because he recognised that the nation needed stories of its origins in order to define its present and future constitution. But as this implies, Cooper also wanted a richer historical sense because he believed that it would foster a conservative respect for established social class and a conservationist respect for natural resources. Kirby, however, stands for the new Democratic man, the day-labourer whose social integration is assured only by his place in the

cash nexus. He is interested in little beyond his earnings and thus
becomes a sort of human locust who will eat up America's natural
abundance with no other motivation than that of personal want.
Here, appearing under the guise of the pioneer, Kirby represents an
attitude which Cooper evidently detested since he was to return to a
similar characterisation in Ishmael Bush in *The Prairie* and Hurry
Harry in *The Deerslayer*. Each of these characters is concerned to
transform nature into cash without any higher consciousness of the
moral problems involved in the conquest or of the goals it is
supposed to achieve. They represent, in other words, the generality
of the people who have little interest in the rhetoric of the conquest
because they are too enmeshed in its brute activities to conform to
the image of 'civilisation' that is supposed to justify the process.

The point of view from which Temple reproaches Billy Kirby
derives from the Federalist and De Lancey side of Cooper's
sympathies, but there is another side, perhaps furnished by respect
for his father's energetic achievement, that can also come into play.
Kirby's abruptly inconsequential question: 'Do pots hold so that a
man can live by them still?' is sufficient to shift Temple out of his role
as patronising landlord and make him adopt first name terms:
'Thou reasonest with judgement, William', Marmaduke replies. 'So
long as the old world is convulsed with wars so long will the harvest
of America continue.'

Behind this discreet shifting of the moral burden for the
destruction of American nature on to the wars of the old world is the
potent recollection that in *A Guide in the Wilderness* Judge William
Cooper had explained how the sale of potashes made by burning the
forests was a major financial inducement to settlers on the Otsego
patent.[17] It is therefore conceivable that Temple's sudden shift from
'Kirby' to 'William' is more the sign of subliminal recollection of
real experiences than a move towards egalitarian sympathy with
Kirby's need to make a living. Whether the word 'William' has this
significance or not, the idealised landed-gentleman-father is mom-
entarily deflated by the recognition that the harvesting of the
wilderness is necessary if the United States is to develop its national
economy. Temple's movement towards this more Democratic
position, however, does not last for long. No sooner has he admitted
the economic necessity than he returns to 'the consoling reflection
[that] the hour approaches when the laws will take notice of not only
the woods, but the game they contain also' (233).

If we follow the narrative events closely from this point onwards we can observe how Natty moves from minor to major status in Cooper's imagination. In the next chapter, Chapter Twenty-One, Temple tries to justify his ownership of the land by reference to the pain, famine, and disease he suffered in the course of settlement, and by pointing out that his paternalist generosity to the settlers had made the earth bring forth fruit and multiply, a standard white justification for conquest.[18] His disquisition on his own merits leads to his relating the story of his first meeting with Natty on Otsego Lake, and of Natty's hostility to the proposed settlement. Here Edwards interposes, 'said he nothing of the Indian rights, sir? The Leatherstocking is much given to impeach the justice of the tenure by which the whites hold the country'. Temple replies, 'I remember that he spoke of them, but I did not clearly comprehend him and may have forgotten what he said . . .'.

Cooper is at a logical impasse and so resorts to the scare of a falling tree to move the narrative forward. In the next chapters, those concerned with the pigeon shoot and the night fishing, the same conflict recurs between Temple who wants the 'wilderness' to be conserved as a future resource, and Jones who expresses the need to press on with its exploitation. The pigeon shoot contrasts the high-mindedness of the Judge with the idiocy of the populace who indulge in wanton slaughter with cannon and musket. The Judge's position is reinforced by Natty who proposes that one should kill no more than one can immediately eat, but neither the Judge nor Natty is able to address the substantial issue that the pigeons are a source of food which, salted away, will keep the pioneers nourished through the spring.

The same opposition is elaborated in the night fishing. The chapter opens with Temple favouring the catching of the famed Otsego bass with rod and line, whereas Jones favours the seine net. Temple's way of fishing is solitary, genteel, leisured, done for pleasure not out of necessity. Jones's method is communal, democratic, done as much in order to eat as to enjoy collective activity. In constructing this opposition, Cooper again casts Temple as a conservationist, but also as an uncaring snob. To him the seine net results in a 'fearful expenditure of the choicest gifts of Providence' (265) because the poor then waste a food fit for princes. The implication is that the prodigal lower orders need men such as Temple to impose civilising legal restraints if they are not to turn the wilderness into a desert. Jones again voices the Democratic faith that natural resources should be used for the greatest good of the greatest number, and further brings out the veiled politics of Temple's stance:

> But this is always the way with you, Marmaduke; first it's the trees, then it's the deer, after that it's the maple sugar, and so on to the end of the chapter. One day you talk of canals through a country because the water won't run the way you wish it to go; and the next, you say something about mines of coal, though any man who has good eyes like myself – I say with good eyes – can see more wood than would keep the city of London in fuel for fifty years. (266)

Temple is thus placed as a National Republican or Whig who wants to slow the harvesting of natural abundance until more capital-intensive means can be developed to maximise the economic yield and the profits of the élite.[19] The starkness of the opposition at this point may signify Cooper's movement to the Democratic cause, but the narrative importance of Temple's rebuttal by Jones is that it leaves the spokesman of law, historical consciousness and civilised social refinement confronting the inadequacy of his own ideology. In terms of the novel's attempt to establish a materially effective code of 'civilisation', and a system of values which will legitimise white ownership of expropriated land, this exposure has profound consequences. It leaves Cooper with no explanation of settler proprietorship higher than acquisitiveness.

As if in response to Temple's inadequacy, Natty now appears out of the darkness, catching fish with spear and flame, and providing a wish-fulfilling image of harmony with nature that effectively displaces Temple's desire to catch fish with rod and line back into pre-history.[20] Natty scorns Temple's offer of net-caught fish because it is 'sinful and wasty to catch more than can be eat' (272), and refuses to agree with the Judge that if the settlers used a net of half the size matters would be in any way improved. To Natty, Temple's conservationist laws are just so much temporisation with settler ways and cannot provide a radical cure. For that, it would be necessary to abolish history and economy and return to 'wilderness' ways in which there would be no community, no pastures, no laws, no sowing, harvesting, nor storage against the winter. (Such an abolition would of course involve not the going back to pre-conquest times as Natty implies, but the movement out of history into myth. Any student of aboriginal history, Cooper included, could have pointed to Indian laws, sowing, harvesting and storage.)

Observing this confrontation between Natty and the Judge, Richard Jones is quick to intervene. He announces that they make a 'very pretty confederacy', and points out the incongruity of 'Judge Temple, the landlord and owner of a township, with Nathaniel Bumppo, a lawless squatter and professed deer killer, in order to preserve the game of the country' (273).[21] Like so many sentences in Cooper this needs to be understood predictively rather than retrospectively, the sign of fantasy rather than accumulated rational logic. Up to this point Natty has given no evidence of lawlessness and has killed no deer out of season so Jones is not describing events as they have occurred but effecting the recognition that Temple and Natty are conceptually intimate and, in the same instant, discovering the means of forcing them apart: in the ensuing narrative it is precisely these qualities announced by Jones, Natty's lawless deer killing and the imposition of white hunting laws upon 'nature', which will be used to liquidate the problem of Natty's 'squatter' rights to the land. In being victimised in this manner, Natty will suffer a fate exactly parallel to that of the many poor white pioneers who found the land they had improved taken from them by the lawful trickery of large land speculators, and equally that of the Indians who discovered that the passing of a 'law' by distant and alien powers could remove their right to live on the land of their forefathers (the Cherokee, for example).[22] The novel translates this logic of everyday life into a moral drama in which Natty's high-minded but voluntaristic response to nature (he kills when he wants but his desires are always just) will be repressed so that the low-minded voluntarism of the pioneers (who kill unjustly when they want) can be kept in 'civilised' bounds. In this moral drama the law becomes a frontier of censorship between desire and fulfilment that has the obvious practical function of organising social existence, and the deeper ideological function of distinguishing the civilised from the savage condition. As Temple advises his daughter when explaining his harsh sentence upon Natty, 'try to remember, Elizabeth, that the laws alone remove us from the condition of the savages; that he has been a criminal, and that his judge was thy father' (397).

It is in moving from the perception (attributed to Richard Jones) of a fundamental sympathy between Natty and the Judge to this state of alienation that we see the cause of Leatherstocking's mythologisation. When Judge Temple declares Natty a criminal, and exacts an impossible fine in order to squeeze from him the secret of the rumoured silver mine, he abandons the moral self-awareness that troubled his conscience about his rights to the land and declares himself in favour of repression and the arbitrary use of the law for personal gain. He thus relieves the anxiety that has so far undermined his confidence by admitting the law's material and historical function as an instrument of theft. Conveniently, his only interlocutor is Elizabeth, his daughter, and the creature of naive sentiment, and she must keep dutiful silence, pressing her '*pocketbook*' to her bosom. Since, in the very act of judging in the name of the law, Temple has exposed the law's real functions, the moral conscience which he has previously symbolised must be transferred to Natty who will henceforth fulfil the wish that there should be some ethical justification for the white man's occupation of the land, however fugitive. In effect, what happens in the trial scene is the sundering of moral superiority from any credible social-material bearer and its projection on to a figure who stands half way between the whites and those people who have the only possible claim to innocence in the history of the conquest, the North American Indians.

The remainder of the novel occurs in the de-realised geography of spectacular event which will come to seem characteristic of the Leatherstocking Tales. For all its drama its function is to close the space of guilt created by Temple's (Cooper's) expropriation of Effingham (Croghan/Indians) by providing an imaginary restitution of the ill-gotten gains to Oliver Edwards/Effingham, the descendant of a man accepted into the Mohegan tribe.[23] Even in the realm of the imaginary, the land remains in the Temple line of descent, so in order to preserve the fragile status of this restitution the voices of conscience must be expelled or die. Indian John dies, whilst Natty effects the condensation of the now rootless signified of white moral superiority with those qualities by means of which the white psyche de-realises the North American Indian: he burns down his house and becomes a nomad in the wilderness, a propertyless, illiterate (i.e. cultureless) child of the forest, a noble white civilised savage. Necessarily opposed to the civilisation whose contradictions have given him birth, he comes to provide an alibi for the conquest by virtue of the fact that his supposed innocence and nobility represent the true communion with nature, whilst in fact they conceal the violence of an unjustifiable expropriation. As the inverse image of Billy Kirby, the true pioneer, he denies what white men are in reality by abolishing history, economy and political belief. He is thus able to resolve the contradiction between white men's possession of stolen land and their desire to believe themselves morally redeemed. He becomes the honest, innocent, non-exploitative American, living in harmony with the natural, and going into the West to conquer with the best will in the world.

4.2 *THE LAST OF THE MOHICANS:* THE LAST OF THE IROQUOIS

That neither the United States nor any individual state, has taken possession of any land that, by usage or construction, might be declared the property of the Indians, without a treaty and a purchase is, I believe, certain.[24]

In *The Pioneers*, Cooper says that Indian John is a Mohegan, that he is the sole descendant of the original inhabitants of the Otsego Lake, and that it was the Mohegans who ceded the land to the Effinghams.[25] Allowing that Effingham is in part a fictional substitute for Croghan, this is again a curious rearrangement of history, for Croghan received his Otsego patent by way of the Treaty of Fort Stanwix of 1768 which Sir William Johnson concluded with the Iroquois. The Otsego was a Mohawk hunting ground. It had never belonged to the Mohegans, a Connecticut tribe who by 1700 were broken, scattered and largely forgotten. Cooper's desire to attribute ownership to the Mohegans, and his resurrection of Indian John as the type of noble savage in his next Leatherstocking Tale, would therefore seem to bear investigation.

In 1926 Gregory Lansing Paine established that Cooper derived most of his knowledge of Indian tribes from John G. Heckewelder's *An Account of the History, Manners and Customs of the Indian Nations*.[26] It was in this work that Cooper discovered the paradigmatic opposition of noble Delawares and ignoble Iroquois which structures the four Leatherstocking Tales he set in New York State. Heckewelder was a Moravian missionary who had lived with the Delaware for long periods between 1762 and 1786 and held them in high regard. For this reason his *History* represents Indian experience from the Delaware point of view, relating in particular how the Delaware had been the proudest and most civilised of Indian nations until their northern neighbours, the Iroquois (Mengwe, in the Delaware tongue), tricked them into laying down their arms and accepting the subordinate status of 'women'. In the 1826 Preface to *The Last of the Mohicans* Cooper takes up this story and tells the reader that

> There is a well-authenticated and disgraceful history of the means by which the Dutch on one side, and the Mengwe on the other, succeeded in persuading the Lenape to lay aside their arms, trusting their defence entirely to the latter, and becoming, in short, in the figurative language of the natives, "women" . . . From that moment may be dated the downfall of the greatest and most civilised of the Indian nations, that existed within the limits of the present United States.[27]

It was this story of the innocent Delaware having been tricked into military impotence by a conspiracy of the Dutch and Iroquois that licensed Cooper's representation of the Delaware as noble allies of the Anglo-American whites and allowed him to contrast Delaware nobility with the treacherous savagery of their ancestral enemies, the Iroquois. In fact Heckewelder's *History* was an inversion of the historical truth. All contemporaneous and subsequent accounts agree that the Iroquois conquered the Delaware in warfare during the sixteenth and seventeenth centuries when they were consolidating their dominion over neighbouring tribes. It was the Six Nations of the Iroquois (the Seneca, Cayuga, Onondaga, Oneida, Mohawk, and, from 1711, the Tuscarora) which constituted 'the greatest and most civilised of Indian nations' for through their superior military, political and agricultural development they were able to establish an Indian empire centred upon the southern shores of Lake Ontario.[28]

For Gregory Lansing Paine, as for most subsequent critics, Cooper's inversion of this history has required no more elaborate explanation than that Heckewelder's work had been published and favourably reviewed shortly before Cooper began writing his novels.[29] However, this explanation encounters several difficulties when it is noticed that the publication of *The Last of the Mohicans* touched off a concerted attack on both Heckewelder's *History* and Cooper's adoption of it. In 1826 the most respected journal of the day pointed out that Heckewelder had related the Delaware legend of Iroquois trickery 'with all the gravity of history' when it was known to be 'utterly irreconcilable with the most authentic accounts, . . . and with well known circumstances'.[30] The same review made passing criticism of Cooper's adoption of Heckewelder and referred the reader to other works which gave the generally respected account. Of particular significance is that one of these works had been written by an associate of Cooper, De Witt Clinton, the Governor of New York State, under whom Cooper served as a Colonel in the state militia in 1823 and from whom he was to receive a letter of recommendation when he applied to become United States Consul in Lyons in 1826. In 1814 Clinton had published an essay on the Iroquois which is one of the most detailed and accurate studies of their history and customs to appear before the modern period, and which would certainly have corrected Heckewelder's erroneous view.[31] Since Clinton's authoritative knowledge was available to Cooper we can only conclude that his reliance upon Heckewelder was not a matter of necessity, but an act of choice determined by the desire to transpose historical experience into Heckewelder's inverted mythological frame. As Cooper was committed at this stage in his career to the convention that the historical novel should be 'true' to its historical materials, and as the transformation of history into myth can only be achieved by violating the historical record, we can expect to find in his texts both instances of distortion and attempts to cover the traces of the deed.[32]

In the 1826 Preface to *The Last of the Mohicans* there is evidence of these contradictory intentions. On the one hand there are implied claims to historical veracity, and on the other there are preparations for the distortions which are to come. Through the subtitle, 'A Narrative of 1757', and the prefatorial remark that the reader who picks up the book expecting 'an imaginary and romantic picture of things . . . will probably lay it aside disappointed',[33] the author implies that his work will be faithful to the historical events it intends to recast in fictional form. The particular event which Cooper chose for his pre-text was a famous massacre of the French and Indian wars. In 1757 a British-American force commanded by Colonel Munro was invested in Fort William Henry at the southern end of Lake George by the French under Montcalm. Having been persuaded to surrender under guarantee of safe conduct, Munro led his troops from the fort, but the baggage train was attacked by Montcalm's Indian allies and many of the wounded and accompanying women were killed. Cooper's novel consists of two parallel captivity narratives, the first of which culminates in this massacre, the second of which proceeds from it. The novel begins improbably enough with Cora and Alice Munro leaving the safety of the southerly Fort Edward and journeying north to join their father in the threatened Fort William Henry. Ignoring the protection offered by a body of troops who are taking the wagon road, they plunge into the wilderness with Major Duncan Heyward as escort and Magua as Indian guide. Magua is a Mohawk who had once been flogged by Colonel Munro for drunkenness and then exiled among the Hurons, allies of the French.[34] However, he has recently returned to the British and, again improbably, is entrusted with this delicate mission. When the party meets Hawk-eye, Chingachgook and Uncas they quickly divine Magua's treacherous intentions, but Magua captures the girls and makes for the Huron camp. Hawk-eye and the Delaware/Mohicans manage to rescue the girls and take them to Fort William Henry, but in the confusion of the massacre they are again captured. The second narrative begins at this point, the girls being taken to the Huron camp whilst Hawk-eye and his companions track them through the wilderness. Finding that Cora has been transferred to a neighbouring group of Delawares, Uncas is able to enlist their support and succeeds in saving Alice. Magua, however, murders both Cora and Uncas before being shot by Hawk-eye.

As became an historical novelist, Cooper researched the history of the Battle of Fort William Henry with some thoroughness. One literary historian who has examined this aspect of the novel has concluded that Cooper is not only faithful to 'the main lines of the campaign but to many of the minutiae as well'.[35] However, as far as Indian history is concerned, Cooper was not so scrupulous. Because he maintains that the Delawares are 'good' and the Iroquois are 'bad', he tries to give the impression that Montcalm was supported at Fort William Henry by both the Hurons and the Iroquois. This representation runs counter to the historical facts as reported by historians from Cadwallader Colden in the eighteenth century, through Heckewelder and De Witt Clinton, down to modern authorities: all agree that the Iroquois were either pro-British or neutral throughout the eighteenth century.[36]

The weight of history that Cooper is trying to invert perhaps needs emphasis. The association of the Iroquois with British interests may be said to have begun when Champlain entered the St Lawrence in 1603 and formed an alliance with the Hurons who then lived on the northern shore of Lake Ontario. Having been forced out of their original homelands by the Iroquois, the Hurons enlisted French help against them, thereby forcing the Iroquois into alliance with any European power to the south. First the Dutch, then the British, benefited from Iroquois-Huron antagonism, for the Iroquois had vested interests in preventing the French and Hurons moving down Lakes Champlain and George onto the Hudson. In the French and Indian wars this was especially apparent, the Iroquois in general trying to stay out of Franco-British conflict but the Mohawks in particular siding with the British and saving the colonies from a thrust at Lake George in 1755. In the same years the Delaware, who were normally pacific, decided to seize the opportunity of revenging themselves on both the dominant Iroquois and the expansionist British, and joined the French side. Thus, if Cooper's novel was to be basically concordant with the historical record of 1757, it should represent an alliance of the French, the Hurons and the Delawares arrayed against the Iroquois and the British. Since even Heckewelder himself tells us that the Iroquois favoured the British at this time, and that the Delawares had gone over to the French and Hurons, it is evident that Cooper has reversed historical alliances in a manner yet more extreme than that allowed by his principal historical source.[37]

If, as the archetypal school of criticism would have us believe, the mythologist had no other intention than openly to represent his text as the product of his personal desires, then it might have been a simple matter for Cooper to invert historical alliances and represent the Delaware as pro-British, the Iroquois as pro-French. However, as Roland Barthes has argued, mythology is never so innocent: it seeks above all to naturalise its desires in the world of historical experience and to manifest itself as authentic representation. Accordingly, Cooper cannot displace the Iroquois in a manner which will permit ready denial but must move them from an historical to a mythological location by a process which will appear 'natural'.[38]

It is in the Preface that this process of naturalisation begins. Having implied a claim to historical truth and named the principal tribes with which the narrative will be concerned, Cooper explains that

> The greatest difficulty with which the student of Indian history has to contend, is the utter confusion that pervades the names. When, however, it is recollected, that the Dutch, the English, and the French, each took a conqueror's liberty in that particular; that the natives themselves not only speak different languages,

and even dialects of those languages, but that they are also fond of
multiplying their appellations, the difficulty is more a matter of
regret than surprise. It is hoped, that whatever other faults may
exist in the following pages, their obscurity will be thought to
arise from this fact.[39]

The 'difficulty' to which Cooper here refers is that presented by the
fact that 'the Iroquois' may be signified by the signs 'Six Nations',
'Mengwe/Mingo', 'Maquas', as well as 'Iroquois', depending upon
whether the speaker is English, Delaware, Dutch or French.
Similarly, tthe Lenni Lenape were named Delaware by the English,
and the Mohegans were also called Mahiccani, Mahigans and
Mohuccans. Such variations might seem adequate reason for
'confusion' were it not for the fact that all contemporary accounts
list the same variants in the names of the tribes, and since, with one
unimportant exception, this multiplicity of signifiers gives rise to no
confusion about which tribe was being signified, nor about where
they lived and with whom they were allied.[40] In the sketch of Indian
history given in *The Pioneers* and repeated in the 1826 Preface to *The
Last of the Mohicans*, Cooper explains these variants and de-
monstrates that there is no confusion in his own mind about which
sign signifies which tribe. In his text, however, as we will now see,
this multiplicity of signifiers is used to create an 'obscurity' about
Indian history, an obscurity behind which the Iroquois can be
displaced into alliance with the French and Hurons.

The main textual agency of this displacement is the treacherous
double agent, Magua. Having begun life as a Mohawk, become a
Huron, and then returned to the Mohawk as a spy, he is able to
confuse the eye of the reader by obliterating distinctions between
the names of the tribes. Since the name 'Magua' is visually and
phonetically proximate to the Dutch name for Mohawk, 'Maqua',
and since Hawk-eye frequently curses the iniquity of both the
individual 'Magua' (the Huron), and the 'Maquas' (the
Mohawks), his name allows the Iroquois and the Hurons to be
established as allied and equally abominable tribes. One can see this
process at work in the following passage in which Hawk-eye
explains to Major Heyward that his guide, Magua, is probably a
traitor.

"A Huron!" repeated the sturdy scout, once more shaking his
head in open distrust; "they are a thievish race, nor do I care by

whom they are adopted; you can never make any thing of them but skulks and vagabonds. Since you trusted yourself to the care of one of that nation, I can only wonder that you have not fallen in with more."

"Of that there is little danger, since William Henry is so many miles in our front. You forget that I have told you that our guide is now a Mohawk, and that he serves with our forces as a friend."

"And I tell you that he who is born a Mingo will die a Mingo," returned the other, positively. "A Mohawk! No, give me a Delaware or a Mohican for honesty; and when they will fight, which they won't all do, having suffered their cunning enemies, the Maquas, to make them women – but when they will fight at all, look to a Delaware or a Mohican for a warrior!" (35)

Here, by implication, Hurons become condensed into the same entity as Maquas, Mingoes and Mohawks and contrasted with the superior virtue of the Delawares and Mohicans. If we follow the process of condensation through the first part of the novel we notice that in Chapter Eight the hostile Indians are called Mingoes, Hurons, Maquas and then Hurons again. In Chapters Nine, Ten and Eleven we have the double agent Magua leading a band of Hurons, then, in Chapter Twelve, Hawk-eye appears shouting 'no quarter to the accursed Mingo' and the same hostile Indians are successively referred to as Hurons, Maquas, and Iroquois. The effect of these displacements is to give the impression that the British are fighting an alliance of the Iroquois, the Hurons and the French at an historical moment when the Iroquois were actually on the British side. The principal means of the displacement of the Iroquois is the transformation g/q in Magua/Maqua, a transformation which allows the signifieds of 'Hurons', 'Magua' and 'Maquas-Mingoes-Iroquois' to be condensed into one term, meaning 'hostile Indian allies of the French', when the historical referents of these signs are known to have been long-standing enemies.

Once one has noticed this process of condensation and displacement it is possible to suggest certain conclusions. Firstly, Cooper's assertion that the names of the Indian tribes are 'confused' and his hope that any 'obscurity' in the novel will be 'thought to arise from this fact' is not the result of 'confusion' but is the consequence of the imagination at work in his writing of fiction. The unexplained but logical shifting of names would seem to confirm that Cooper knew how the Indian nations stood in their actual historical relations and that he wished to erase historical distinctions by changing the Iroquois from friendly into hostile Indians. Since the process by which the change is achieved resembles the work of condensation found in dreams, it seems valid to suggest that the text of *The Last of the Mohicans* is heavily determined by an unconscious desire to invert historical relations. As Freud pointed out, 'turning a thing into its opposite, is one of the means of representation most favoured by the dream-work . . . It serves to give expression to the fulfilment of a wish . . . "if only it had been the other way around"'. The suggestion that the displacement of the Iroquois is achieved by a process which resembles the dream-work may be given support by recalling that the novel was conceived when Cooper was suffering from a fever, that Chapter Twelve was first drafted as notes of a waking-dream, and that contemporary and modern critics have noticed the novel's feverish and obsessive characteristics.[41]

It is not hard to find a superficial reason why Cooper should have wished to represent the Iroquois as the enemies of British America. During the War of Independence most of the Iroquois Nations remained loyal to the British and launched a series of bloody attacks on upper New York State before being destroyed by the American forces. At the time Cooper was writing it may thus have seemed more agreeable to represent the Iroquois as having been in 1757 the enemies they were to become in 1779. But any such desire would have run counter to the commitment to historical accuracy exemplified in Cooper's detailed research of the Battle of Fort William Henry. Since there is no reason to suppose that this commitment was shallow, we need a more profound explanation for the conflict between the desire to accord with history, and the desire to displace the Iroquois.

Evidently the beginnings of such as explanation consist in Cooper's awareness that his father had made the family fortune by selling lands that had once belonged to the Iroquois. This awareness was doubtless enriched by the knowledge that the Iroquois were a settled and cultured people whose granaries, orchards and homesteads had been systematically destroyed on Washington's orders only a few years before the author was born. In Cooperstown, during the author's lifetime, there was the evidence of Indian artefacts regularly turned up by the plough, Indian burial mounds and Indian apple orchards, the latter phenomenon being in itself quite sufficient to make it impossible to naively accept that United States continental expansion consisted simply in the displacement of a savage nomadism by a superior civilisation.[42]

To have written a thoroughly accurate history of the year 1757 would have involved representing the Iroquois as a settled agricultural and arboricultural people, as a people with sufficient political development to be treated as a nation by the British, and as the loyal defenders of British America against French attack. Such a representation would obviously have entailed quite convoluted agruments about the legitimacy of United States expansion. It would therefore seem probable that Cooper's representation of the Iroquois as the most savage of Indians, and his tendency to displace them into allies of the French and Hurons, results from two factors: from the need to repress knowledge of their cultural attainments so that the ideology of expansion may remain unquestioned, and from the desire to remove them from their homelands so that the patriarchal estate would appear to have been a wilderness before the arrival of the white man.

There is one striking and perturbing scene in the novel which, when analysed and restored to its historical context, provides concrete exemplification of this latter desire. Between the two narratives of captivity and release which comprise the novel there is an interlude in which Colonel Munro, Hawk-eye, Uncas, Chingachgook, and Major Heyward return to the corpse-strewn ruins of Fort William Henry and cast about for traces of the route along which Magua has fled with Cora and Alice. In the darkness of night a lone Indian fires at Chingachgook. Uncas slips away and returns with the scalp of the assailant. The party gathers around Uncas and debates the identity of the dead Indian. It turns out that he is an Oneida, one of the Iroquois Six Nations, and the mention of his name has the effect of provoking an admission of the historical truth that the text has attempted to deny.

> "What has become of our enemy, Uncas?" demanded Duncan; "we heard your rifle, and hoped you had not fired in vain."
>
> The young chief removed a fold of his hunting shirt, and quietly exposed the fatal tuft of hair, which he bore as the symbol of his victory. Chingachgook laid his hand on the scalp, and considered it for a moment with deep attention. Then dropping it, with powerful disgust depicted in his strong and expressive features, he exclaimed –
>
> "Hugh! Oneida!"

"Oneida!" repeated the scout, who was fast losing his interest in the scene, in an apathy nearly assimilated to that of his other associates, but who now advanced with uncommon earnestness to regard the bloody badge.

"By the Lord, if the Oneidas are outlying upon our trail, we shall be flanked by devils on every side of us! Now, to white eyes there is no difference between this bit of skin and that of any other Indian, and yet the Sagamore declares it came from the poll of a Mingo; nay, he even names the tribe of the poor devil, with as much ease as if the scalp was the   20 leaf of a book, and each hair a letter. What right have christian whites to boast of their learning, when a savage can read a language, that would prove too much for the wisest of them all! What say you, lad; of what people was the knave?"

Uncas raised his eyes to the face of the scout, and answered, in his soft, musical voice –

"Oneida."

"Oneida again! when one Indian makes a declaration, it is commonly true; but when he is supported by his people,   30 set it down as gospel!"

"The poor fellow has mistaken us for French," said Heyward, "or he would not have attempted the life of a friend."

"He mistakes a Mohican, in his paint, for a Huron! You would be as likely to mistake them white coated grenadiers of Montcalm, for the scarlet jackets of the 'Royal Americans'," returned the scout. "No, no, the sarpent knew his errand; nor was there any great mistake in the matter, for there is but little love atween a Delaware and a Mingo,   40 let their tribes go out to fight for whom they may in a white quarrel. For that matter, though the Oneidas do serve his sacred majesty, who is my own sovereign lord and master, I should not have deliberated long about letting off 'kill-deer' at the imp myself, had luck thrown him in my way."

"That would have been an abuse of our treaties and unworthy of your character."

"When a man consorts much with a people," continued Hawk-eye, "if they are honest, and he no knave, love will grow up atwixt them. It is true that white cunning has   50 managed to throw the tribes into great confusion, as respects friends and enemies; so that the Hurons and the Oneidas, who speak the same tongue, or what may be called the same, take each other's scalps, and the Delawares are divided among themselves; a few hanging about their great council fire, or their own river, and fighting on the same side with the Mingoes, while the greater part are in the Canadas, out of natural emnity to the Maquas – thus throwing everything into disorder, and destroying all the harmony of warfare. Yet a red natur is not likely to alter with every shift   60 of policy! So that the love atwixt a Mohican and a Mingo is much like the regard between a white man and a sarpent."

"I regret to hear it; for I had believed those natives who dwelt within our boundaries had found us too just and liberal, not to identify themselves, fully, with our quarrels."

"Why," said the scout, "I believe it is natur to give a preference to one's own quarrels before those of strangers. Now, for myself, I do love justice; and therefore – I will not say I hate a Mingo, for that may be unsuitable to my colour and religion – though I will just repeat, it may have been   70 owing to the night that 'kill-deer' had no hand in the death of this skulking Oneida." (233–35)

Aside from the present argument, this passage should attract the attention of any reader of the novel because the episode seems gratuitously motivated, erupting into the hiatus between the two narratives as if merely to add a frisson of violence. Since the Oneidas have not been active in the novel until this point, and indeed have only been named twice (once in the Preface and once in one of Hawk-eye's asides), it is with good reason that the characters are at pains to explain what is happening.[43] Major Heyward's recognition (line 32) that the Oneidas are friendly Indians only makes matters worse and provokes Hawk-eye's confession that he is fully prepared to kill a loyal servant of the king for reasons of personal animosity. This confession contradicts Hawk-eye's general posture of impartiality, and as the episode proceeds contradiction piles upon contradiction. In lines 50–51 Hawk-eye allows that it is 'white cunning' which has confused relationships between the Indian tribes and goes on to admit that in truth only a few Delawares are fighting with the Mingoes (and presumably the British) whilst the majority have gone to Canada (where they may be presumed to be allied with the French and Hurons.)[44] Evidently this admission belies the reversal of Indian alliances which has so far structured the novel and reveals that in part of Cooper's mind there resides a more accurate knowledge of white and Indian alliances then he is normally prepared to admit. What seems to have happened here is that the knowledge of the truth has for a moment returned from the repressed and briefly illuminated the 'confusion' and 'obscurity' with which Cooper shrouds Indian history.[45] That the agency of this admission is the name 'Oneida' would seem to indicate that there is a special problem attached to this name and that the Oneida have a highly charged function in Cooper's imagination. Closer examination of the special history of the Oneidas, and of Cooper's relationship with them, will be seen to clarify the pertinence of the Oneida in this crucial scene and also provide a new perspective on several recurrent features of the Leatherstocking Tales.

When the Iroquois Confederacy decided to support the British in the War of Independence two of the Six Nations demanded the suspension of the principle of unanimity which had held the Confederacy together for more than one hundred years. These two nations were the Oneida and the Tuscarora, most of whom, largely through the influence of the Congregationalist missionary, Samuel Kirkland, had been persuaded to favour the American side. As a result of their loyalty to the American cause the Oneida and Tuscarora suffered the attacks of the other Iroquois Nations and had to move from their homelands to safeguard their lives. Some of the Oneida warriors acted as invaluable guides for the American forces, leading them through the Iroquois heartlands that they knew so well. The loyalty of the Oneidas was to draw fulsome praise from nineteenth-century historians and was also to provide Thomas Campbell, then one of Britain's most famous poets, with the subject for a poem. His 'Gertrude of Wyoming' was published in 1809 and was well known in the United States in the 1820s since it told the story of a Mohawk massacre of white settlers which occurred at Wyoming, Pennsylvania in 1788. In the poem an Oneida brave, Outalissi, helps a 'buskin-clad' white man, Henry Waldegrave, fight off the Mohawk attack. We know that Cooper was familiar with 'Gertrude of Wyoming' because he appends an epigraph from the poem to Chapter Thirty-Six of *The Pioneers*, the chapter in which Mohegan John complains that the whites have taken Indian lands by violent means. It thus seems probable that the poem provided Cooper with a model for the relationship between Chingachgook and Hawk-eye, but that for some reason Cooper felt impelled to change Campbell's Oneida, Outalissi, into his own Mohegan, Chingachgook.

This intertextual suggestion gains in significance the more one researches the place of the Oneida in history. Although the loyalty of the Oneidas was a subject for praise in the nineteenth century, and although Article II of the Treaty of Fort Stanwix of 1784 announced that 'The Oneida and Tuscarora Nations shall be secured in the possession of the lands on which they are settled', they suffered much the same fate as the rest of the Iroquois Nations, their lands being illegally purchased by unscrupulous land agents. In 1821, four years before the writing of *The Last of the Mohicans*, there was a notable scandal when the Ogden Land Company succeeded in persuading the Oneidas to sell a large tract of what was left to them of their land. This purchase was illegal since only government agents were empowered to purchase Indian lands. In 1861 the official historian of these transactions noted that 'every Consideration of Justice demanded that we should deal generously with our late Allies', and in one eight-page footnote to the official record he felt impelled to remark that 'History will attach a Stain of Dishonour, for which no apologies can atone' to the names of those New York State officials who were appointed to treat justly with the Indians but who only swindled them of their lands for personal gain. Since Cooperstown was but five miles from the original boundary between Mohawk and Oneida lands, and since Susan Cooper tells us that one of the few Indian tribes with which Cooper had any personal contact was this very same Oneida, there may be both biographical and conceptual reasons why it should be an Oneida who initiates the admission of the true complexity of Indian history in *The Last of the Mohicans*. Firstly, the loyalty of the Oneidas to the Americans in the War of Independence contradicts Cooper's distorted representation of the Iroquois *as a whole* as having been the enemies of the Americans either in 1757 or in 1779. Secondly, the eventual removal of the Oneidas from their homelands constitutes embarrassing evidence of the fate of those Indians who were constantly loyal to American forces.[46]

If we can now see why Cooper should have wished to repress knowledge of Oneida history, we have yet to understand the reason why the name 'Mohican' should have presented itself as an appropriate substitute within the structure of Thomas Campbell's poem. This logic is again uncovered by examining the place of the Mohegans in history. In the passage in which the Oneida is abruptly murdered Cooper relies upon the idea that, because 'there is but little love atween a Delaware and a Mingo' (line 40), it is logical for a 'Mohican' to want to kill an Oneida.[47] In the long historical view this suggestion has some validity. The Delaware and the Mohegans were generally subject to Iroquois attacks, and, in the seventeenth century, the Mohegans had especially good reason to fear the Mohawks. The Mohegans lived around the mouth of the Thames River in Connecticut and as the pressure of colonisation increased along the coast they found themselves driven towards the Mohawks who guarded the eastern flank of the Iroquois Confederacy. Finding themselves trapped between two equally implacable forces the Mohegans joined with the whites in Connecticut and helped them defeat the Pequots and the Narragansetts in 1637 and 1676. As the work of Francis Jennings has revealed, they were, like the Oneida, highly praised for their loyalty, but they eventually sold their lands and dispersed among the Delawares. Some of the Mohegans were left on a reservation at Norwich, Connecticut, and one group which had been Christianised by the Moravians lived at Stockbridge, Massachusetts until the War of Independence. Then, having helped the colonists against the British around Boston, they were sent to persuade the Oneida not to join with the other Iroquois Nations but to take the American side. The Mohegans were successful in their embassy and in 1784 they settled with the Oneida on their reservations in upper New York State. Between 1818 and 1830 their lands were sold and they moved to Indiana and Wisconsin. The sale of Oneida lands thus resulted in the removal of three Indian tribes, the Oneidas, Tuscaroras and Mohegans, all of whom had been consistently loyal to the American colonists, and all of whom recur in Cooper's Indian novels. Since we know that Cooper met with the Oneida it seems probable that at the same time he met with the remnants of the Mohegans who were then living in harmony with them and that to some extent he must have been aware of the moral problems involved in their removal. The names Mohegan and Oneida may thus be seen to be linked in Cooper's imagination for both experiential and political reasons.[48]

I believe that here we approach an important psychological origin for the Leatherstocking Tales. As a Mohican, Cooper's Chingachgook is able to represent the good and the loyal in the Indian precisely because the historical experience of Mohegan removal is sufficiently distant in time and space to allow the moral complexity of the more recent removal to be safely negotiated. The word 'Mohican' is, in effect, an alibi, a sign which can stand in the place of the more immediately pressing case of the Oneida and allow into consciousness a distorted form of history which will assuage Cooper's anxieties over his possession of Indian lands. Cooper's return to Indian–white relations in *The Pathfinder*, *The Deerslayer* and *Wyandotté* might thus be understood in the Freudian terms of a repetition compulsion: on each occasion Cooper attempts to allow the real history of Indian–white relations into consciousness, and on each occasion he succeeds only in perpetuating a mythic form of history. Like dreams, the Leatherstocking Tales succeed in translating the wish 'if only things had been like that' into the reassuring statement 'that's how things were'. The result of this transformation is a series of novels in which the historical order is not so much 'confused' as logically distorted, in which signs stand in foreign places in order to reduce the complexity of the past towards the schematic and desired opposition of nobility and ignobility, civilisation and savagery. Their social function as mythic histories may be said to correspond to Freud's opinion that 'myths . . . are the distorted vestiges of the wishful phantasies of whole nations'.[49]

As far as *The Last of the Mohicans* was concerned, Cooper seems to have had some consciousness of the kind of distortion his novel had performed. On 29 May 1826, shortly before he left the United States to take up residence in France, he gave an address to the 'Bread and Cheese Club' in which he touched on the subject of history and truth:

> But Sir, if there be a man in this community who owes a debt to the Muse of History, it would seem to be the one who has now the honour to address you. No writer of our country has invaded her sacred precincts with greater licence or more frequency. Sir, I have not yet been unmindful of the weight of my transgressions in this particular, and I have long and seriously reflected on the means of presenting an expiatory offering before the altar of the offended Goddess. The apparent tardiness of this repentance ought not to be ascribed to want of diligence or want of inclination, but is merely an additional evidence of the vast disparity which is known to exist between truth and falsehood.[50]

It is evident that this speech was intended as a droll concession to the contemporary preference for histories rather than historical novels, but it is difficult not to hear in it a tacit reference to the displacements we have noticed in *The Last of the Mohicans*. Such a concern with the truth is one of the exemplary features of this novel which strives more painstakingly towards historical authority than any other Leatherstocking Tale, and which correspondingly reveals all the ambiguities of its doubled genre, the historical romance. What has become abundantly clear in this reading is the contingent opposition of these modes in the early nineteenth century, and the justice of established approaches to early American fiction in terms of the wish-fulfilling forms, romance and myth. But rather than representing the romance as effectively sundered from its material circumstances, this reading displays the romance as a mode of organising those same materials under the sign of unconscious desire. In the process are confirmed two observations by Barthes which at first sight appear distinct, but which on inspection can be seen as complementary. The first is the postulate that myth is 'speech *stolen and restored* . . . only the speech which is restored is no longer that which was stolen: when it was brought back it was not put exactly in its place'. The second is that whilst myth is experienced as an innocent, factual system, it is a semiological system which naturalises its own intentions.[51] We can see the continuity between these two propositions in Cooper's representation of the Iroquois, for the sign 'Iroquois' has not been merely 'stolen and restored'; it has picked up something else along the way. What has been picked up is the intentionality 'evil' that has no more to do with the Iroquois-in-history than 'civilisation' has to do with the colour of one's skin. This intentionality is a function of the Iroquois' positional relationship vis-à-vis Cooper: since they are opposed to expansion they become Other; since they are Other they become evil. In history this Otherness is political, but in the romance it becomes ethical, a quality made to appear as grounded in Iroquois 'nature' that legitimises their removal. That this process occurs in reverse with the defunct Mohegans is evident: helping the whites is a premise of their nobility. But what then is the status of the innocent white man, Hawk-eye? We are told, with a repetitiousness that invites inspection, that he is 'a man without a cross', a man with no 'cross' of miscegenation in his blood, pure white, and impartial in his judgements. In this sanitised neutrality he is the very alibi of imperialism, the pathfinder who is expert with the means of conquest but who does not approve the ends, the exile from civilisation who disowns the dispossession. He soliloquises admirably enough, but surely we are now more ready to believe the denied, than the denial:

I am not a prejudiced man, nor one who vaunts himself on his natural privileges, though the worst enemy I have on earth, and he is an Iroquois, daren't deny I am genuine white . . . and I am willing to own that my people have many ways of which, as an honest man, I can't approve. It is one of their customs to write in books what they have done and seen, instead of telling them in the villages, where the lie can be given to the face of the cowardly boaster, and the brave soldier can call on his comrades to witness for the truth of his words. (26–27)

This can so easily be read the other way around.

4.3 *THE DEERSLAYER*: SCALPS AND THE MYTH OF WHITENESS

In the present state of our country one of two things seem to be necessary, either that these sons of the forest should be moralized or exterminated.

House Committee on Indian Affairs, 1818.[52]

. . . eye like Lochiel's; finger like a trigger; nerve like a catamount's; and with but two little oddities – seldom stirred without his rifle, and hated Indians like snakes.

Herman Melville, *The Confidence Man*.[53]

When trying to understand the representation of historical experience in Cooper's Indian novels we should remember that in 1840 the United States elected as President a man whose *soubriquet*, 'Tippecanoe', referred to his prowess against the Indians, and that the previous incumbent but one, Andrew Jackson, had spent part of his early life fighting Indians and speculating in frontier lands. From the election of such men to the highest public office it is evident that in political as well as economic terms, the 'frontier' was not a marginal condition but was at the centre of social life and that attitudes towards the Indians who were being killed on that frontier were centrally important in defining the national culture. Cooper's difficulties and achievements in representing the Indian can therefore be seen not as a minor aspect of his work to which they have often been relegated but as one of the points at which his work engages most closely with the fundamental issues of the period.

Notable among these issues are the concept of civilisation, the legitimacy of territorial expansion, and the production of wealth from the land.

Cooper's difficulties, as has been implied, were generated by the conflict between the desire of the landed-gentry to legitimise its social power by developing a conservative, historical ideology, and Cooper's personal knowledge of the techniques of expropriation with which that class had created its wealth. But it is important to recognise that in the resulting anxiety about whether white civilisation was in fact superior, Cooper was relatively alone. To the majority of his contemporaries the Indians were evidently sub-human and the conquest of the West was unproblematically justified as the expansion of a superior civilisation over an inferior order of savagery. As there were no clearly alternative social fractions and ideologies which opposed the destruction of the Indians, the only direction for Cooper's anxiety to take was to confuse history with myth. The extremity of his situation can perhaps be judged by recalling the apologetic self-defence he felt required to make when he wrote his Preface to the Leatherstocking Tales in 1850.

> It has been objected to these books that they give a more favourable picture of the redman than he deserves. . . . It is the privilege of all writers of fiction, more particularly when their works aspire to the elevation of romances, to present the *beau idéal* of their characters to the reader. This it is which constitutes poetry, and to suppose that the redman is to be represented only in the squalid misery or in the degraded moral state that certainly more or less belongs to his condition, is, we apprehend, taking a very narrow view of an author's privileges. Such criticism would have deprived the world of even Homer.[54]

Since Cooper reserves idealisation for a few solitary survivors of friendship with the whites and degrades those Indians who showed military vigour and cultural sophistication, the fact that he should have felt defensive about having idealised even his tokens of racial guilt indicates the difficulty of his position. Even when resorting to an entirely imaginary view of Indian history, the writer was required to show all Indians as living in a 'degraded moral state'.

In *The Deerslayer* Cooper seems to go as far as possible towards admitting the moral dubiety of the conquest but he is, in the end, unable to admit its economic rationale (which of course structures his life) and so he is retained in an imaginary circuit in which history has to be repressed. The resulting mythic text attempts the impossible satisfaction of the desire that the conquest has been just.

The route from *The Last of the Mohicans* to *The Deerslayer* led through the burial of Natty at the end of *The Prairie* and his resurrection in *The Pathfinder*, a novel which renegotiates the mythic New York State of the *Mohicans* without deriving the same invigorating tension from contradicted history. Natty's resurrection in 1840 appears to have been occasioned by a decline in Cooper's earnings, a decline which derived in part from a fall in book prices and in part from disaffection in Cooper's readers who disliked the author's recently acquired tendency of lecturing them on the errors of their ways. Returning in 1833 from a stay of seven years in France, Cooper had first outraged public opinion in the Three Mile Point affair and then by expressing his reservations about the state of the nation in *Home as Found* and *The American Democrat* (1838). In these works his explicit defence of the established landed gentry played directly into the hands of the Whigs who had tired of being labelled aristocrats by well-to-do Jacksonians and had found their own log-cabin and hard cider candidate for the 1840 election. William Henry Harrison won the election partly by appealing to the popular vote as a backwoodsman Whig and Cooper found himself the victim of a libellous campaign which held him up as the epitome of a Democratic aristocrat. When he resurrected Natty Bumppo he was thus in literary retreat from the aggression of political life and from the contradictions of his own ideological situation. He was also involved, in a way which cannot be incidental to novels concerned with 'nature', in the re-purchase of some of his father's Otsego lands that had been lost at the time of writing *The Pioneers*.[55]

As we have seen when considering the theory of the romance, although Cooper's early aesthetic pronouncements had indicated a desire to claim the authenticity of history for his works, the opening lines of *The Deerslayer* indicated his surrender to the subjectivist credo of the romancer. If one begins a novel with the generalisation that 'on the human imagination events produce the effects of time' then it follows that there is nothing to be gained by understanding the past as it actually was – since the past is mere imaginary effect – nor in probing its relationship with the present. The past in effect becomes a pageant of usable materials which the artistic imagination can work up as it will.

The direct result of this movement towards romance in the last

Leatherstocking Tale is that Cooper makes scant effort to found his text in historical facts. He ends his Preface to *The Deerslayer* by saying that 'the legend is purely fiction, no authority existing for any of its facts, characters, or other peculiarities, beyond that which was thought necessary to secure the semblance of reality' (p. x). Despite this disclaimer it is important to note that Cooper still ambiguously wants to hold on to the shreds of the historian's status. The novel is not set in the never-never world of romance but in a real geography and at a dated historical moment so that although it is not history it is capable of appearing as such. In a futile stab at material foundations, Cooper tells us that 'the scene of this tale . . . is intended for, and believed to be, a close description of the Otsego prior to the year 1760', and goes on to emphasise the accuracy with which geography of the lake is drawn. He makes a point of confessing that the shoal on which Hutter's 'castle' is said to stand has been 'misplaced' a little from where it is in fact to be found on the actual lake, but having made his confession concludes that 'in a word, in all but position, even this feature of the book is accurate' (p. x). In a symptomatic reading such attention to small honesties can only indicate a greater lie. It seems to suggest that beneath the conscious surface of the text is an awareness that the Iroquois have been much more radically displaced than the foundations of Hutter's house, the more so since this house bears the same name ('castle') as Judge William Cooper's original house in Cooperstown.[56] When we recall that at the end of *The Pioneers* Natty was able to cast his eyes around the Otsego hills and remember the time when the smokes of Delaware encampments could be seen rising from the forests, and now see in *The Deerslayer* that on his first arrival these lands are 'untouched by the hands of man' (33) we realise that there is nothing in Cooper's historical geography that has any guarantee of permanence, nothing except possibly his hatred of the Mingoes. The narrative is dated as occurring between 1740 and 1745, a vague enough period to accommodate its few days of events, and a period throughout which the Delaware remained unhappily subjected to Iroquois dominance and to the Iroquois policy of British alliance.[57] As in *The Last of the Mohicans*, however, the enemy is signified by Mingoes, Iroquois and Hurons, without regard to political distinctions and here without the neurotic displacements that were necessitated by a desire for historical accuracy in the earlier novel. There are in fact trace suggestions that the Iroquois might *not* be the enemy (' . . . the Iroquois, or the enemy, whoever they are . . .' (70); 'the Iroquois, or the Hurons, as it would be better to call them . . .' (172) but in general they are represented as allies of the French who live, like dogs, in 'kennels' (174) and who are only on the Glimmerglass (Otsego) because they have moved down from their *Canadian* homelands.[58] In a transparent piece of shifting Cooper remarks that 'this particular party of the Iroquois were posted on the shores of the Oneida, a lake that lies some fifty miles nearer to their own frontier than that which is the scene of our tale' (173).[59] Given that *The Deerslayer* is set in the paternal lands which Cooper is actively engaged in re-purchasing, this denial of the original owners of the land can be seen as a mental act that parallels the economic reconstitution of William Cooper's estate: as the author buys up the ground he mentally removes the Indians. This act also provides the boundary condition of James Fenimore Cooper's imagination, for whatever else will be admitted about white men in *The Deerslayer*, colonial land speculation and Iroquois rights will not.

Since these facts are central to any understanding of the white man's relationship to the land, it follows that their denial must entail a loss in materiality and leave us only with a mythical 'nature', a moral essence which has been divorced from historical reality and returned to 'the semblance of reality' by secondary revision. As Freud has told us, illogicality must be the mark of such a text, so it is hardly surprising that Mark Twain should have been able to lampoon Cooper's utter implausibility in *The Deerslayer* and mock his 'very limited powers of invention' (secondary revision often working crudely and with some desperation).[60] In his essay on Cooper's 'Literary Offences' Twain analyses with some care the scene where Deerslayer and Hurry Harry March first meet up with Tom Hutter on board the 'ark'. Twain notes that the river which flows out of the Glimmerglass is at first thirty feet wide at the lake, narrowing to twenty feet further down stream. Later the river becomes twenty feet wide at the lake and this is then the narrowest part of the stream! If the ark is to be as capacious as it needs be for the action which will occur on it Twain suggests it must be one hundred and forty feet long and sixteen feet wide, but the river bends have a radius of only thirty to fifty feet according to Cooper, so either Hutter's ark is flexible or its bow and stern must occasionally be on dry land. Numerous other implausibilities can be found in this scene (as elsewhere in Cooper),[61] notably that 'no less than six Indians' climb 'a sapling' which later becomes a 'trunk' and then develops into a 'tree' and then try to drop from this rapidly changing piece of nature on to the ark as it passes beneath them. Even though the ark must be moving slowly (because it is being pulled by two men against the current and is a considerable size) the first Indian to leap from the sapling/tree contrives to wait until the vessel has nearly passed from under him before making the leap, and his fellows then proceed to emulate his stupidity by leaping into the water behind him.

> Perceiving that they were discovered, the Indians uttered the fearful war whoop and, running forward on the tree, leaped desperately toward their fancied prize. There were six on the tree, and each made the effort. All but their leader fell into the river more or less distant from the ark, as they came, sooner or later, to the leaping place. The chief, who had taken the dangerous post in advance, having an earlier opportunity than the others, struck the scow just within the stern. (67–8)

The transformation of a sapling into a tree large enough for six Indians to run about on, and the fact that the river changes size from one paragraph to the next, can only be appreciated in their full significance when one realises that Cooper penned this scene at a desk in Cooperstown not many yards from the actual place he was supposed to be describing with great 'precision'. From this fact alone it is evident that the transformation of geography in *The Deerslayer* is radical in the extreme, and that any appearance of material order in the text is superficial. Of the nineteen rules 'governing literary art in the domain of romantic fiction', Twain says that Cooper broke eighteen. The more pertinent are rule two, that 'the episodes of a tale shall be necessary parts of a tale, and shall help to develop it', rule four, that 'the personages in a tale . . . shall exhibit a sufficient excuse for being there', and rule seven, that 'when a person talks like an illustrated, gilt-edged, tree-calf, hand-tooled, seven dollar *Friendship's Offering* in the beginning of a paragraph, he shall not talk like a negro minstrel in the end of it'.[62] Such lapses cannot be simply ascribed to the prerogatives of the romance because although the romance is free from the need to be literally verisimilistic, it is still under the aesthetic requirement to be internally consistent. Unmotivated episodes, characters changing character with no apparent cause, ships too big for the rivers they are on; these are ruptures with any conceivable code of expectations and point to the text's construction by private fantasies that have failed to establish authority over reality.

It is tempting to suggest that the inconsistencies derive from the speed at which Cooper wrote and from his deep dislike of revision.[63] Cooper's manuscripts were often at the printers before the novels were finished, a form of literary production which left the heroine of *The Pathfinder* with an embarrassing and entirely unaccountable change of name in the middle of the first edition. However, since Scott, Dickens and Balzac could pen six hundred pages in as many weeks and achieve both mimetic verisimilitude and internal consistency, we must conclude that speed of composition itself was not the cause of Cooper's imaginative confusions. Brief reflection on the narrative structure of any of the last four Leatherstocking novels would seem to indicate a more persuasive explanation in the theory of dreams, for, like dreams, the narratives seem to be constructed by tableaux of hallucinatory violence which represent the conflict of good and evil, nature and civilisation, civilisation and savagery, white man and red man.[64] These tableaux are given narrative extension by means of the psychologically reductive devices of pursuit, capture, escape, and attack. Our willingness to believe is enlisted by the spurious factuality of a prose that pays obsessive attention tó inches and feet, to minutes elapsed, to all the mechanical agencies of canoeing, killing, building, tracking, escaping. These very data, with which Twain was able to expose Cooper's hand (although he himself was to write not such dissimilar rules and detections into *Huckleberry Finn*), were, as we have seen, the authorised language of Common Sense, the verisimilitude of factualism. Here, in *The Deerslayer*, it is applied as secondary revision to restore the appearance of logicality to a text that dramatises all the desires and repressed contradictions of that same world-view.

In personal terms, the setting of the novel in 1740–5 on the Otsego Lake clearly satisfies the wish that the land had been a peopleless 'wilderness' one hundred years before the time of writing. The desire is so exigent that it overrides not only the history of white expropriation and Mohawk (Iroquois) agricultural settlement, it overrides even the fictitious chronology established in the previous Leatherstocking novels. A process of colonisation which began with commissioned surveys and proceeded through the issue of warrants and patents to result in the creation of vast fortunes by a small section of society, is de-realised and reduced to Natty's communion with the forest, his love of the noble Delaware and his hatred of the ignoble Mingo. A binary opposition of moral categories has been substituted for the real conditions. The only obvious relic of repressed history that remains is the mystery at the bottom of Tom Hutter's chest – a gentleman's finery and surveyor's instruments – that unconsciously alludes to the 'Deputy Superintendent of Indian Affairs' mentioned in the Preface, a gentleman surveyor whose name we know to have been George Croghan, the original hutter on Otsego Lake, the true father of Judith and Hetty.

It is not, however, for its personal function that the novel is interesting, although understanding its personal function provides a guide to its wider significance. The interest of this text which has so de-materialised historical experience that it no longer has any secure ground on which to stand is that its narrative seems to be generated by a discussion of the mythic sign 'whiteness'. As J. P. McWilliams has observed, Hurry Harry March and Tom Hutter provide the central theme of the novel in allowing the admission that white men took Indian scalps for money and that they behaved in general with all the savagery that they exclusively attributed to their enemies.[65] The importance of this admission for Cooper can be seen by reference back to *The Last of the Mohicans* (Chapter Twelve) where Chingachgook slips off to butcher an unsuspecting French sentry and comes back with his reeking scalp. Hawk-eye comments that it 'would have been a cruel and inhuman act for a white-skin; but 'tis the gift and natur of an Indian, and I suppose it should not be denied!' (141). Hawk-eye might not *deny* scalping to an Indian 'nature' but until *The Deerslayer* Cooper has certainly kept silent on its practice by white men. It is, at least by implication, not part of 'white nature'. When later in the same novel Uncas comes back to the camp with the scalp of the Oneida, only Uncas and Chingachgook are capable of deciphering the tribe to which the assailant belonged. Improbably enough, neither Hawk-eye, the experienced hunter and backwoodsman who can tell an Indian by his 'paint' at considerable distances, nor Heyward, the professional soldier, are capable of recognising the tribe of an Indian from his scalp. Impressed by the skill of his Indian friends, Hawk-eye feels compelled to redress the white man's notions of his innate superiority to the red by posing the rhetorical question 'what rights have christian whites to boast of their learning, when a savage can read a language that would prove too much for the wisest of them all' (233). The complex deceit involved in this question consists firstly in the implication that it is only the savages who can read scalps when colonial governments had given bounties for the scalps of enemy Indians since the beginning of the conquest. (Since the bounties were paid on a scale of declining value for men, women and children, and since colonial officials can be presumed to have preferred not to pay for the scalps of their allies, we can deduce that white men must have had some abilities in 'reading' not just the tribe but also the age and sex of the bounty hunter's victims.) The second and more complex deceit is the implication that the Indian could read only the language of scalps and no other form of script. The very fact that Cooper should have implicitly denied Indian literacy raises the question whether he was really unaware that the Delaware had a hieroglyphic script of their own, and that the Cherokee had developed a written alphabet and widespread literacy in their aboriginal language. Knowledge of these scripts was available in the nineteenth century, even though the general tendency was to deny the Indian all forms of cultural development, especially literacy, numeracy, agriculture and husbandry, so as to generate the illusion of white civilisation's superiority.[66] Cooper's denial here may be simply part of the general tendency, but coupled as it is with a denial of the white man's practice of reading scalps, it may be that a series of condensations and displacements have converted two significant denials into a discrete assertion of 'civilised' values. Like so much about Cooper's knowledge of the Indians one cannot be finally sure of its extent; one can only surmise from its extraordinary completeness in some respects (for example, the thorough knowledge of Iroquois torture rituals displayed in *The Deerslayer*) that an absence or denial is more likely to be a sign of repression than of simple ignorance.[67]

Between 1826 and 1841 it is evident either that Cooper's knowledge of the Indians had increased, or that his conscience had become more active, for in *The Deerslayer* we have not only a belated and brief admission of Indian agriculture (511) and, in Rivenoak, the portrait of an Iroquois chief as a credible and humane human being, we also have the frequent admission of white savagery towards the Indians, as much in the arguments of Hurry Harry and Tom Hutter as in their actions. Harry in particular allows into the world of the Leatherstocking Tales the contemporary idea that the Indians were only half-human, and ought to be exterminated like any other verminous pest. Natty replies to this argument on two heads, firstly that 'the red men [are] quite as human as we are ourselves', secondly, that they have different 'gifts' (i.e. social

customs) which need to be respected as valuable in their own right,
however different they are from 'white gifts'.[68] Natty's attitude is
obviously more in sympathy with that of the growing number of
anthropologists in the United States who were beginning to take a
serious interest in Indian culture, but it is eventually as fatal as
Hurry Harry's obvious racism.[69] Let us look closely at Natty's
distinctions.

> God made us all – white, black, and red – and no doubt had his
> own wise intentions in colouring us differently. Still, he made us,
> in the main, much the same in feelin's, though I'll not deny that
> he gave each race its gifts. A white man's gifts are Christianized,
> while a redskin's are more for the wilderness. Thus, it would be a
> great offense for a white man to scalp the dead, whereas it's a
> signal vartue in an Indian. Then ag'in, a white man cannot
> amboosh women and children in war, while a redskin may. 'Tis
> *cruel* work, I'll allow, but for them it's *lawful* work, while for *us* it
> would be grievous work. (36)

According to the avowed ethics of white society these distinctions
are perfectly valid: white men are not supposed to scalp and to
butcher women and children whereas Cooper presumes that
everyone knows that such behaviour is permitted, if not actually
esteemed, in Indian societies. Unfortunately, however, this conventional opposition is not supported by history, not even today.[70] To
quote but a few examples that Cooper can scarcely have been
ignorant of: in his *History, Manners and Customs* Heckewelder
reported that in 1782 sixty-four men and women, and thirty-four
children of a Christianised Delaware group living at Gnadenhutten,
Pennsylvania, were butchered in cold blood for no other reason than
that some unrelated Delawares had taken the British side; in 1725, in
an orgy of scalp hunting, one John Lovewell of Dunstable,
Massachusetts, made three raids for Indian scalps and netted
himself something over one thousand pounds in bounty before being
killed by the Indians. This latter event, like the famous seventeenth-
century captivity of Hannah Dustin (and her eventual escape
carrying the scalps of her captors home for bounty), had given rise to
a great many literary and sub-literary productions by the time
Cooper came to write his Indian novels.[71]

The Deerslayer's argument about 'white gifts' is not undermined
by these historical facts because it is here made at the level of 'ought'

rather than 'is', and it is immediately countered by Harry March who interjects the historical facts that 'the Colony' offers a bounty for Indian scalps 'all the same as it pays for wolves' ears and crow's heads' so he looks on 'scalping, or even skinning a savage . . . much the same as cutting off the ears of wolves for bounty'. Deerslayer's reply to this is that scalping is

> . . . ag'in a white man's gifts. I do not pretend that all that white men do is properly Christianized . . . but I will maintain that tradition, and use, and colour, and laws make such a difference in races as to amount to gifts. (37)

The same argument is repeated several times in the novel, Natty arguing that scalping is against 'white gifts', Hurry Harry countering with the fact that bounty payments are made by the colonial authorities, and Natty replying that 'the King's Majesty, his governors, and all his councils, both at home and in the colonies, forget from what they come, and where they hope to go' when they break God's law in such a manner.

The argument is as circular and frustrating as the narrative it animates because it attempts to justify in logical and historical terms the arbitrary assertion of white superiority. (In theoretical terms it is an attempt by secondary revision to restore logicality to the mythical concept of whiteness, an attempt which is spurious in so far as the desire which animates the novel will override any gain in apparent rationality, the desire being to justify James Fenimore Cooper's material possession of the Otsego Lake.) What Natty is saying in effect is that there is a moral essence, 'white gifts', which is naturally part of white flesh, just as there is a contrary moral essence, 'red gifts', which inheres in red flesh. These naturalised moral essences are by now familiar to us as mythic signs which have the function of de-politicising ideological assertions and making arbitrary values appear to constitute the material world-in-itself. In each of these confrontations with Hurry Harry, Natty's belief in the mythic sign encounters the resistance of history: since white men hunt scalps for bounties paid by white government how can white men claim a superior status to that of the Indians? How can 'white gifts' signify moral goodness, innocence, purity, nobility of spirit?

Natty's answer is that white men 'forget from where they come' when they try to take the scalps of sleeping men, women, and children (even when aided by the piously contradictory Natty).

Such an answer is not so much satisfactory as revealing of mythic thought. We noted above that the mythic sign functions through the ease with which it changes its signified, now signifying abstract essence, now signifying concrete phenomenon. As a virtue of this mobility the behaviour of white men can never logically contradict any theoretical 'whiteness': it can only reveal 'whiteness' as an essence they have temporarily rejected like a soldier going into plain clothes in order to accomplish a dirty job. (Similarly, as we shall see, noble red men can never cease to be ignoble savages under the skin.) Trapped in the basin of the Otsego Lake, the narrative oscillation of *The Deerslayer* between castle, ark, and Indian camp, between civilisation and nature, freedom and captivity, dramatises the unstable circularity of such terms, the futile attempt of the narrative being to prove white nobility against the contradictory evidence of white savagery. What is maintained by the whites in the Indian camp, even when the scalp-hunters are captive there, is their essential purity, whereas in the ark and in the castle disagreements occur in which it becomes apparent that the connections between whiteness as moral essence and its material manifestation in the white skin can be broken and restored so that white men can undertake savage acts without violating essential white superiority. When scalping, Tom and Hurry do not cease to be white, they merely forget their own 'true nature'.

The problem which lies behind the narrative can be seen as Cooper's longstanding concern to justify the white man's possession of the land. Evidently, if white men behaved according to their highest principles 'whiteness' would represent the historical advance of a morally superior order over the morally inferior order of savagery. Through their scalp-hunting Tom and Hurry prevent a narrative which would exemplify such an advance of civilisation, just as Billy Kirby in *The Pioneers* and Ishmael Bush in *The Prairie* posed a similar obstacle by refusing to treat the land as anything more than an object to be turned into ready cash. The signal difference between these earlier characters and Tom and Hurry Harry is that the march of the Hutters is now seen to entail the same attitude towards human beings (albeit Indian human beings) as Kirby took towards the Otsego forests: they are worth so much a head. As several critics have observed, the brutality of this perception in *The Deerslayer* is a sign of Cooper's disaffection from the direction America is taking, a disaffection which doubtless both permits and motivates Cooper's questioning of the premises of

Christian civilisation.[72] Cooper, however, has such investments in the land that he is incapable of admitting the real motivations of the conquest, and so his Indian novels attempt to satisfy the questioning of the moral conscience by inventing a world of imaginary replies. Usually the end-point of any interrogation is a resort to violent event, description of nature, or practical action because there can be no satisfactory reply to such a question.

It is usually between the Indian and the good, white female that the interrogation becomes most direct. In *The Pioneers* Indian John reproaches Elizabeth Temple with the hypocrisy of white arguments, and in The *Deerslayer*, when Hetty Hutter takes the Christian gospel of 'turn the other cheek' into the Iroquois camp to plead for the life of her father, she encounters the unanswerable logic of Rivenoak, the Iroquois chief:

> If [the paleface] is ordered to *give* double to him that asks only for one thing, why does he *take* double from the poor Indians, who ask for *no* thing? He comes from beyond the rising sun, with his book in his hand, and he teaches the red man to read it; but why does he forget himself all it says? When the Indian gives, he is never satisfied, and now he offers gold for the scalps of our women and children, though he calls us beasts if we take the scalp of a warrior killed in open war. (193–4)

As the almost dematerialised voice of pure white Christian conscience, Hetty has blissfully insufficient intelligence even to comprehend this question which, Cooper authorially admits, has puzzled far wiser heads than Hetty's. Taunted by Hist, who points out that paleface reason (like mythic whiteness) is always good for the paleface and always bad for the Indian, she collapses into tears. To console her Hist remarks the obvious truth that there is 'wicked red man and wicked white man – no colour all good – no colour all wicked'.

In a certain sense, as much is admitted by the narrative, for Hutter and March are white and bad, Natty and Hetty are white and good, Chingachgook and Hist (and perhaps even Rivenoak) are red and good, whilst the Mingoes are evidently bad reds. There is thus, as Marius Bewley observed, a quadratic equation of moral and material qualities in the novel with which narrative can be generated. But there is also an overriding scheme that needs to be taken into consideration – the division between civilisation/essential whiteness and savagery/essential redness constitutes an apartheid which dictates that for all their savagery Hutter and March will always be civilised whilst for all his goodness Chingachgook will always be a savage. If one aggregates the meanings of 'red gifts' throughout the novel one finds that 'red gifts' are treachery, vengefulness and senseless brutality.[73] By this definition, Hutter and March have 'red gifts' and Chingachgook has the antithetical 'white gifts' of loyalty, nobility and modesty. However, both of these conceptual moves are forbidden by the colour of the skin so for all his idealisation Chingachgook remains red and potentially associated with 'red gifts'. It is significant that whilst he is called 'the Big Sarpent' the venomous Mingoes are called 'riptyles': thus, Chingachgook's superior qualities entitle him to soubriquet in capital letters and a genus-specific name, whereas the Mingoes qualify for the lower case 'r' and description only by the kingdom *reptilia* but under the skin both Mingoes and Chingachgook are venomous reptiles, 'divils', serpents in the Garden of Eden. Natty makes this fundamental association embarrassingly apparent when, in a passage which clearly illustrates the operation of Common Sense philosophy when applied to the Indians, he tells Judith Hutter that even his loyal and esteemed Delawares are at base natural scalpers, no more highly evolved than dogs on the scent of blood.

> I judge not, Judith; yes, I judge not. An Injin is an Injin, gal, and it's pretty much hopeless to think of swarving him when he's got the scent and follows it with his nose in the air. The Delawares, now, are a half-christianized tribe –not that I think such sort better than your whole-blooded disbelievers – but, nevertheless, what good half-christianizing can do to a man some among 'em have got, and yet revenge clings to their hearts like the wild creepers here to the tree!   (398)

It is at moments such as this that one sees Natty slipping the mask of idealisation and revealing the real logic behind his existence. It is of course an inconsistent logic because, as the resolution of repressed contradictions, Natty must serve many desires and make the best vector he can at any particular moment. Protesting against the desecration of nature by senseless white men at one instant, he is at the next shooting a free-flying eagle to show what a good shot he is. Sometimes honest, modest and innocent, at other times boastful and murderous, he seems in the end nothing less than the bad conscience of a conqueror.[74]

Warrior I may now call myself, I suppose, for I've both fou't and conquered, which is sufficient for the name; neither will I deny that I've feelin's for the callin', which is both manful and honorable, when carried on accordin' to nat'ral gifts – but I've no relish for blood. Youth is youth, howsever, and a Mingo is a Mingo. If the young men of this region stood by and suffered the vagabonds to overrun the land, why, we might as well turn Frenchers at once and give up country and kin. (564)

(Let us not forget that it is white men who have overrun Mingo land and not vice versa.)

With such straightforward 'feelin's for the callin'' in mind it is as difficult to accept Cooper's claim that Natty's reputation was achieved with 'a total absence of mystification and management', as it is to accept Judith Hutter's declaration that 'there is no lie about the Deerslayer' (296–7, 320). His author may inform us that:

He loved the woods for their freshness, their sublime solitudes, their vastness, and the impress that they everywhere bore of the divine hand of their Creator. He rarely moved through them without pausing to dwell on some peculiar beauty that gave him pleasure, though seldom attempting to investigate the causes, and never did a day pass without his communing in spirit, and this, too, without the aid of forms or language, with the infinite source of all he saw, felt, and beheld. (283)

But we must balance this poetry of unconscious oneness and sublimity against the real conditions of genocidal conflict and theft that are ever likely to erupt through the depopulating reverie. Like a crucifix directing the eye towards heaven whilst marking a battlefield of carnage, this 'nature' with which Natty enters sublime communion is the transcendental sign of expropriation and death, it is the alibi of all that has to be denied if the honest man is to go on living whilst the nation continues to extend the 'area of freedom'.[75]

5 Nathaniel Hawthorne

5.1 *THE SCARLET LETTER*: THE ADULTEROUS ALLEGORY OF AMERICAN ART

In the 1840s Hawthorne wrote three stories explicitly concerned with American regeneration. 'The Celestial Railroad' suggested that material progress was not producing heaven on earth but leading the human spirit towards damnation. In the same year, 1843, 'The New Adam and Eve' represented the need for the reborn to avoid the culture of the cities and the learning of the library if they were to find their way to salvation. In 1844 'Earth's Holocaust' implied that their hope had been foolish, for until the 'foul cavern' of the human heart had been consumed in the flames it would be 'the old world yet' (x, 403).[1]

The publication of the first two of these stories in *The Democratic Review* at the time when it was promulgating the doctrine of Manifest Destiny may be read as a political gesture. Against the tendency to justify territorial expansion by declaring the United States regenerate, Hawthorne was registering his critical disbelief in American perfection. His objection, however, was delivered from within the Democratic fold as that of a moralist who was sure that redemption had not been achieved, but who agreed that it was in terms of America's redemption that judgement should be made. Many of his representations of the Puritan past seem designed to exemplify precisely this failure, the pure in heart being repressed by a social discipline that denies their regenerative possibility. But the verdict is always ambiguous, for the pure in heart, like the couple at Merry Mount, need the logic of repression if they are to comprehend the full complexity of being human. The Fall, like the Crucifixion, is necessary if they are to understand the goodness of a world they once inhabited and to which they hope one day to return. This is true Edenic thinking: paradise must always be an elsewhere that mankind is not yet good enough to inhabit.

In a culture that justified its existence by the idea of earthly regeneration there was only a notional separation between the religious and the political. Hawthorne's exploration of the Edenic theme, his interest in myths of metamorphosis, and his reading in the Protestant tradition and the history of New England can be seen as a consistent exploration of the central ground of American ideology. The form of his tales, combining myth, parable, history and allegory in constantly changing relationships, may be seen as an accurate trace of the form of the ideology in itself: secular and quasi-rational, founded in history, and yet structuring all belief by reference to a grand Providential design. It is because Hawthorne's stories had for so many years been representing the form and content of American belief that *The Scarlet Letter* becomes such an ideologically significant text. Begun as a story for a volume to be called *Old Time Legends, together with Sketches, Experimental and Ideal*, it is easy to imagine the original intention as being to re-present the Edenic couple within New England history and thus show how the Pilgrim Fathers would have denied their regenerate love. The innocent lovers and their child, 'the infant that was to redeem the world' (90) are condemned by the satanic Chillingworth, and by a society more interested in preserving old world hierarchy than in discovering the possibilities of the new.[2] Such a story would seem the logical next step in Hawthorne's research of history and myth. It also has the crucial effect of confronting America's mythical historical origin (the Puritan emigration) with its central a-historical myth, that of Eden. The confrontation of these key modes of national definition is a major reason for the text's enduring interest.

To criticise the Puritans for having denied the Edenic possibility of the New World is evidently anachronistic since the Puritans believed in working to build an exemplary city, not in the spontaneous discovery of Eden. However, the fact that they did repress those who believed that regeneration was immediately available allowed Hawthorne to display the Puritan past as an historical origin and analogical frame for the failure of regeneration in his own day. Many of the keys to the analogy are contained in 'The Custom-House', the prose sketch which Hawthorne made introductory to *The Scarlet Letter*, and which serves to locate the entire work within the Common Sense demand that there should be a definite knower who accepts responsibility for the knowledge of the text. Because the sketch belongs to the probable genre of autobiography the author's discovery of the originating letter can be thought to belong to the world of documentary fact. The main narrative can then be accepted as a speculative historical romance, an imaginative investigation of the possible circumstances of the letter's production. The potential readers' reservations about the status of fiction are allayed by assuring them that in the world of contemporary customs there is no ambiguity about the relationship of signifier to signified, writer to reader, or knower to the known, whereas the task of an historical speculation is to discover the elusive signifieds of a 'mystic symbol'. On closer examination, however, the comfortable dichotomy seems but a mask that conceals analogical connections between the past-to-be-narrated and the author's actual situation, connections which undermine the security of 'factual' prose and the conventional piety that the present is a vast improvement on the past.

The first level of connection is the obvious analogy between the surveyor's situation in the custom-house and Hester's situation in Boston. In his opening paragraph Hawthorne observes that 'thoughts are frozen and utterance benumbed, unless the speaker stand in some true relation with his audience' (4), a testimony to his own artistic isolation in the custom-house of contemporary life that will constitute a dominant theme in the introductory sketch. Like Hester, also an artist and stigmatised by her emblematic 'A', Hawthorne is forced to inhabit a 'circle of seclusion' (95) because he feels that his society is antipathetic to the creative temperament. There are evident changes between New England past and present, but underlying them there is a continuity of institutions and attitudes that provides a sense of historical belonging, a 'home feeling with the past' (9), and also implicitly denies the contemporary belief that with independence a radical regeneration has occurred. Society in the nineteenth century might no longer be inclined to stand the artist literally on the scaffold, but as Hawthorne had discovered in his own career, it was nonetheless capable of pillorying the artist in the market-place. Indeed, Hawthorne's situation was in many ways worse than Hester's because whilst Hester achieved a dignity correspondent to the open severity of her oppression, Hawthorne was considered largely irrelevant to a society that wanted to restrict critical representation of its ideology. He says that his literature is 'utterly devoid of significance' beyond 'the narrow circle in which his claims are recognised' (27), a sentiment which doubtless informs the ambivalence of Hawthorne's writing when Hester is forced to expose the emblem of her sin in the market-place. There, whilst the author expresses a certain gratification that the Puritan crowd 'had none of the heartlessness of another social state, which would find only a theme for jest in an exhibition like the present', there is a countervailing bitterness at their silence: Hester longs 'to behold all those rigid countenances contorted with scornful merriment' (57). This ambiguity seems to imply that a hostile reception is a preferable fate for the artist than anonymity.

If the problematic relationship of the artist to society provides one level of analogical connection between the introductory sketch and the main narrative, a further level of connection is to be found in a vein of satire by which the surveyor insinuates the failure of New England to live up to its proclaimed high destiny as a New World. When he remarks that the social geography of contemporary Salem extends from 'Gallows Hill and New Guinea [the immigrant quarter] at one end' to 'a view of the alms house at the other' (8) he establishes a phenomenological field of prisons, immigration and poverty that is resumed in the opening sentences of the novel. There, in the second paragraph, we receive a bleak historical truth which contradicts all naive reformist zeal: 'the founders of a new colony, whatever Utopia of human virtue they might originally project, have invariably recognised it among their earliest practical necessities to allot a portion of virgin soil as a cemetery and another portion as the site of a prison' (49). The denial of social ideals by social practice (a denial of the Imaginary by the Actual) remains a constant between the Puritan past and the Democratic present in which the federal eagle seems to offer asylum to the poor and oppressed of Europe, but when they arrive merely flings off 'her nestlings with a scratch of her claw, a dab of her beak, or a rankling wound from one of her barbed arrows' (5). The pervasive meaning of 'The Custom-House' seems to be that in a time of mounting immigration the idea of America as a New World is an imaginary construct belied by its shallow and commercial actuality. 'Neither the front nor the back entrance . . . opens on the road to Paradise' (13).

The recognition that 'The Custom-House' provides an implicit denial of contemporary utopianism as an introduction to a narrative concerned with the disparity between the pious intentions of the Pilgrim Fathers and their actual behaviour, may prepare us to accept a more subtle series of analogies between the inhabitants of the introductory sketch and the characters of the main narrative. In 'The Custom-House' we are introduced to three representatives of contemporary society, the patriarch or Inspector, the old General or Collector, and the businessman or Deputy Collector. As Larzer Ziff has pointed out, the patriarch resembles Hester in that both are creatures of instinct rather than of thought, the Inspector being 'a rare perfection' of 'animal nature [with] a very trifling admixture of moral and spiritual ingredients' (17).[3] This analogical similarity may be extended by recognising that like Chillingworth, the Deputy Collector is a type of the mind who, 'by the merest touch of his finger', is capable of 'making the incomprehensible as clear as daylight' (24). Whilst these two characters represent body and mind, the old General typifies the national spirit, kindly, equable, authoritarian and militaristic. His features, those of 'stubborn and ponderous endurance' (22) resemble 'the ponderous sobriety, rather than activity of intellect' (238) with which Hawthorne characterises the 'primitive statesmen' (238) of the Puritan colony. Since the old General also has such a kindly heart 'as would never have brushed the down off a butterfly's wing' he may be further taken as condensing in his personality the opposition between Bellingham/Wilson and Dimmesdale in the main narrative.

As is properly the case with analogies, this pattern is subtle rather than strict; and we have no way of knowing whether it is consciously intended or whether it is an incidental effect of Hawthorne's having written his introductory sketch in parallel with the main narrative.[4] The implication, however, is clear: in Hawthorne's mind the past and the present are linked by the continuity of attitudes and institutions; no gulf of radical regeneration intervenes; history amounts to a diffusive liberalisation of established structures, not their replacement by the New.

Without development this point tells us little beyond what we would have been led to expect by Hawthorne's earlier stories where the past is a 'neutral territory' (36) which facilitates the representation of contemporary political and moral issues. But if we accept the invitation to read *The Scarlet Letter* as at one level an allegorical commentary on the present, then it opens up other meanings in the text. It has often been noticed as discordant in a novel supposedly so 'Puritanical' that Hester, on her first appearance on the scaffold, is likened to 'the image of Divine Maternity . . . whose infant was to redeem the world' (56). Hawthorne attributes this simile to a hypothetical 'Papist in the crowd'. He later has the Reverend Wilson liken Hester to the Whore of Babylon or Church of Rome, and on another occasion she is likened to a nun (110, 163). These references associate the Puritan oppression of Hester with their oppression of all heterodox religionists, but also imply that Hester's suffering may be read as an analogy of hostility to Catholicism in Hawthorne's own time. Contemporary readers of *The Scarlet Letter* would have been well aware that anti-Catholic hysteria had been rife in Boston in the 1830s, and that on one notorious occasion an anti-Catholic mob had burnt down a convent in order, as they believed, to save the inmates from 'priestly debauchery'. Through this subtle association of Hester and Catholicism, Hawthorne may have been insinuating that in the land of the free, now advertising its religious toleration, hostility to heterodox belief continued much the same as it had in Puritan times.[5]

The association of Hester and Catholicism begins to take on greater significance when one realises its connection with one of the dominant thematic and symptomatic motivations of *The Scarlet Letter*, the desire to confess. Dimmesdale's desire throughout the novel is to escape his self-torturing seclusion by confessing his crime to the great democratic multitude. Within the text he thus signifies the text's personal function as a confession of the part of Hawthorne's ancestors in the destruction of America's Edenic promise, and its national function as a reminder to contemporary readers of the iniquitousness of the national past. We know that when Hawthorne was writing the novel he considered having Dimmesdale make his confession not on the scaffold in the market-place, but to a Catholic priest. That such an idea should have occurred to Hawthorne would seem to indicate that along with Emerson, Brownson, and other descendants of the Puritan tradition he saw in Catholicism a more charitable religion and a potential release from the isolating self-examination of the Puritan mind.[6] That it is Hester who is associated with Catholicism (rather than Dimmesdale, who could easily have become the type of debauched Jesuit featured in contemporary anti-Catholic fiction), would also seem to imply that Hawthorne appreciated Catholicism's respect for artistic representation, its abundant use for the sumptuary which Hester produces, and its sanctioning of the expression of spiritual and moral sentiments in symbolist art. Indeed, there is throughout the novel an implicit association of Catholicism, paganism, and 'merry Old England' (110) that projects the idea of artistic activity as having received greater respect in the much maligned Old World than it had ever received in New England past or present.

This sequence of associations may indicate that in establishing aesthetic licence for his text Hawthorne has relied upon authorities that appear to him catholic in the more general sense of the word. The influence of Spenser on Hawthorne's work has often been noticed, but it may well be that in the multi-levelled allegorical method of *The Scarlet Letter* the author is going back through Spenser and the Puritan allegorical tradition to Augustine's *City of God*, a work which suggests that the Eden story is susceptible to three-fold symbolic interpretation, alludes to the Trinitarian nature of humanity, and discusses whether there could be a guiltless sexual intercourse in Paradise.[7] Although there is no direct evidence that Hawthorne read Augustine, it is improbable that he would have ignored a philosopher of such seminal importance to Calvinism and to the conception of the Puritan American task, especially when writing a novel concerned with the founding of the earthly City. But whether there is a direct or mediated influence, it is remarkable that the allegories of *The Scarlet Letter* seem almost to have been constructed around the scriptural hermeneutics practised by the medieval church, exemplified by Augustine, and present in a diffused form in such literary texts as *The Faerie Queene* and *The Divine Comedy*. This hermeneutic system distinguished four complementary levels of meaning, the literal or historical level being the *sensus literalis*, and three further allegorical levels (christological, tropological, and eschatological) forming the *sensus spiritualis*, the text's spiritual or allegorical significance.[8] In *The Scarlet Letter*, as previous critics have shown, a story of New England history can be interpreted as being concerned with Christian myth, or with the dichotomy of head and heart, or with the problems of artistic production.[9] By reference to the medieval hermeneutic tradition it seems possible to display these separate concerns as providing simultaneous allegorical structures. The characters of the historical drama, Chillingworth, Dimmesdale and Hester, may be said to figure at the mythological level as allegorical types for Satan, Adam and Eve, whilst figuring at a tropological level as Mind, Soul and Body, and, at a tertiary artistic level, as Analysis, Morality and Creativity. To this structure may be added the analogical level already noted in 'The Custom-House', as shown in the table.

Such a structure can doubtless be enriched by other levels of interpretation, but its main virtue is to show that because Hawthorne has coded the historical with the typical and emblematic, he has created an allegory that needs multiple acts of

		Chillingworth	Dimmesdale	Hester	Pearl
Sensus literalis	Character				
	Familial relationship	Husband	Father	Mother:Wife	Child
	Role	Scientist	Priest	Artist	
Sensus spiritualis	Christological	Satan	Adam	Eve	'Reedemer'
	Tropological	Mind/Head	Soul/Heart	Body/Breast	
	Artistic	Analysis (Thought + Morality)	Morality (Morality + Compassion)	Creativity (Compassion + Thought)	'Imagination' 'The Created'
	Analogical	Businessman Deputy Collector	Old General Collector	Patriarch Inspector	

interpretation. As in a dream, each of Hawthorne's symbols seems to allude to several different chains of association and his text therefore needs to be over-interpreted if its full significance is to be understood.

Our modern understanding of dream interpretation is not foreign to *The Scarlet Letter*: not only was the author a student of dreams, he also initiates his story with the discovery of a 'mystic symbol' whose many meanings, precisely like those of dream symbol, evade the analysis of his mind. The narration that supposedly tries to specify the meanings succeeds only in enriching the interpretative problem, not in resolving it. It is the reader who must decide whether 'A' is for Adam, Adultery, Angel, Admirable, or for any of the other possibilities which the text seems to allow. What we may be sure of is that in its material nature the scarlet letter itself points to repression, not because it brands Hester as criminal but because it reveals the Puritans as denying the body (of the word, as of Hester) and thereby creating the emblem, the type, the sin, and its penalty: to display oneself as repressed.[10]

The function of repression in forming the text's unifying symbol can be understood by glossing each of the interpretative levels in turn and observing how they are integrated. As I remarked above, Hawthorne's rewriting of metamorphic myth in the late 1840s, along with his commentaries on the idea of American regeneration, gives support to the idea that at the mythological level *The Scarlet Letter* is concerned with the failure of the Puritans to recreate Eden in the New World. The meditation on Adam and Hester's 'crime' has far more powerful authority than that provided by Milton, for Saint Augustine had already specifically concerned himself with the problem of whether sexual intercourse could occur in Paradise, or whether it was only the consequence of the Fall. He had concluded in terms which Hawthorne seems to adopt: 'if there had been no sin, marriage would have been worthy of the happiness of paradise, and would have given birth to children to be loved, and yet would not have given rise to any lust to be ashamed of'.[11] Accordingly, by shaming Hester the Puritans only confirm their own fallen condition and deny the regeneration of America, for the love of Hester and Adam is indeed without lust and gives birth to a child who should be loved, not introduced into the world as a living token of shame.

In this ironic *Paradise Lost* Chillingworth acts the part of Satan, tempting Adam and Hester by his absence, then holding

Dimmesdale's soul in purgatory when he returns (128, 252). The energy of his characterisation, however, seems more inspired by his function within the artistic allegory, for Chillingworth exemplifies the analytic mind which seeks to expose the workings of the unconscious (sexual instincts, imaginative associations) and to brand them with the signifieds 'adultery' and 'guilt'. These are the identities which society imposes, and society, as the description of Bellingham's mansion makes clear, is in itself a product of the Old World that frustrates American regeneration by imposing hierarchy and restraint upon nature. The mythological level can thus be seen to repeat the structures we have observed in Cooper's novels but with far greater lucidity. The union of Hester and Dimmesdale would, if allowed, produce a rhapsodic fusion of nature and morality, a spontaneous being-in-the-wilderness-of-the-New-World that would admit of no consciousness, no literary expression, no sense of difference. In order for this mythological union to have form and expression it needs the prohibitory boundary provided by consciousness and the Law, Chillingworth and Bellingham, for only these agencies of repression are capable of translating unconscious desire into the differential system of linguistic communication.

The function of Pearl at the mythological level is problematic since it is only by condensing Eden and Bethlehem that one can provide a birthplace for the child of Adam and Eve. The association of Hester with the Virgin Mary to some extent allows for this, Pearl paradoxically symbolising the 'infant that was to redeem the world' (56), the pearl of great price (the knowledge of good bought dear by knowing ill), and 'the infant worthy to have been brought forth in Eden' (90). By collecting these descriptions Pearl can be seen as the symbolic offspring of New World intercourse, but by her conduct she also dramatises the need for repression by being ungovernable until acknowledged by her sinful father. Just as Adam and Eve need the Fall in order to join myth to humanity, so Pearl discovers the moral need for crucifixion on the scaffold. By her redemption into humanity when acknowledged by her father in the market-place, Pearl further symbolises the need for nature (the 'natural' child) to be brought into sorrow (husbandry/patriarchy: agriculture/possession) in order for the disciplines of civilisation to be established.

Pearl's symbolic functions, as I have said, appear confused, perhaps because the deeper motivation of Pearl's behaviour seems to belong to the artistic allegory of the text. In the chapter devoted

to her characterisation we find Pearl playing beside her mother in a
'circle of seclusion from human society' (94) which resembles that
occupied by surveyor Hawthorne in the custom-house. The chapter
seems almost transparently autobiographical, Hester at her needle
being a slight metaphorisation of Hawthorne at work on his text (or
of Sophia, his wife, at her domestic labour), and the child, the
daughter Una, playing at his feet. What is truly remarkable about
the textual child, however, is the fecundity of her imagination and
the contradictory hostility she evinces to the forms of her own
imagination.

> It was wonderful, the vast variety of forms into which she threw
> her intellect, with no continuity, indeed, but darting up and
> dancing, always in a state of preternatural activity, – soon
> sinking down, as if exhausted by so rapid and feverish a tide of
> life, – and succeeded by other shapes of a similar wild energy. It
> was like nothing so much as the phantasmagoric play of the
> northern lights. In the mere exercise of the fancy, however, and
> the sportiveness of a growing mind, there might be little more
> than was observable in other children of bright faculties; except
> as Pearl, in the dearth of human playmates, was thrown more
> upon the visionary throng which she created. The singularity lay
> in the hostile feelings with which the child regarded all these
> offspring of her own heart and mind. She never created a friend,
> but seemed always to be sowing broadcast the dragon's teeth,
> whence sprung a harvest of armed enemies, against whom she
> rushed to battle. It was inexpressibly sad. . . . (95)

Since Pearl is 'the scarlet letter endowed with life' (102), and is here
characterised with Hawthorne's ambiguous feelings about the
imagination, it seems valid to treat Pearl as the emblem of the
literary text itself, as the typical paradox of Hawthorne/Hester's
creativity. The difficulty posed by Pearl to both author and reader
can then be seen to derive from her contradictory functions at the literal,
mythological and artistic levels. At the literal level she has to learn
about sin in order to mature. At the artistic level she has to
dramatise the need of the imagination for the restraint of the
analytic mind (Chillingworth) if it is to achieve meaningful form.
But at the mythological level Pearl should need no discipline,
knowledge, or society, for if America is a second Eden then its child
should exemplify the return to primal innocence. Pearl's failure to

exemplify this achievement would then seem to suggest that truly *American* art is a contradiction in terms, for art is product of the Fall, and the Fall is the sign of the Old World. Pearl's eventual emigration to Europe thus symbolises the impossibility of achieving an art which, whilst being highly wrought, is at the same time concordant with the American mythology of regeneration. (It also prefigures Hawthorne's own later artistic emigration in *The Marble Faun*.)

We can now begin to define the integration of the different allegorical levels. True American art, like Hester's innocent relationship with Dimmesdale, would be non-reflective, spontaneous, unconstrained, a literal enactment of transcendentalist precepts of communion and oneness. It would be as anarchic and fulsome as Thomas Morton's festivities around the maypole, as incoherent as the babble of the stream that defines the boundary between Pearl and the lovers in the forest grove. Whitman comes close to such a Bacchanalian art in *Leaves of Grass*, as does Melville in the allusively scabrous passages of *Moby-Dick*, but Hawthorne works in greater deference to prevailing codes of the seemly and the verisimilar.[12] His art needs boundaries, repressions, the marketplace and the knowledge of sin to make it grow. In the forest Hester must take up the emblem of her crime before Pearl will recognise her: *The Scarlet Letter*, whether as text or as initial sign, can only be produced by the fall into fixed emblematic identities and allegorical knowledge, into society and law, convention and contract.

There is, however, a continuing ambiguity. The stigmatisation of Hester is the cruellest part of her suffering for it forces her to give up her individuality and 'become the general symbol at which the preacher and moralist might point' (79). The complexity of her personality is thus reduced to the signified 'adulteress', condensing all her creativity, maternity, passion and spontaneity into the singularity of a *crime*. Yet the typing of Hester for the purposes of social order is in a sense the basis of Hawthorne's activity as allegorist: the constant desire is not to deny Hester's freedom by admitting that she is, in fact, what she is set out to be, an adulteress, because whilst Hawthorne's art needs her to be a type, it also needs her to have the apparently autonomous and unpredictable quality of a character in a novel. The set of tensions gathered around the emblematisation of Hester can thus be seen to include Hawthorne's shift from allegorical tales to more realistic novels (a shift Poe had recently urged),[13] his indebtedness to the Puritan tradition and his desire to escape it, as well as the fundamental dilemma of the sometimes anarchic and utopian author that in ascribing identities he conspires in fixing the inherently fluid relationship of signifier to signified and becomes bound to the dominant ideology.

Hawthorne's awareness of the latter dilemma is implicit in his handling of Pearl and is clearly exemplified at two moments in the novel. In 'The Minister in a Maze' when Dimmesdale has decided to admit his love for Hester and escape the repressive orthodoxy of the Puritan colony, he finds himself rehearsing all the blasphemous and lewd suggestions that arise when one inverts or lets slip the conventional. (Presumably it was in similar mood that he seduced Hester Prynne and the whole narrative began.) In an earlier moment, when Hester first stands on the scaffold at the end of Chapter Two, her mind escapes into a stream of unstructured recollections and then returns almost with relief to the oppressive gaze of the Puritan community and the secure identity of the scarlet letter. The question of which state of mind is the true or real, and which the dream, had been posed by Hawthorne's work since 'Young Goodman Brown' and indicates the contradiction between a utopian desire for signifying without repression and a conservative need for society to fix the bounds of sense. The contradiction cannot be resolved, only elaborated. In his writing Hawthorne searches for escape, confession, release; yet the more he writes the more he inscribes himself in the oppressive environment of the market-place, and the more he denies the spontaneous production of signs which should characterise the art of an Edenic America. The climax of the novel, in Dimmesdale's confession on the scaffold, may be read as an attempt to close the gap through an outpouring of Dimmesdale's instinctual self to the *demos*. However, the real admission of his instinctual self had occurred in 'The Minister in a Maze' and the confession on the scaffold only serves to acknowledge that Dimmesdale's sexuality and love are criminal and that the mystic symbol means no more than adultery. Thus, although in confessing Dimmesdale believes he has escaped the tormenting voice of Chillingworth (the super-ego) and achieved full-speech, he has only succeeded in repressing his instinctual self by equating its activities with the signified of a repressive social law. His death is consequent because he has agreed with the dominant ideology and reduced both himself and Hester to the status of types.

Dimmesdale's confession that his intercourse with Hester was illicit has further significance for Hawthorne's art because

Hawthorne had previously defined his writing as 'an imperfectly successful attempt to open an intercourse with the world' (ix, 6). The word 'intercourse' is used with some frequency in the novel to describe human relationships, following the sense of Webster's 1828 definition as 'communication, commerce . . . either in common affairs and civilities, in trade, or in correspondence by letters'. Excluded from this definition is the sexual signification which appears in Webster's definition of 'adultery' as 'the sexual intercourse of any man with a married woman; . . . in *scripture*, idolatry, or apostasy from the true God'. The word 'intercourse', then, is one point in an associative chain involving adultery and idolatry, sexual intercourse and art.[14] Lusting after women not one's own, like the worship of false gods, threatens the stability of the social order: as adultery consists in sexual intercourse escaping the bounds of the licit, so art runs the risk of making illicit meanings, graven images, or questioning the dominant ideology.

The importance attached to this chain of associations in *The Scarlet Letter* may be illustrated by returning to the contradiction between the history of New England and its mythological representation. In showing that the Puritans failed to build a New World because they had not abandoned the Old World need for hierarchy and repressive order, Hawthorne evidences his agreement with contemporary Democratic ideology. He sees the past as a fallen Eden needing only Independence and Democracy to redeem it. But in representing the disparity between the ideal and the actual in the past he reveals his doubts about the contemporary regeneration of America. Brook Farm had taught him that utopianism, however seductive, did not produce a viable social organism because human relationships, like art, need regulations that can only seem oppressive to the utopian point of view. Hawthorne's art is therefore formed by the contradiction between a desire for regeneration and a knowledge that history has proved regeneration to be a mythological project. Because the myth has been so thoroughly instilled, Hawthorne resorts to a conservative morality of original sin to explain regeneration's failure. Yet this morality conflicts with his Democratic belief in America and its people. Since his art is formed by this circle of contradictions it must always seem from some point of view to be adulterous, impure, an apostasy; it is always establishing illicit meanings, always fracturing the consensus ideology. Like the badge of shame which Hester embroiders, it will always be a warning that only by keeping intercourse within limits

can one achieve great art, and that the need for such limits denies
the possibility of regeneration.

5.2 *THE HOUSE OF THE SEVEN GABLES* AND THE TAKING OF NABOTH'S VINEYARD

In Hawthorne's lifetime Massachusetts experienced the industrial
revolution which would affect most other states only after the Civil
War. An economy which in the 1820s had been based on overseas
commerce and agriculture was rapidly transformed to manufacture
commodities in factories and workshops. Textiles, for example,
which had been an important contribution to household and state
economies in Hawthorne's childhood, were by mid-century being
mass produced in the purpose-built factory towns of Waltham and
Lowell.[15] Hester's art of embroidery, once a major occupation of
Massachusetts women, was capitalised. The overseas trade, once the
mainstay of the state, dwindled, centralised on Boston, and left
Salem to decline into the sleepy neglect which Hawthorne so
eloquently describes in 'The Custom-House'. The revenue of its
Surveyor declined in proportion. Just to the south, the small town
of Lynn expanded to become the centre of the state's third largest
industry, shoe manufacture. Its workers were predominantly the
Irish immigrants who would soon turn Protestant Massachusetts
into a Catholic state.

As we have seen, one of Hawthorne's responses to these changes
was to search for a utopian model of social intercourse against which
other forms, many of them new and threatening, could be measured.
Another was to experience as an acute dilemma the eighteenth-
century distinction of the analytic mind from the passional body,
and to desire a return to the whole human being. In this Hawthorne
evidences the crisis of the mercantilist world-view which had
cultivated the idea of a Reason divorced from Fancy and Passion in
order to found society upon contract and calculation. When
industrial capital displaced mercantile capital, this balanced separation of head and heart became an alienated opposition, partly
because industrial capital segregates mental and physical labour
into distinct social classes.[16] A yet more important effect on
Hawthorne's work, as on Melville's, was that industrialisation
emphasised the importance of labour, self-improvement and
upward social mobility through the acquisition of skills and capital,

ideas which had played a minor role in the myth of yeoman self-sufficiency and which now tended to relegate the idea of a bounteous nature to subordinate status.[17] These changes of rank within the constellation of Democratic beliefs allowed Hawthorne and Melville a perspective on the agrarian component of dominant ideology not available to writers at previous historical moments. Economic changes also exerted increasing strain on party loyalties, for the growing emphasis on free labour (the ideology of a capitalising labour market in which each worker 'freely' sells his labour time) illuminated the differences of political economy between a North transforming to capitalism and a South trapped in a pre-capitalist mode of production. Some Northern Whigs and Democrats began to see their differences as less important than their shared opposition to the extension of slavery. In the 1848 elections anti-extension Democrats broke ranks and formed the Free Soil party behind Van Buren. This split the Democratic vote and lost the Democrats the election, but although the Free Soil party disappeared within a few years, it was the first indication of the new ideological opposition between the Republican North and the agrarian Democratic South.[18]

A small consequence of the Democratic failure in 1848 was that Hawthorne was removed from the post of Salem's Surveyor of Customs and was precipitated into writing *The Scarlet Letter*. The campaign to have him evicted, despite Zachary Taylor's promise not to implement a wholesale spoils system, was led by the Reverend Charles Upham, a prominent Salem Whig and erstwhile friend who stooped to accuse Hawthorne of financial irregularities in his capacity as Surveyor. In 'The Custom-House', Hawthorne relates the circumstances of his dismissal in a passage that gives a useful perspective on his political position:

> The late Surveyor was not altogether ill-pleased to be recognised by the Whigs as an enemy; since his inactivity in political affairs, – his tendency to roam, at will, in that broad and quiet field where all mankind may meet, rather than confine himself to those narrow paths where brethren of the same household must diverge from one another, – had sometimes made it questionable with his brother Democrats whether he was a friend. Now, after he had won the crown of martyrdom, (though with no longer a head to wear it on,) the point might be looked upon as settled. (42)

A later statement that he thought the preservation of the Union to be more important than the abolition of slavery, confirms the impression that he was a Conservative Democrat who found political allegiance essential to his identity of delicately balanced contradictions, and who at the same time experienced the political as a potentially destabilising factor.[19] The child of 'aristocratic' forebears, his own father dead before he could know him, his social status that of poor relation, Hawthorne devoted his life to elaborating the story of his ancestors' importance at the same time as he castigated his ancestors as corrupt and sought to rid himself and his country of the tyranny of the past. Iconoclastic hagiography was perhaps his way of expressing his uncertain relationship to an absent father, and hence his uncertain relationship to authority, the State and the dominant ideology.

One reason why *The House of the Seven Gables* is now judged a lesser novel than *The Scarlet Letter* may be that it is the more direct and therefore more contradictory expression of Hawthorne's ambivalent relationship to the 'aristocratic' past and the Democratic present. The oppositions it manifests are not resolved by myth but are rather left to confront the reader in a text that is irresolute, inconsistent, and yet clearly structured. Clifford, the neurasthenic artist, descendant of a long line of aristocratic Pyncheons, is contrasted with Holgrave, the artist of light and science, the radical reformer and optimist who for political reasons and as a descendant of the expropriated Maules has every reason to be hostile to the Pyncheons. The opposition between these two characters represents that between the radical Democrat and aristocratic Whig: Holgrave inveighs in Jeffersonian manner, demanding an end to hereditary wealth, the reformation of society every twenty years, and every fifty years the merging of the family into 'the great obscure mass of humanity' (II, 184) so that it can purge itself of accumulated sin. The desire to escape the past that was evident in Hester's desire to throw off her letter and escape the colony is here more vigorously expressed. Holgrave is Hawthorne's project for a new kind of artistry, a new relationship to America and Democracy, a relationship which repudiates history and scepticism, the Puritan past and the importance of the family name.

The appeal of Holgrave's position to the introverted Clifford is apparent, but bodes his death. Watching a political procession pass beneath his window (the viewer's position symbolising superiority and apartness) he wants to jump down and merge himself in 'the great centre of humanity' (II, 166). Such an escape would evidently be suicidal. When Clifford does finally flee the house with Hepzibah he is only capable of one sustained outburst of Democratic invective against aristocracy before he collapses helpless at a wayside station. When we next see him, he has returned to the hereditary prison of the Pyncheon house.

Since Clifford has not been represented in political debate with Holgrave and so cannot be said to have been converted by him, and since what Holgrave says against aristocracy in his own voice is also said by Hawthorne in his authorial discourse, it seems reasonable to conclude that the novel *expresses* an acute personal tension but fails to establish sufficient aesthetic distance to be able to *represent* it. Having constructed the Pyncheon dynasty around the Hawthorne family past, Hawthorne is too personally involved in the outcome to view the opposition dispassionately. Evidently he has a strong desire to convert to the radical Democratic position since Holgrave is represented as consistently attractive and no argument is advanced to counter his proposals for the renewal of society. However, to accept Holgrave's position would entail abandoning the genetic guilt with which Hawthorne constructs his literary identity. Hawthorne would then be without a subject, and without a reason for his address to the Democratic readership. He would also have to live in the bland optimism he represents in Phoebe, the creature of the New World's regenerate nature. The dream of release from conceited ancestral status and from the impoverished isolation such conceit now brings may be potent, but when imaged as a clear objective alternative between past and present, aristocracy and democracy, culture and nature, it results in bathos. When Holgrave proposes marriage to Phoebe we are told that

> The bliss which makes all things true, beautiful, and holy shone around this youth and maiden. They were conscious of nothing sad nor old. They transfigured the earth, and made it Eden again, and themselves the two first dwellers in it. (II, 307)

Coming from an author who has always balanced a belief in democracy with a large scepticism about the reformer's belief in Edenic regeneration this must surely indicate an intellectual defeat. (It is certainly an artistic one, since the couple are supposed to be experiencing this state of bliss whilst standing beside a recently discovered corpse.) The system of oppositions, so carefully drawn, has somehow failed to allow the Democratic affirmation that seems intended all along: instead of being destroyed by Holgrave the house takes in the descendant of the expropriated Maules and remains intact, inherited wealth lining the nest. A conservative restitution of the élite resolves personal discords whilst aborting the serious political issues that have motivated the text.

The regression of the ending may perhaps be explained by picking out the covert references to the contemporary political situation with which the novel opens. In the Preface, Hawthorne states his purpose as being to convince the reader of

> the truth . . . that the wrong-doing of one generation lives into successive ones, and, divesting itself of every temporary advantage, becomes a pure and uncontrollable mischief; and he would feel it a singular gratification if this romance might effectually convince mankind . . . of the folly of tumbling down an avalanche of ill-gotten gold, or real estate, on the heads of an unfortunate posterity, thereby to maim and crush them, until the accumulated mass shall be scattered abroad in its original atoms. (II, 2).

The Preface is usually read as merely referring to the genetic wrongdoing of the Pyncheons by ignoring the fact that in 1851 an avalanche of 'ill-gotten gold, or real estate' had just tumbled down upon the United States through the conquest of Mexico and the ensuing gold rush. As Hawthorne began his novel Congress was debating the compromise that was to prevent the Union breaking apart over slavery in the newly acquired lands. Many predicted that national ruin would be the result of the expansionist's greed and cited the story of King Ahab as a parable. In *I Kings 21* all could read how King Ahab coveted his neighbour Naboth's vineyard and how, when Naboth refused to sell, Queen Jezebel had him accused of worshipping false gods and stoned to death. Before Ahab could take possession of his lands God sent Elijah to pronounce sentence upon Ahab that 'in the place where dogs lick the blood of Naboth shall dogs lick thy blood', but because Ahab humbled himself the Lord announced instead that he would bring evil on Ahab's house 'in his son's days'.[20]

The invitation of the Preface to relate the novel to recent national events is clearly reinforced by the parallelism between the story of Ahab and the first chapter of the novel: Matthew Maule refuses to sell his well to his powerful neighbour, Colonel Pyncheon, whereupon the Colonel has him accused of witchcraft and executed. As Maule dies he pronounces the curse upon the Colonel that 'God will give him blood to drink!' (II, 8), a curse which continues to affect subsequent generations of the tyrannical Pyncheons.[21] In this novel Hawthorne would therefore appear to be levelling a far more fundamental critique of the Puritan elect than anything he has previously penned, and to be extending that critique from the past into the present. He is in effect saying that the Puritans' witch-hunting was motivated, at least in part, by the desire to amass wealth; that oppression results from greed masquerading as religious principle; and that this wrong-doing lives into successive generations right down to the present. The conquest of Mexico, and Judge Jaffrey's subversion of the course of justice in order to expropriate his own cousin, are but contemporary instances of a tradition that denies the highest ideals of the New World. This is indeed a bleak example of saying 'nay' to contemporary reformers and sets a question mark beside all the fundamental tenets of American progress, for if the Pilgrim Fathers built their society by expropriating fellow whites, and if such behaviour continues in the present, then how can one maintain the ethical superiority of the United States? This was the question some of Hawthorne's contemporaries were asking during and immediately after the war with Mexico.[22]

By associating himself with Holgrave, Hawthorne adopts a Democratic discourse that blames the Whig élite for the failure of America to fulfil its promise of regeneration. The Pyncheons are consistently represented as greedy 'aristocrats' bent on amassing wealth and as building their houses over the graves of their expropriated victims. They are men who

> possess vast ability in grasping, and arranging, and appropriating to themselves, the big, heavy, solid unrealities, such as gold, landed estate, offices of trust and emolument, and public honours. With these materials, and with deeds of goodly aspect, done in the public eye, an individual of this class builds up, as it were, a tall and stately edifice, which in the view of other people, and ultimately in his own view, is no other than a man's character, or the man himself. Behold, therefore a palace! . . . Ah; but in some low and obscure nook . . . may lie a corpse; half-decayed and still decaying, and diffusing its death-scent through all the palace! (II, 229–30)

This critique is pertinent but inherently unstable because the desire for other people's real estate is far from uniquely Whig; the Democratic party to which Hawthorne owed his place as Salem's Surveyor of Customs had won the 1844 election on an expansionist platform and once in office had proceeded to engage Mexico in a war which was to result in the cession of almost one third of what now constitutes the United States. The radical Democrats whom Holgrave typifies had objected to annexation because it would extend slavery, not because it was inherently immoral to take a neighbour's lands. Furthermore, Holgrave/Maule's self-righteous attack on the owners of hereditary wealth is undermined by the fact that Maule's well was originally taken from the Indians. The basis of the radical's complaint, whether in the recent or distant past, can therefore be seen to be hollow.

Having clarified the political contradiction which lies behind the text's thematic oppositions, we are better placed to understand that the artistic inconsistencies with which so many critics have found fault arise from the attempt to resolve the contradiction between the history of expropriation and the desire for regeneration at a moment when expropriation is threatening to tear the nation apart. The ending which Hawthorne wrote to flood with sunshine an otherwise too sombre tale may be seen as the realisation that the disgreement between Democrats and Whigs on such questions as the distribution of wealth and power is less important than their basic agreement about the expansion of the American empire. When, as the exponent of regenerating Democracy, Holgrave marries Phoebe Pyncheon, country cousin of the expropriating élite and personification of regenerating nature, and then settles in a house of stone which until a few weeks previously he had wanted to destroy, there is an admission of a unity which the text has tried to keep at bay: the marriage occurred long ago between an ideology that has legitimised the expropriation of the Indians and a myth of nature that has stood as an alibi for building farms on another people's ground.

In an obscure way, the lifting of Maule's curse points towards such an understanding. In its pragmatic aspect the curse consists in the Maules having concealed the Pyncheons' deed to Indian lands in Maine, thereby condemning the family to the illusion that they own great wealth to which they cannot produce the title. With some improbability this deed is recovered when Clifford recalls 'an old dreamy recollection haunting [him] . . . of unimaginable wealth' (II, 185). Holgrave touches a hidden spring and the portrait of

Colonel Pyncheon comes crashing to the floor to reveal the deed's hiding place. Covered with the 'hieroglyphics of several Indian Sagamores' it is a 'truth that history has let slip . . . out of the evidence' (II, 17–18). By placing this deed behind the image of the patriarchal founder of the Pyncheon dynasty, the Maules have at the same time alluded to the origins of all white wealth and concealed the larger history of expropriation to which their own expropriation gives only metonymic expression. They have also cursed the Pyncheons to believe themselves properly entitled to land to which they can prove no right of possession, the cursed belief of all the expansionist Ahabs in American history.

6 Herman Melville: Writing as Whaling

The abundance of criticism that is now gathered around *Moby-Dick* is sufficient evidence that like *The Scarlet Letter* it is also an over-determined text. However, where much of the over-determination in Hawthorne seems unconscious, we know that at least initially Melville's allusiveness was deliberate. Much critical industry has been devoted to bringing these allusions to light and as a result we now know that *Moby-Dick* was inspired by the Bible, by Milton, Rabelais, Cervantes, Shakespeare, Thomas Browne, Robert Burton, Pierre Bayle, and by contemporary whaling texts. We know that Ahab was modelled upon Satan, Faust, Lear, Prometheus, Oedipus, Narcissus; and that the voyage of 'The Pequod' is symbolic of Western man's quest for truth, and, via the Biblical story of Ahab, a political allegory of the American belief in Manifest Destiny.[1] Criticism has thus enabled a consensus view of the text as a more or less knowing symbolic commentary on the Christian heritage of literary forms and beliefs, and as a commentary on how those beliefs motivate Americans in their relationship to nature. This view is generally helpful, but it fails to explain why the text that gives condensed expression to these themes should be composed in such an evidently heterogeneous collection of discourses. As Nina Baym has recently observed, most criticism has been content to acknowledge briefly the discursive variety of the text, and has then extracted the plot and proceeded to interpret *Moby-Dick* as if it were a largely conventional whaling narrative with some poetic passages and symbolic characterisation. In this, modern criticism has been less sensitive than contemporary reviewers who inventoried the various discourses of *Moby-Dick* as 'naval observation, magazine article-writing, satiric reflection . . . rhapsody, romance and matter-of-fact . . . '.[2]

One can, as Baym has done, draw up one's own list, adding sermons, short stories, moral essays, prose sketches, political speeches, satirical thrusts, dramatic soliloquies, stage directions, anatomical and zoological descriptions, technological manual writing, travelogue, encyclopaedic digests et cetera, et cetera. Alternatively, one can, as James Guetti has done in the single essay to place Melville's language at the centre of critical concern, discriminate basic modalities of discourse (factual or circumstantial, figurative allusions, and figurative prose which is ultimately uncertain as to its meanings) and use these modalities to illuminate the fundamental epistemological conflict between an Ishmael who refuses to conceptualise the whale and an Ahab intent on establishing the signified of the whale as 'cosmic malignancy'.

We shall return to consider the merits of Guetti's approach shortly, but it is first helpful to glance at *Typee* where the same heterogeneity of discourse is latent, the text moving between history writing, travelogue, anthropological observation, adventure narrative, romantic natural description, and a kind of proto-symbolic discourse that Melville will later develop into rippling sexual innuendo.[3] Of these one might exemplify the following:

(*Geographical history*)

This island, although generally called one of the Marquesas, is by some navigators considered as forming one of a distinct cluster, comprising the islands of Ruhooka, Ropo, and Nukuheva; upon which three the appellation of the Washington Group has been bestowed. They form a triangle, and lie within the parallels of 8° 38′ and 9° 32′ South latitude and 139° 20′ and 140° 10′ West longitude from Greenwich. (11)

(*Travelogue/romantic description*)

The beautiful aspect of the shore is heightened by deep and romantic glens, which come down to it at almost equal distances, all apparently radiating from a common centre, and the upper extremities of which are lost to the eye beneath the shadow of the mountains. Down each of these little valleys flows a clear stream, here and there assuming the form of a slender cascade, then stealing invisibly along until it bursts upon the sight again in larger and more noisy waterfalls, and at last demurely wanders along to the sea. (23–24)

(*Anthropological observation*)

In the manufacture of the beautiful white tappa generally worn
on the Marquesan Islands, the preliminary operation consists in
gathering a certain quantity of the young branches of the cloth-
tree. The exterior bark being pulled off as worthless, there
remains a slender fibrous substance, which is carefully stripped
from the stick, to which it closely adheres. When a sufficient
quantity of it has been collected, the various strips
are . . . .   (147)

(*Adventure narrative*)

Satisfied by his scrutiny, my light-limbed companion swung
himself nimbly upon it, and twisting his legs round it in sailor
fashion, slipped down eight or ten feet, where his weight gave it a
motion not unlike that of a pendulum. He could not venture to
descend any further; so holding on with one hand,
he . . . .   (60–61)

(*Proto-symbolic*)

After a long interval . . . 'The Perseverance' . . . was spoken
somewhere in the vicinity of the ends of the earth, cruising along
as leisurely as ever, her sails all bepatched and bequilted with
rope-yarns, her spars fished with old pipe staves . . . . I suppose
she is still regularly tacking twice in twenty-four hours somewhere off Buggerry Island, or the Devil's-Tail Peak.   (22–23)

(*Polemic*)

The Anglo-Saxon hive have extirpated Paganism from the
greater part of the North American continent; but with it they
have likewise extirpated the greater portion of the Red race.
Civilisation is gradually sweeping from the earth the lingering
vestiges of Paganism, and at the same time the shrinking forms of
its unhappy worshippers.
    Among the islands of Polynesia, no sooner are the images
overturned, the temples demolished, and the idolators converted
into *nominal* Christians, than disease, vice, and premature death
make their appearance. The depopulated land is then recruited
from the rapacious hordes of enlightened individuals who settle
themselves within its borders, and clamorously announce the
progress of the Truth.   (195)

Bakhtine has taught us to see that the novel is a genre composed of heterogeneous discourses, each of which expresses the interests of differing social fractions, different social practices. The integration of these discourses in most fictions is assured by a central voice of authority – that of the 'author' – that accords each discourse its appropriate value in relation to the dominant ideology.[4] In the first-person narration of *Typee* this integration is assured by the conventional system of autobiographical, 'true-life' adventure. Tommo officially invents nothing, reports only what happened to him and his companion, Toby, on the island, or repeats matters of public record (the history of the islands' discovery, for example.) Tommo constitutes a naive experiencer/perceiver of events/facts and makes clear distinctions between what he has observed and the deductions that may be drawn from it. As he says in the narration, 'those things I have stated as facts will remain facts, in spite of whatever the bigoted or credulous may say or write against them. My reflections, however, on those facts may not be free from error' (199). In the Preface this sentiment becomes more emphatic. Melville acknowledges that 'a few passages in the ensuing chapters . . . may be thought to bear rather hard upon a reverend order of men' (the Protestant Missions), but declares that 'such passages will be found . . . to be based upon facts admitting of no contradiction . . . . The conclusions deduced from these facts are unavoidable . . . . He has stated such matters just as they occurred, and leaves every one to form his own opinion concerning them . . .' (xiv).

Melville's confidence in the true perception of 'the facts', and in the ability of his readers to arrive at rational, unprejudiced deductions from those facts, reveals the extent of Tommo's agreement with the dominant epistemology of Common Sense and allows us to see why the different discourses of *Typee* are not evidently heterogeneous. Since the narration derives its authority from this epistemology, and from the simple appropriation of the material world which it facilitates, the trenchant criticism of the effects of Christianity on the pagan islanders are effectively marginalised as 'speculation'. Despite Melville's confidence, his comments remain no more than one man's view and leave his readers to reach their own, possibly different, conclusions.

It is not surprising that whilst the religious press objected to Melville's polemics, the real issue around which contemporary opinion divided was the 'factual' status of *Typee*. Harper's likened the manuscript to *Robinson Crusoe* and then decided 'it was impossible that it could be true and therefore was without real value'. In London, John Murray considered it for his 'Home and Colonial Library', a collection of 'true-life' imperial adventures intended for sale throughout the British colonies, but was at first suspicious of its truth and only accepted it after Melville had removed some of that 'taint of fiction'. When it was eventually published in the United States – the second edition purged of critical and sexual embarrassments – reviewers again divided on the question of its truth, the issue only being settled when 'Toby' appeared in the mid-West and corroborated the first part of the narrative. From that moment *Typee* was considered a reliable report of life among the cannibals and remained Melville's most popular book throughout the nineteenth century.[5] Now, however, thanks to Charles Anderson's researches and to more recent accounts, we know that Melville's representation of Marquesan life owes as much to wish-fulfilment as it does to historical experience.[6] What Melville saw in *Typee* was an earthly paradise where the Calvinist tenets he had learned in the Dutch Reformed Church were inverted. As in Transcendentalism, nature ceased to be malign and was revealed as benign; communion with nature rather than its repression became the means to grace. Since in any mythic vision there must be elements which prohibit fulfilment of the desire, so in *Typee* the enticing horror of cannibalism, the fear of the Happars, Tommo's unhealing injury and imprisonment, and the threat of tattooing, provide the necessary boundaries of the dream world. Within these boundaries, however, life is represented as a calm felicity in the bosom of spontaneously productive nature.

That the purpose of this representation is to criticise the presumptive superiority of Christian civilisation needs no emphasis, but what has crucial bearing on Melville's later work is that because he remains true to the dominant ideology of 'the facts' he is incapable of acknowledging that his own conversion to a benign view of nature merely substitutes a new myth for an old. Because the problem of knowledge is denied so is the actual complexity of Marquesan civilisation. Melville's savages, like Cooper's, are ennobled, but they are still 'savages'. Whilst Melville describes their domestic and marital customs with the accuracy of an amateur anthropologist, he is so intent on painting a picture of luxurious indolence and natural goodness that he attributes the construction of vast edifices of stone to an ancient civilisation (when in fact they were public works of recent date), denies the careful husbandry and science that went into Marquesan agricultural production, and ignores the periodic famines and bouts of genocidal warfare that wrecked the islands.[7] As we have seen in reading Cooper, this denial of historical culture is the fundamental work of myth and so, even against his intentions, Melville becomes a cultural imperialist: as a reformed Protestant his mission is to convert his readers to the true religion of nature, even if this leads him to deny the humanity of the people he offers as example.

It is scarcely conceivable that Melville was aware of this when he was writing the novel. Although he was only in the valley for four weeks he supported his initial experience by extensive reading in contemporary accounts and seems to have thought of his work as autobiography transformed in accordance with reasonable poetic licence. This said it would appear that Melville discovered his own predisposition towards the Edenic myth whilst trying to correct Christianity's belief in the superiority of civilisation to savagery. This paradoxical fate seems the origin of the dilemmas he was to confront in his later writing. Certainly foreshadowed in *Typee* is the narcissus theme of *Moby-Dick*, the self-delusion of the Protestant missions who see the Marquesans as only the savages they expect to see, being more profoundly represented in Ahab's inability to see the whale as merely a whale, and in his mythologisation of it as the essence of cosmic malignancy. Equally and more subtly fore-shadowed is the alternative case, Ishmael's attempt to refuse all mythologies standing as an implicit criticism of the earlier Tommo who innocently abandoned the Ahab position only to adopt the equally destructive (if more sympathetic) myth of the noble savage.

It is this tension between a mythological view of the world and the question of its alternative that I wish to explore in this chapter, but before leaving *Typee* I want to draw attention to a linguistic incident which has relevance to the later work. In Chapter Two of *Typee* Melville introduces his reader to the historical geography of the islands, giving their latitude and longitude, their size, and the manner of their discovery by the whites (p. 11, quoted above). He then moves on to the kind of travelogue discourse that serves up the 'desert' isles as romanticised objects for Western consumption. In passing he notes that 'this island is about twenty miles in length and nearly as many in breadth. It has three good harbours on its coast; the largest and best of which is called by the people living in its vicinity "Tyohee", and by Captain Porter was denominated

Massachusetts Bay' (11). Despite the many polemics against imperialism in the book, the politics of this change of name are not taken up by Melville. They can be illuminated by recalling the words of the Bishop of Avila when he presented Queen Isabella of Spain with the first grammar of a modern European language. To the Queen's demand, 'What is it for?' the Bishop replied, 'Madam, language is the perfect instrument of empire'.[8]

In the writing of *Moby-Dick* Melville seems to have discovered this more insidious aspect of imperialism. The first section of the novel opens with an 'Etymology' which has been prepared by a 'pale Usher . . . [who] was ever dusting his old lexicons and grammars with a queer handkerchief, mockingly embellished with all the gay flags of all the known nations of the world' (1). There then follows a quotation from Hakluyt, compiler of that most compendious guide to colonisation, the *Principall Navigations, Voiages, and Discoveries of the English Nation*. The quotation warns the reader to be sure 'to school others' in the correct spelling of 'whale' for without 'the letter H, which almost alone maketh up the signification of the word, you deliver that which is not true'. Two quotations follow from Webster's and Richardson's Dictionaries, both of which provide etymologies that naturalise the original meaning of 'whale' as expressions of the movement of 'rolling' or 'wallowing'. To complete the section we then have the list 'חר, χητos, Cetus, Whoel, Hvalt, Wal, Hwal, Whale, Baleine, Ballena, Pekee-Nuee-Nuee, Pehee-Nuee-Nuee' (1).

The underlying meanings in this introduction to 'the whale' are, firstly that linguistic definitions are nationalist; secondly that attempts are made to assert the normalcy and natural truth of names; and thirdly that, as Mallarmé and Saussure were later to observe, words are arbitrary strokes and arbitrary sounds that become attached to signifieds only through their function in social codes.[9] Although Webster would suggest that the English word 'whale' expresses the original essence of the referent more effectively than any other sound, Melville's bland list places the English word on the same level as the seemingly risible and barbarous 'Pekee-Nuee-Nuee'. The distance between this recognition and Melville's innocent repetition of linguistic colonialism in *Typee* is testimony to the growth of his understanding in the intervening years. In *Mardi* he had explored the production and function of mythical beliefs, and he had also delivered himself of some stridently critical remarks on the ethics of the conquest of Mexico, but not until *Moby-Dick* did he apply his perceptions to his own practice as a writer and to the central issues of Jacksonian ideology.[10] Ahab, as many critics have observed, is not only modelled on mythological figures such as Prometheus, he is a myth-believer who ascribes to the world all the vengefulness of his own character ('the sum of all the general rage and hate felt by his whole race from Adam down' Ch. 41, 160) and who then mistakes these ascribed qualities for the objective essence of the extra-linguistic 'whale'. Ahab's mental operations thus typify the procedure we have previously outlined in the production of the mythological sign, Melville's double irony being that he makes Ahab, the symbolic leader of white civilisation, invest the white whale with all those qualities that white civilisation must deny about itself if the conquest is to be justified. The whale becomes the mirror of Ahab's guilt.

The position of Ishmael is superficially more simple, but ultimately more complex. In James Guetti's reading he functions both as a character who attempts to refuse the dominion of Ahab's mythological view, and as the narrator whose adoption of one discourse after another constitutes a refusal of the text to assert that there is any *one* language which has superior rights in the expression of 'the whale'. From the introductory 'Etymology' and 'Extracts' onwards, Ishmael researches available classificatory schemes and linguistic codes, frequently contradicting one with another or describing them as 'superstitious' or 'erroneous', often introducing their knowledge by an explicitly speculative tag ('as if' or 'seemed'). He thereby makes it apparent that all discourse comes under the sign of Narcissus: in language we stamp our own image on the world and believe that we have expressed objective reality. There are complex tensions within this procedure since the enchantment of metaphorical richness is great, but even when Ishmael has yielded to the spell of the poetic he always undercuts the effect in the next phrase, sentence, or paragraph, refusing to 'establish one vocabulary as more central than another'.[11]

Guetti's commentary clarifies the mode of integration between discursive heterogeneity, dramatic action, and ultimate meanings, but there are several problems to which his analysis provides only partial explanations. One of these is the idea that 'the final effect of all these languages . . . is to turn back upon themselves as artificial forms, as language, and in doing so to assert the existence of something ineffable beyond themselves'.[12] Certainly the text leaves us with this impression, the whale remaining ineffable and uncapturable to the end. But in this the text encounters the irreducible dilemma of language for in signifying the ineffability of the whale it has assigned a meaning to it: 'the whale' signifies 'the ineffability of the real'. Language, no matter how valiantly the user tries, can neither escape the reproduction of meanings nor avoid the assignation of identities. To say, as Guetti does, that Ishmael is 'voiceless because he is all voices' is to fall into the illusion of innocent repetition: in speaking the whale Ishmael may pretend that it is not *he* who speaks but *others* who speak through him – 'I am the architect', he says, 'not the builder' (Ch. 32, 229) – but in thus disowning responsibility for the linguistic materials of the text he falls into the alternative myth, the myth of the impartial producer.

In order to explore this more subtle mythology in the text we need to question Guetti's central contention that the difference between Ishmael-as-narrator and Melville-as-author is 'only nominal'.[13] Scholars who have examined the genesis of *Moby-Dick* agree that the novel first took form as a relatively straightforward whaling narrative similar in style to Melville's previously successful 'true-life' adventure fictions. Melville had more or less completed this text, which Charles Stewart has helpfully called the *Ur-Moby-Dick*, when he met Hawthorne in August 1850 and abruptly set about the rewriting which was to occupy him for a further year. Discrimination of the *Ur-Moby-Dick* material from later additions must mainly proceed by conjecture from internal evidence, but, taken together with what slight external evidence we have available, it would seem that the ur-text was a fictionalised version of Melville's own experiences aboard the *Acushnet*, the whaling vessel on which he shipped to the Marquesas Isles. Stewart suggests that the ur-narrative was to end where *Typee* began, with Melville's (Ishmael's) desertion from the whale ship, possibly as a result of the exactions of a tyrannical captain. Revising the text Melville added the Shakespearian soliloquies and dramatic chapters, the classificatory and allusive matter, the character of Ahab and the obsessive pursuit of Moby-Dick. Melville may also have added the name 'Ishmael' and awarded Queequeg the role of Ishmael's companion.[14]

This information concerning the genesis of *Moby-Dick* helps to explain why there seem to be two distinct authorial positions in the novel, one in which Melville works through the narrative persona of Ishmael and adopts the limited colloquial style of an ordinary seaman, and another in which Melville acts as a highly literate author who is interpolating his own pre-existing text. The provision of this second, more speculative, episteme to the text, implies a critical attitude on Melville's part towards the 'true-life' convention he had previously adopted, a desire to go beyond the limits of the approved and financially rewarding bounds of probable knowledge and to 'dive deeper than Ishmael can go' (Ch. 41, 162). Leon Howard and Randall Stewart have suggested that this change of tack was inspired by Melville's discovery of the dark allegorical meanings which lie beneath the surface of Hawthorne's *Mosses from an Old Manse*, and, interfusing the inspiration of Shakespeare, from a renewed desire to demonstrate that a 'Young American' could achieve the heights of genius more commonly associated with masterpieces of the European tradition. Such a view seems entirely justified by Melville's expression of these sentiments in the review he wrote of *Mosses* at the precise moment of transition between the two versions of *Moby-Dick*.[15]

Following up the suggestions I made in the preceding chapter concerning the Ahab story, urgent literary nationalism seems to have been only the surface of Melville's political intentions at this crucial moment. Once the connection between *The House of the Seven Gables* and *Moby-Dick* has been noticed, then the suggestions of textual scholars that the characters of Ahab and possibly Ishmael and Queequeg were added after the meeting with Hawthorne can be seen in a new light. Melville's discovery of the potential of Hawthorne's allegorical method coincided with the discovery of a framework of political allusions that would allow his whaling narrative to pass comment on recent national events. Thanks to Alan Heimert's painstaking study of the political allusions, we know that the narrative relies upon the frequent use of the 'ship of state' as a metaphor in political controversy surrounding the 1850 compromise measures. The history of the Republic was likened to a voyage, and its wreck at the hands of hungry 'Ahabs' who coveted Mexico's 'vineyards' was greatly feared. Melville's voyage of 'The Pequod' gives allegorical expression to the radical Free-Soil fear that Democracy's monomaniacal urge to dominate nature will at worst destroy the Republic and at best contravene the libertarian principles enshrined in the constitution. To embroider the point, the ship is crewed by three mates, one of whom represents New England (Starbuck), one the West (Stubb), and one the South (Flask); each mate is served by an appropriate harpooneer, Starbuck by the islander Queequeg, Stubb by the Indian Tashtego, Flask by the black Daggoo upon whose shoulders he rides. Ahab, whom Heimert deciphers as John C. Calhoun, the southern Democrat and arch-proponent of expansion and slavery, is served by his own special team of 'dusky spirits'.[16]

In the light of our previous observations on *Typee* it seems significant that it is when this political allegory is added to the original whaling narrative that its discursive heterogeneity becomes apparent. It is also significant that all of the aesthetic aspects of the text which today command critical attention also appear at this time. We may therefore make two important suggestions: firstly, that the questioning of the political justifications for expansionism is associated with the questioning of the centralising authority of Common Sense narration; secondly, that the interrogation of the original whaling narrative proceeds from a contradiction in the politics of nationalism, for on the one hand Melville aspires to produce a work of national literary genius, and on the other hand he becomes sceptical of nationalist activity. The Lukácsian premise that a literary work achieves significance in proportion to its articulation of dominant ideological contradictions seems entirely justified.

If one focuses attention on the first twenty-two chapters of the novel where Ishmael is securely placed as the narrator it is relatively easy to exemplify these contradictions, and also to see why it is that the disrupted narrative method of the rest of the book should be associated with the politics of the Ishmael point of view. Portents, loomings, and rare disruptions excepted, the consistent intention of the first phase of the narrative is to satirise the supposed superiority of Christian civilisation and to propose the alternative view that all men, whatever their colour or creed, are created equal. Ishmael-as-narrator expresses this view in quick thrusts against contemporary prejudice ('as though a white man were anything more dignified than a whitewashed negro', Ch. 13, 60), and Queequeg dramatises the point by behaving like a good Christian in saving from drowning a man who has just mocked his 'cannibal' ways. Ishmael's gloss on this event might stand both as summary of his own point of view, and as index of the strategy of inversion used in his satire: Queequeg seemed 'to be saying to himself – "It's a mutual, joint-stock world, in all meridians. We cannibals must help these Christians", (Ch. 13, 61). To communicate this radical levelling message is the trans-parent function of Ishmael's relationship with Queequeg, their going to bed together serving to elicit the predictable reader-response of horror at such miscegenation, and Ishmael's bowing down before Yojo, Queequeg's pagan idol, serving to scandalise dogmatic obedience to Jehovah, the one 'true' God. Ishmael here defends his worship of 'false' gods with a destructive argumentation in Christian ethics:

> I was a good Christian; born and bred in the bosom of the infallible Presbyterian Church. How then could I unite with this wild idolator in worshipping this piece of wood? But what is worship? thought I . . . – to do the will of God – *that* is worship. And what is the will of God? – to do to my fellow man what I would have my fellow man to do to me – *that* is the will of God. Now, Queequeg is my fellow man. And what do I wish that this Queequeg would do to me? Why, unite with me in my particular Presbyterian form of worship. Consequently, I must then unite with him in his; ergo, I must turn Idolator. (Ch. 10, 54)

This inversion of the Protestant mission originates in the same concern with Christian hypocrisy that will satirise the relationship between other-worldly piety and the profit motive in the characterisation of Captains Bildad and Peleg, Bildad urging '*Lay* not up for yourselves treasures upon earth . . . ' (Ch. 16, 74) whilst Peleg tries to decide what tiny fraction of the profits Ishmael will receive for his labours. It is also consistent with the critical representation of Ahab's monomaniacal desire to limit the meanings of the whale to those which his Calvinist ideology has projected onto it, but it is important to notice that although Ishmael satirises Christian hypocrisy he does so from within a unified discourse, a unified world-view. Whilst he turns Christianity back on itself to make its contradictions apparent, he remains true to its higher universalist values. His narration is in fact not far removed from that used by Tommo in *Typee*, a narration which could either record in all innocence that the name 'Tyohee' had been changed to 'Massachusetts Bay', or which could allow satirical or polemical attacks on missionary behaviour. Limited by the convention of probable first person knowledge, the representation can hardly address the wider questions of imperialism, and cannot question the assumption of its narration that the individual who names has a privileged authority. Put another way, how could Ishmael represent social history whilst a first-person narrator? And how could he imply that the language he uses is neither derived from experience, nor from his own consciousness, but is a social institution that pre-conditions his meanings?

It is tempting to extend Guetti's argument and suggest that in deciding to rewrite the *Ur-Moby-Dick* Melville was in some way aware of these questions and had sensed that his earlier narratives were innocently guilty of inscribing the dominant values his narrators often attacked. The 'Etymology' section would certainly support the contention that in adopting the method of discursive heterogeneity he was in effect extending Ishmael's critical position from one contained within the epistemic individual to a self-reflective criticism of his own textual politics. Ishmael, the true democrat in his social relations, becomes Melville, the true democrat in linguistic relations. Or, alternatively, Melville becomes a proto-modernist, lucidly revealing the arbitrariness of all semiological systems; a man, such as Bruce Franklin has him, who knows that all human knowledge is myth.[17]

This is an attractive picture, but it can only survive by denying Melville's contradictory commitment to some of his discourses. How, for example, does it square with 'The Advocate' section?

> For many years past the whaleship has been the pioneer in ferreting out the remotest and least known parts of the earth. She has explored seas and archipelagoes which had no chart, where no Cook or Vancouver had ever sailed. If American and European men-of-war now peacefully ride in once savage harbors, let them fire salutes to the honor and glory of the whale-ship, which originally showed them the way, and first interpreted between them and the savages. (Ch. 24, 99)

How does it square with the 'Postscript' to 'The Advocate' where Melville boasts the use of sperm oil as 'coronation stuff'? (209) These chapters clearly 'advocate' the interests of the text to writer and reader, advertising the central importance of whaling to the national economy and deriving from this importance (by good base-superstructure logic) a claim to the literary importance of *Moby-Dick*.[18] Elsewhere Melville will praise the Enderbys of London as founding fathers of whaling (Ch. 101) and will even go so far as to make helpful suggestions as to how the industry can be made more efficient (Ch. 62). Clearly this advocacy of whaling requires that we complement the critique of imperialism with the recognition that

Melville-as-author has his own investments in the whaling industry, and that his writing, like the whale ship itself, is engaged in establishing the system Ishmael nominally opposes. Where the whale ship goes, there follows the missionary and the national flag; and the whaling narrative inscribes the mental operations of the process.

The bulk of the book (Chapters 58–108), as Howard Vincent has established, is composed of technological descriptions derived from contemporary sources.[19] Most critical commentaries tend to give these sections cursory acknowledgement, but arguably it is these matter-of-fact materials which are the most enthralling part of the book, the Ahab-Ishmael drama serving to articulate the political and metaphysical issues that lie behind the business of whaling. Many chapters in themselves exemplify the lure of factualist description, beginning in Ishmael's narration or in a narrative event and becoming engrossed in the mechanics of whaling, then ending in the authorial attempt to suggest analogies between the event-world of the narrative and a more general level of significance. The movement owes something to the sermon form of *exemplum-exordium* but also expresses the profound dichotomy between probable and possible knowledge, between fact and speculation. Melville himself refers to this dichotomy in the famous image of 'The Pequod' freighted on the one side with a sperm whale's head and on the other with a right whale's head. 'So, when on one side you hoist in Locke's head, you go over that way; but now, on the other side, hoist in Kant's and you come back again; but in very poor plight. Thus, some minds for ever keep trimming boat. Oh, ye foolish! throw all these thunderheads overboard, and then you will float light and right' (Ch. 73, 277). The desire of the writing may well be to throw both heads overboard and produce an alternative discourse in which the dichotomy between empiricist and idealist persuasions will not be apparent, but the irony is that this moment in itself constitutes the development of a 'Kantian' analogy out of 'Lockean' whaling materials. Though brilliant with wit, the rather forced nature of this analogy (there being no inherent similitude between the whale's heads and the philosophers, only a punning connection between 'right' and 'Locke' and an association between sperm whales and Plato established earlier in the text) serves to foreground the alienation of concept from experient. As Melville had already announced, with typically contradictory skill, 'O Nature, and O soul of man! how far beyond all utterance are your linked analogies!

not the smallest atom stirs or lives in matter, but has its cunning duplicate in mind' (Ch. 70, 264). Parsed out, this analogical coda to the chapter entitled 'The Sphynx' protests that analogies exist but cannot be expressed, a paradox which points to the central contradiction between an Ishmaelite belief that the whale-world is ineffable and an Ahab/authorial desire to find higher literary and philosophical meaning in the 'blubber' of whaling.[20]

Reading the classificatory discourses of *Moby-Dick* with this paradox in mind, we can see that whilst *in toto* they expose the arbitrariness of all semiological systems, in themselves they are often searching for a reliable basis of meaning. The 'Cetology' chapter which classifies whales as 'Folio, Octavo, Duodecimo' is offered as a self-referential parody of the use of books to divide up the world into knowable classes, but also needs to be read for its paradoxical intentions: beginning with the fearful phrase 'Already we are boldly launched upon the deep; but soon shall be lost in its unshored, harborless immensities', it essays to recuperate the sense of an oceanic and nameless 'chaos' through 'the classifications of its constituents' (Ch. 32, 116). Having worked out a classification of whales as literary genera, Melville finally encounters the problem of all imperial systems: certain elements cannot be incorporated. 'The Bottle-Nose Whale; the Junk Whale; the Pudding-Headed Whale; the Cape Whale; the Leading Whale . . . ' these have to be obliterated if the totalising function of the system is to be maintained. Melville omits them 'as altogether obsolete; and can hardly help suspecting them as mere sounds, full of Leviathanism but signifying nothing'. We can scarcely ask for more eloquent testimony to the fact that signs are defined differentially against other signs and that when they are not part of a system they become empty, 'mere sounds'. Melville recognises this problem and ends his chapter with the explanation:

> It was stated at the outset, that this system would not be here, and at once, perfected. You cannot but plainly see that I have kept my word. But I now leave my cetological System standing thus unfinished, even as the great Cathedral of Cologne was left, with the crane still standing upon the top of the uncompleted tower. For small erections may be finished by their first architects; grand ones, true ones, ever leave the copestone to posterity. God keep me from ever completing anything. This whole book is but a draught – nay, but the draught of a draught. Oh, Time, Strength, Cash, and Patience! (Ch. 32, 127–28)

Without the last six words the paragraph would end on a bathetic note. It is the implication of a contradictory desire to finish the systematisation that provides the tension.

Critical self-awareness and economy are clearly at odds. The invocation to be kept from imperial systematisation (notice the passive) has led to the complaint that there are insufficient resources for completing the task. This contradiction of thought and desire is at the centre of the textual dilemmas, for the contemporary concept of the novel was of an enclosed and enclosing system, publishers paying on the nail of narrative conclusion. Not until modernism was the desire to write in prose liberated from the desire to specify, to dominate, to mine the depths and yield up meanings. The thought of Ishmael-Melville seems compatible with the later tendency to refuse to make the world into its own petty imperium, but the authorial desire dominates: 'Some certain significance lurks in all things, else all things are little worth, and the round world itself but an empty cipher, except to sell by the cartload, as they do the hills around Boston, to fill up some morass in the Milky Way' (Ch. 99, 358). Melville thus confesses his own desire to 'extract from the world's vast bulk its small but valuable sperm' (Ch. 98, 358): the rare and valuable commodity that author-Melville seeks is a higher literary value than the blubber a factualist whaling narrative offers in its unrefined state.

Rather than intending to flaunt the arbitrariness of all systems of knowledge, then, it seems more accurate to recognise that Melville's encyclopaedic tendency is motivated, at least in part, by the desire to produce a spermatic literary significance. Inspired by Pierre Bayle's *Dictionnaire historique et critique*, the rational documentation of the whale's anatomy and the citation of historical authorities offer an Enlightenment demythologisation of Ahab's monomaniacal delusion, but because the encyclopaedic method strives to discover the whale 'as it really is' it can offer no solution.[21] Here we must remember that as the first fruit of the Enlightenment the encyclopaedia assaulted the Christian mythos of transcendent unity by striving to represent the world as exhaustibly knowable in its parts. The authority of the encyclopaedia comes not from above but from below, from the materials with which it deals and from the knowledge of them which human authorities have established. The only unity in the encyclopaedic view is the purposive belief that in its exploded condition of measured fragments the world can be known as *items*, and that, through such knowledge, it can be put to use. The product of secularisation, the encyclopaedia sets to one side the question of transcendent unity and presents the world as a *combinatoire* whose mythos is pure knowledge, existing independently of the knower because distilled from the totality of authoritative descriptions. Democratic in its replacement of hierarchy by alphabetic serialisation, it cannot explain ultimate meanings, rather it condemns all meaning to the status of provisionally factual information.[22]

The encyclopaedic approach to whaling thus raises the dilemma it seeks to resolve: it makes the elusiveness of truth the more apparent the more exhaustive it becomes. Only Ahab, the Democrat tyrant, can limit this endless differentiation by binding the crew to the one unitary vision which orders all others. This higher significance, the malignancy of the whale, is a mythological conversion of biological matter into the essence of a quality he has ascribed. It is effectively parallel to the de-politicising naturalisation of ideology that facilitates the continental conquest, for if nature is naturally iniquitous its subjugation becomes a sanctified task. Taken in this sense, the unifying transcendent signified that Ahab supplies is also the unacknowledged signified of whaling itself, for in order to exploit the material world and turn it to profit, man perceives it as an Otherness God has predestined for his use. The entry of the encyclopaedia into this system appears intended to demystify the mythological whale by producing the 'real' whale, but this it cannot do for the whale can never be other than our consciousness of it. In effect, despite its seeming neutrality, the encyclopaedia is but another myth, a categorising system that appears to present the world-in-itself but which is constantly splitting it into arbitrary distinctions of human use. In it, the world is pure intentionality masquerading as indifferent objectivity.

Once encyclopaedic categorisation has been seen not as alternative to Ahab's monomania but as an antithetical mythology of the objectively significant, the dialectic of Melville's narrative can be understood. The democratic Ishmael-Melville may relativise all beliefs, represent Christianity as in no way superior to paganism, and make manifest the insufficiency of cetological accounts, but as the writer of a whaling narrative intended for public consumption Melville must finally produce 'the whale' from within his differentiating system of discourses. This Melville, the Ahab-Melville, is not immune to the Ishmael point-of-view: he expresses the desire, also found in Melville's letters, to give up the chase and sleep 'in the new-mown hay' (Ch. 132, 445).[23] As dollars damn the author into wresting significance from the world, so in spite of his own rural utopian tendency Ahab is driven by the fear that a lack of 'cash would soon cashier Ahab' (Ch. 46, 184) to stamp a final identity on Moby-Dick.

Melville's search for the whale thus oscillates between two poles that seem more antagonistic than they actually are: the recognition that language and identities have no natural basis, and the recognition that culture is only held together by the tyrannical decision to fix meanings on the world. The radical Democrat in Melville attempts to find an end to arbitrariness that does not involve Ahab's striking through the mask: he yearns to abolish social, political and linguistic differences by merging self and other in a pre-lapsarian communion. Even as he voices this yearning, however, he realises that differences will incapacitate utopia:

> Oh! my dear fellow beings, why should we longer cherish any social acerbities, or know the slightest ill-humor or envy! Come; let us squeeze hands all round; nay, let us all squeeze ourselves into each other; let us squeeze ourselves universally into the very milk and sperm of kindness.
>
> Would that I could keep squeezing that sperm for ever! For now, since by many prolonged, repeated experiences, I have perceived that in all cases man must eventually lower, or at least shift, his conceit of attainable felicity; not placing it anywhere in the intellect or the fancy; but in the wife, the heart, the bed, the table, the saddle, the fire-side, the country; now that I have perceived all this, I am ready to squeeze case eternally. In thoughts of the visions of the night, I saw long rows of angels in paradise, each with his hands in a jar of spermaceti. (Ch. 94, 348–49)

In a rebound that echoes the textual reluctance to limit the signified of Moby-Dick, the writing moves from its conceit of an amorphous felicity to admit that felicity in the actual world is restricted to privileged sites and cannot, therefore, be disseminated across all human relations; the thought then moves back to an angelic vision of an eternal squeezing of sperm that is unattainable on earth. This unresolved movement between a desire to abolish all differences, and the fall into privileged locations, is the consistent movement of the book. Ishmael climbs the mast, enters his pantheistic grass-growing mood, then his shout goes up with the rest (Ch. 41, 155) and he rejoins a crew bent on profiting from sperm. In adopting whaling as his subject, and then in striving to give it higher literary and political significance, he has engaged with the central ideological issues of his time and exposed the mythologisation entailed by the conquest of the continent. He has realised that there is no natural or necessary relationship between human language and the world, neither one that the encyclopaedia may find nor one that the despot may impose. He has also, perversely, repeated the essential operation of Western ideology: because his text will not sell if it represents whaling as being no more than the conversion of nature into dollars, he has produced a representation that gives material exploitation a transcendent, epic value. The despair with which Ahab casts his last harpoon ('*Thus*, I give up the spear!' Ch. 135, 468) is that of a text which has inevitably imposed a meaning on the world, even though it represents the world refusing to accept it as its own.

The escape of the whale, like the resurrection of Ishmael from the wreck buoyed up by the Indian's coffin, is poetically pleasing and perhaps ethically just. It is, however, wish-fulfilment, for behind these pleasing alibis the historical process of naming, conquering and exploiting goes unabated. Melville's text charts the interior logic of mythogenesis and through complex allegory indicts its contemporary political function, but because the writing proceeds from and is addressed to the critical conscience of white society it remains myth's victim. Melville is not an Indian and cannot tell what it is to be named what one is not, and exterminated in this other name. He shows the people giving up their freedom to serve the false gods of those who possess economic and rhetorical power, and he reveals the myth of an essentially malignant nature as being no more than a convenient mania to unite the crew. His alternative, however, is but another version of the myth, the idea of a primitive democracy which naturally inheres in all men and which can be conjured into being by an act of moral will rather than by any fundamental change in economic and political relations. This idea has of course been projected onto the world as a fundament of Democratic ideology since the time of Jefferson. Melville's resort to it is characteristic of the Ishmaelite Free Soilers who opposed the conquest of Mexico by pitting the myth that defined the regeneration of the body politic against the myth that legitimised continental conquest. The text that tears and exposes the ideological-discursive paradigm of Common Sense is a text which represents

Democratic thought fractured against itself, just as the party of continental conquest, slavery and the rights of man was to continue to be until the outbreak of the Civil War.

Notes and References

The following abbreviations are used in citing periodicals:

AL	*American Literature*
AQ	*American Quarterly*
ELH	*English Literary History*
JAH	*Journal of American History*
JAS	*Journal of American Studies*
MLN	*Modern Language Notes*
NAR	*North American Review*
NEQ	*New England Quarterly*
NCF	*Nineteenth Century Fiction*
NLH	*New Literary History*
NLR	*New Left Review*
NYH	*New York History*
MP	*Modern Philology*
PMLA	*Publications of the Modern Language Association*
PQ	*Philological Quarterly*
YFS	*Yale French Studies*

References to the works of Freud are to the *Standard Edition of the Complete Psychological Works of Sigmund Freud*, 23 vols, ed. James Strachey (London: The Hogarth Press, 1953–73).

Unless otherwise specified, references to the works of Cooper, Emerson, Hawthorne, Melville and Poe are to the editions listed below.

James Fenimore Cooper, *The Works of James Fenimore Cooper*, 32 vols, *The Mohawk Edition* (New York: G. P. Putnam, 1896).
—, *The Letters and Journals of James Fenimore Cooper*, 6 vols, ed. James F. Beard (Cambridge, Mass.: Harvard University Press, 1960–68).
Ralph W. Emerson, *The Complete Works of Ralph Waldo Emerson*, 2 vols (London: George Bell, 1876).
Nathaniel Hawthorne, *The Centenary Edition of the Works of Nathaniel Hawthorne*, 13 vols, eds William Charvat, Roy Harvey Pearce, Claude M. Simpson (Columbus: Ohio State University Press, 1962–1977).
Herman Melville, *The Letters of Herman Melville*, eds Merrell R. Davis and William H. Gilman (New Haven: Yale University Press, 1960).
—, *Typee: A Peep at Polynesian Life. The Writings of Herman Melville*, The Northwestern–Newberry Edition, eds Harrison Hayford, Hershel Parker, G.

Thomas Tanselle (Evanston, Ill.: Northwestern University Press, 1968) vol. I.
—, *Mardi, and a Voyage Thither. The Writings of Herman Melville*, The Northwestern-
Newberry Edition, eds Harrison Hayford, Hershel Parker, G. Thomas Tanselle
(Evanston, Ill.: Northwestern University Press, 1970) vol. III.
—, *White Jacket, or The World in a Man of War. The Standard Edition of the Works of
Herman Melville* (New York: Russell and Russell, 1963) vol. IV.
—, *The Piazza Tales, The Standard Edition of the Works of Herman Melville* (New York:
Russell and Russell, 1963) vol. X.
—, *Billy Budd, and Other Prose Pieces. The Standard Edition of the Works of Herman
Melville* (New York: Russell and Russell, 1963) vol. XIII.
—, *Moby-Dick, or The Whale, The Norton Critical Edition*, eds Harrison Hayford and
Hershel Parker (New York: W. W. Norton, 1967).
Edgar A. Poe, *The Complete Works of Edgar Allan Poe*, ed. James A. Harrison, 17 vols
(1906; rpt. New York: AMS Press, 1965).

I THE NATIONAL TASK

1. Herman Melville, *White Jacket, Standard Edition*, IV, p. 189.
2. See Louis Hartz, *The Liberal Tradition in America: An Interpretation of American
   Political Thought since the Revolution* (New York: Harcourt Brace, 1955) pp. 89–
   96; J. Barrington Moore Jr., *The Social Origins of Dictatorship and Democracy:
   Lord and Peasant in the Making of the Modern World* (Harmondsworth:
   Penguin, 1969) pp. 111–58. On the relationship of literary production to
   efforts to establish a national consciousness see Benjamin T. Spencer,
   The Quest for Nationality: An American Literary Campaign (Syracuse
   University Press, 1957); Howard Mumford Jones, *The Theory of the American
   Novel* (New York: Cornell University Press, 1966) pp. 18–38 and *O Strange New
   World* (London: Chatto and Windus, 1965) pp. 331 *et seq.*; Daniel Boorstin, *The
   Americans: the National Experience* (New York: Random House, 1965) pp. 275–
   346.
3. Noah Webster, *Dissertations on the English Language, with Notes Historical and
   Critical* (Boston: Isaiah Thomas, 1789) pp. 397–8. See also his *Sketches of An
   American Policy* (Hartford, Conn.: Hudson and Goodwin, 1785) p. 47. On the
   politics of Webster's work see Richard M. Rollins, 'Words as Social Control',
   AQ, 28 (1976) pp. 415–30.
4. Cooper, letter to Horatio Greenough, 21 May 1831, quoted Robert E. Spiller,
   James Fenimore Cooper: Critic of his Time (New York: Russell and Russell, 1963)
   p. viii. Poe, 'Marginalia to Godey's Lady's Book, September 1845', *Complete
   Works*, XVI, p. 78.
5. O'Sullivan's preface is reprinted in Edwin C. Rozwenc, *Ideology and Power in the
   Age of Jackson* (New York University Press, 1964) pp. 300–19. The passage
   which Poe echoes may be found on pp. 317–18 and seems in turn to be a
   repetition of De Tocqueville, *Democracy in America*, 2 vols, trans. Henry Reeve
   (1835; rpt. New York: Schocken Books, 1961) II, pp. 65–6.
6. Robert Rantoul Jr., *Memoirs, Speeches and Writings of Robert Rantoul Jr.*, ed.
   Luther Hamilton (Boston, 1854) pp. 184–5, quoted Rush Welter, *The Mind of
   America, 1820–1860* (New York: Columbia University Press, 1975) p. 5. The
   publishing situation is fully discussed in Chapter 2 below.

7. The most thorough commentary on political and social beliefs in the period is Rush Welter, *The Mind of America, 1820–1860* (New York: Columbia University Press, 1975); Marvin Meyers, *The Jacksonian Persuasion: Politics and Belief* (1957; rpt. Stanford University Press, 1976) is still of great value. Cf. Michael A. Lebowitz, 'The Jacksonians: Paradox Lost?' in Barton J. Bernstein (ed.), *Towards a New Past: Dissenting Essays in American History* (New York: Random House, 1968) pp. 65–89; Arthur M. Schlesinger, *The Age of Jackson* (Boston: Little, Brown, 1953); Glyndon Van Deusen, *The Jacksonian Era* (London: Hamilton, 1959). The classic study of attitudes to the Indians is Roy Harvey Pearce's *Savagism and Civilization: A Study of the Indian and the American Mind* (1953; rpt. Baltimore: Johns Hopkins Press, 1967). More chilling, however, is Albert K. Weinberg, *Manifest Destiny: A Study of Nationalist Expansionism in American History* (1935; rpt. Chicago: Quadrangle Books, 1963). Michael Paul Rogin, *Fathers and Children: Andrew Jackson and the Subjugation of the American Indian* (New York: Alfred A. Knopf, 1975) offers a stimulating psychohistory of Jacksonian attitudes.

8. Welter, pp. 61–6. Ironically, as the nation was being represented as an asylum for the oppressed it was rapidly constructing asylums in which to incarcerate its own misfits. See David J. Rothman, *The Discovery of the Asylum: Social Order and Disorder in the New Republic* (Boston: Little, Brown, 1971). The irony is exploited by Hawthorne in 'The Custom-House' and Chapter One of *The Scarlet Letter* in references to the dialectic of freedom and incarceration which critics like to take back to the Puritan experience at the expense of its contemporary political relevance. The theme of imprisonment runs from *The Pioneers* through Poe to 'Bartleby'. On the pre-visioning of the United States as an asylum see Marcus Lee Hansen, *The Atlantic Migration: A History of the Continuing Settlement of the United States*, ed. Arthur M. Schlesinger Jr. (New York: Harper and Row, 1961) pp. 146–71.

9. The paradox of an already achieved perfection being postulated in the same breath as a growth towards even greater perfection, is characteristic of the period. See R. W. B. Lewis, *The American Adam: Innocence, Tragedy and Tradition in the Nineteenth Century* (Chicago University Press, 1955) p. 5n. Cooper's *Notions of the Americans* seemed to a British contemporary the complete expression of this belief: 'According to [Cooper's] dicta, [the Americans] are a people not only "Adorned with every virtue under heaven," but without vice, fault, blot or blemish. According to his *Notions*, they are not only as perfect as it is possible for human nature to be already, but they are becoming every day more perfect. . . .' *Literary Gazette*, 12 (June 1828), quoted G. Dekker and J. P. McWilliams, *Fenimore Cooper: The Critical Heritage* (London: Routledge & Kegan Paul, 1973) p. 151. By 1847 Cooper had changed tack: describing the Crater, he produced this fine specimen of Whig thought: 'The policy adopted by the government of the colony was very much unlike that resorted to in America, in connection with the extension of the settlements. Here a vast extent of surface is loosely over-run, rendering the progress of civilization rapid, but very imperfect. Were the people of the United States confined to one half the territory they now occupy, there can be little question that they would be happier, more powerful, more civilized and less rude in manners and feelings, although it may be high treason to insinuate that they are not all, men, women and children, already the *ne plus ultra* of each of these attainments.' *The Crater,*

Mohawk Edition, p. 398. When Melville was not trying to conform to conventional pieties, as he was in *White Jacket*, he too could be acid about American perfection: 'the grand error of your nation, sovereign kings! seems this: the conceit that Mardi is now in the last scene of the last act of her drama; and that all preceding events were ordained to bring about the catastrophe you believe to be at hand, – a universal and permanent republic.' *Mardi, Writings*, III, p. 238.

10. Of the more distinguished, one might mention Loren Baritz, *City upon a Hill: A History of Ideas and Myths in America* (New York: John Wiley, 1964); Sacvan Bercovitch, *The American Jeremiad* (Madison: University of Wisconsin Press, 1978) and *The Puritan Origins of the American Self* (New Haven, Conn.: Yale University Press, 1975); Perry Miller, *Errand into the Wilderness* (Cambridge, Mass.: Harvard University Press, 1975); Charles L. Sandford, *The Quest for Paradise: Europe and the American Moral Imagination* (Urbana: University of Illinois, 1961); Cecilia Tichi, *New World, New Earth: Environmental Reform in American Literature from the Puritans through Whitman* (New Haven, Conn.: Yale University Press, 1979).

11. See Paul W. Gates, *The Farmer's Age: Agriculture 1815–1860* (New York: Holt Rinehart & Winston, 1962) pp. 70–98; Clarence H. Danhoff, 'Farm-making Costs and the Safety-Valve 1850–1860', in Vernon Carstensen (ed.) *The Public Lands: Studies in the History of the Public Domaine* (Madison: University of Wisconsin Press, 1963) pp. 253–96. For general accounts see Louis M. Hacker, *The Triumph of American Capitalism* (New York: Columbia University Press, 1940) and Douglas C. North, *The Economic Growth of the United States, 1790–1860* (New York: W. W. Norton, 1966). The causes of the recession of 1837 have been thoroughly analysed in Peter Temin, *The Jacksonian Economy* (New York: W. W. Norton, 1969). Paul W. Gates, 'The Role of the Land Speculator in Western Development', in Carstensen, *The Public Lands*, pp. 349–67, explains the financial structure of land speculation. For a history of the rationale and procedures of Indian removal in the 1830s see Rogin, *Fathers and Children*, pp. 207–48. Antebellum economic changes have recently been brilliantly summarised and reinterpreted by Charles Post, 'The American Road to Capitalism', *NLR*, 133 (1982) pp. 30–51.

12. See Weinberg, *Manifest Destiny*, pp. 72–99; Pearce, *Savagism and Civilization*, pp. 19–35, 66–73; Tichi, *New World, New Earth*, pp. 8–19.

13. See Henry Nash Smith, *Virgin Land: The American West as Symbol and Myth* (Cambridge, Mass.: Harvard University Press, 1950) pp. 133–73.

14. Quoted Smith, *Virgin Land*, pp. 139–40.

15. The theory of ideology being deployed here is derived from Louis Althusser, 'Ideology and the Ideological State Apparatuses', *Lenin and Philosophy and Other Essays*, trans. Ben Brewster (London: New Left Books, 1971) pp. 123–73. The central thesis is that ideology represents a lived imaginary relationship to the relations of production and serves to perpetuate them.

16. Smith, *Virgin Land*, pp. 141–42.

17. See quotation in note 9 above.

18. R. W. B. Lewis, *The American Adam: Innocence, Tragedy and Tradition in the Nineteenth Century* (Chicago University Press, 1955) p. 5. Frye's dehistoricising theory of myth is clearly expressed in his 'Myth, Fiction, and Displacement', *New Directions from Old* (New York: Harcourt Brace Jovanovich, 1963) pp. 21–38.

19. Myth criticism was invented in the 1950s as a way of divorcing literature's social function from history. Useful analyses of this critical tendency can be found in Philip Rahv, 'The Myth and the Powerhouse', in John B. Vickery (ed.), *Myth and Literature: Contemporary Theory and Practice* (Lincoln: University of Nebraska Press, 1966) pp. 109–18; Robert Weimann, 'Past Origins and Present Functions in American Literary History', *Structure and Society in Literary History* (Charlottesville: University of Virginia Press, 1976) pp. 89–146; and Bruce Kucklick, 'Myth and Symbol in American Studies', *AQ*, 24 (1972) pp. 435–50. The most significant attempt to examine the historical causes and social purposes of mythology in the United States is Richard Slotkin's *Regeneration through Violence: The Mythology of the American Frontier, 1600–1860* (Middletown, Conn.: Wesleyan University Press, 1973). Robert D. Richardson, Jr. surveys historical attitudes towards myth in his *Myth and Literature in the American Renaissance* (Bloomington: Indiana University Press, 1978).

20. I owe this connection to Richard Chase who, despite approaching myth in the usual dehistoricising fashion, provides a persuasive summary of the psychoanalytic method. See his *Quest for Myth* (1949; rpt. New York: Greenwood Press, 1969) pp. viii, 90–7.

21. See Sigmund Freud, *The Interpretation of Dreams, Standard Edition*, IV, pp. 279, 326–7.

22. Freud, 'Revision of the Theory of Dreams', *Standard Edition*, XXII, p. 22; *Totem and Taboo, SE*, XIII, pp. 94–5. Cf. *SE*, V, pp. 478–508.

23. See Roland Barthes, 'Myth Today', *Mythologies*, trans. Annette Lavers (London: Jonathan Cape, 1972) pp. 109–59. The understanding of the sign deployed in this section is informed by Barthes; by Jacques Lacan's reading of Saussure in 'The Insistence of the Letter in the Unconscious', trans. Jan Miel, in Jacques Ehrmann (ed.), *Structuralism* (New York: Doubleday, 1970) pp. 101–37; and by Jean Laplanche and Serge Leclaire, 'The Unconscious: A Psychoanalytic Study', *YFS*, 48 (1972) pp. 118–75.

24. Barthes, *Mythologies*, pp. 130, 142, 143.

25. The sign 'the people' had the same capability in Jacksonian rhetoric, meaning i) a moral good, ii) certain social groups, especially farmers and mechanics, iii) not other social groups, especially not aristocrats. Although 'the people' thus served to fuse value with thing the referent was still clear. The word is capable of including or excluding social groups by covert means. See Meyers, *The Jacksonian Persuasion*, pp. 18–24. In modern discourse 'American' performs similar functions, as in 'un-American activities'. Even in its primary use this word 'American' is well on its way towards myth since whether 'American' refers to one nation or twenty-two is apparent only from context. De Tocqueville had words like these in mind when he observed that a liking for abstract terms was characteristic of democratic societies because 'an abstract term is like a box with a false bottom; you may put in it what ideas you please, and take them out again without being observed'. *Democracy in America*, II, p. 84.

26. Ferdinand de Saussure, *Course in General Linguistics* (1915; rpt. trans. Wade Baskin, Glasgow: Fontana/Collins, 1974) pp. 65–78. Cf. Lacan, note 23 above.

27. Although we arrived at this diagram via Freud and Barthes, retrospectively we see that another route was possible: in 'Nature' Emerson defines language thus: i) Words are signs of natural facts, ii) Particular natural facts are symbols of

particular spiritual facts, iii) Nature is the symbol of spirit. Emerson's theory of language was possibly influenced by theories of ancient myth. See John T. Irwin, 'The Symbol of the Hieroglyphics in the American Renaissance', *AQ*, 26 (1974) pp. 103-26, 112. It is therefore not remarkable to find here a model of mythic speech correspondent to our own: the movement from Emerson's second proposition to the third involves the subtraction of fact, the conversion of qualifiers into substances and leaves a domain of materialised essences.

28. Sir Walter Scott, *The Waverley Novels*, 48 vols (Edinburgh: Constable, 1901) II, pp. 401-2.

29. James Fenimore Cooper, *The Last of the Mohicans* (London: John Miller, 1826) p. x.

30. See Chapter 4.1 below. That this was a *projective* as well as *retrospective* sentiment was made clear in 1828: 'As a rule, the red man disappears before the superior moral and physical influence of the white, just as I believe that the black man will eventually do the same thing, unless he shall seek shelter in some other region'. *Notions of the Americans*, 2 vols (New York: Frederick Unger, 1963) II, p. 277.

31. Cooper discusses precisely these issues in Chapter 3 of *The Deerslayer*. See Chapter 4.3 below. Melville's disquisition on 'The Whiteness of the Whale' can also be read as a commentary on the mythical opposition of white and red: 'yet for all these accommodated associations of whiteness, with whatever is sweet and honourable, and sublime, there yet lurks an elusive something in the innermost idea of this hue, which strikes more of panic to the soul than the redness which affrights the blood'. *Moby-Dick*, p. 164.

32. Barthes, *Mythologies*, p. 130.

33. Hayden V. White, 'The Forms of Wildness: Archeology of an Idea', in Edward Dudley and Maximillian E. Novak (eds), *The Wild Man Within: An Image in Western Thought from the Renaissance to Romanticism* (University of Pittsburgh Press, 1972) pp. 3-38, 30.

34. Natty, Ishmael, Huck Finn and Emerson's self-reliant ideal, all boast their freedom from schooling. Only the woods and the whale ship are sufficient to teach the American innocent. On the one hand an expression of Democratic suspicion that educational institutions were centralising and élitist, on the other an expression of the desire to escape the past, the American hero's lack of learning also signifies the need to neutralise the intellectual capacities which are capable of deconstructing his mythic identity.

35. Thus, for example, scalping becomes the 'nature' of the savage, but a vice taught to naturally innocent white men by corrupt civilisation. Scalping is not part of a white man's 'nature'. See Chapter 4.3 below. Weinberg, *Manifest Destiny*, p. 77, provides a nice example of this shifting: in the 1780s it was argued that *the law of nature* enjoined man to stake a claim to the soil and plant it; hunting somehow became less than natural.

36. John Armstrong, *The Paradise Myth* (Oxford University Press, 1969) pp. 104-23.

37. See the discussion of the famous denials of American reality by Cooper, Hawthorne and James in Chapter 3 below.

38. See Emerson's comment to this effect, note 22 to Chapter 3 below.

39. Freud, *Standard Edition*, v, p. 500. 'Those parts of a dream on which the secondary revision has been able to produce some effect are clear, while those on which its efforts have failed are confused.'

2 WRITER TO READER

1. Orestes Brownson, 'Address to the United Brothers Society of Brown University' (1839), rpt. in Richard Ruland (ed.), *The Native Muse: Theories of American Literature* (New York: E. P. Dutton, 1976) p. 280.
2. William Charvat, *Literary Publishing in America, 1790–1850* (Philadelphia: University of Pennsylvania Press, 1959) pp. 55–7; James D. Hart, *The Popular Book: A History of American Literary Taste* (New York: Oxford University Press, 1950) pp. 85–105.
3. Charvat, pp. 36–7.
4. Charvat, pp. 38–60. Cooper, *Notions of the Americans*, 2 vols (1828; rpt. New York: Frederick Ungar, 1963) II, 106–7. William Charvat, 'Cooper as Professional Author', *The Profession of Authorship in America, 1800–1870: The Papers of William Charvat*, ed. Mathew J. Bruccoli (Columbus: Ohio State University Press, 1968) pp. 68–83.
5. See Charvat, *The Origins of American Critical Thought, 1810–1835* (New York: Russell and Russell, 1968) pp. 1–26. Quotation from p. 7. Charvat's history of critical thought does not extend to the antebellum period but he argues that the common denominators of early nineteenth-century criticism become the main current of American criticism. Terence Martin, *The Instructed Vision: Scottish Common Sense Philosophy and the Origins of American Fiction* (New York: Kraus Reprint, 1961) extends Charvat's work to the 1860s and confirms the suggestion. Perry Miller, *The Raven and the Whale: The War of Words and Wits in the Era of Poe and Melville* (New York: Harcourt Brace Jovanovich, 1956) provides a comprehensive study of periodical publishing. For a political history, see John Ashworth, *The Democratic Review: A Study of a Radical Jacksonian Journal, 1837–1851* (M. Litt Dissertation, University of Lancaster, 1973) pp. 8–9.
6. *Mardi, Writings,* III, pp. 512–13.
7. 'Benito Cereno', *Standard Edition*, X, p. 105; 'Billy Budd', *Standard Edition*, XIII, p. 29.
8. I take the word 'factualism' from Hubert Hoeltje who uses it to describe the critical predilections of Samuel Taylor Goodrich, editor of *The Token* in which Hawthorne's first prose sketches and tales appeared. See Hubert H. Hoeltje, *Inward Sky: The Mind and Hearty Nathaniel Hawthorne* (Durham, NC: Duke University Press, 1962) p. 98.
9. Cf. Charles Feidelson, *Symbolism and American Literature* (Chicago University Press, 1962) p. 89 *et passim*; Sacvan Bercovitch, *The American Jeremiad* (Madison: University of Wisconsin Press, 1978) esp. pp. 176–210; and Ursula Brumm, 'Christ and Adam as "figures" in American Literature', in S. Bercovitch (ed.), *The American Puritan Imagination* (Cambridge University Press, 1974). My purpose is not to deny the perceptions achieved from this premise but to indicate the way towards more materialist explanations. For a commentary on the errors of Feidelson's approach when used to make Melville, Hawthorne and Emerson into both symbolists *avant la lettre* and latterday Puritans, see René Wellek, 'The Term and Concept of Symbolism in Literary History', *Discriminations: Further Concepts of Criticism* (New Haven Conn.: Yale University Press, 1970) pp. 90–121, 101.
10. Cf. Cecilia Tichi, *New World, New Earth*, pp. 18 *et seq.*; Sacvan Bercovitch, *The*

Puritan Origins of the American Self, pp. 8, 100, 110–11; Larzer Ziff, 'The Literary Consequences of Puritanism', in S. Bercovitch (ed.), *The American Puritan Imagination*, p. 47.

11. This is very much the burden of Henry Nash Smith's latest study, *Democracy and the Novel: Popular Resistance to Classic American Writers* (New York: Oxford University Press, 1978). In the 1840s critical antagonism was so heated that many writers chose to publish under pseudonyms. See Perry Miller, *The Raven and the Whale*, p. 124.

12. Cooper, Preface to *Home as Found*, rpt. George Perkins, *The Theory of American Novel* (New York: Holt, Rinehart and Winston, 1970) p. 26. On Cooper's income see note 4 above.

13. Hawthorne's relationship with the publisher, James T. Fields, is described by Charvat in *Literary Publishing*, pp. 57–9, in a manner which provides a valuable perspective on Hawthorne's writing.

14. Melville to John Murray, 25 March 1848, to Lemuel Shaw, 23 April 1849 and 6 October 1849, *Letters*, pp. 70, 85, 91. Cf. also *Letters*, p. 165 for balance of account with Harpers, and Charvat's *Profession of Authorship*, pp. 190–203 for an illuminating discussion on the effects of the publishing economy on Melville's writing. In April 1854 Hawthorne returned an 1846 copy of *Mosses from an Old Manse* to Ticknor and Fields with the comment, 'Upon my honour, I am not quite sure that I entirely comprehend my own meaning in some of these blasted allegories'. Quoted J. Donald Crowley, 'Historical Commentary' to *Mosses from an Old Manse, Centenary Edition*, x, p. 522.

15. Melville to Nathaniel Hawthorne, 1 June 1851, *Letters*, p. 127; 'Hawthorne and His Mosses', *Literary World*, 7 (1850) pp. 125–7, pp. 145–7, rpt., J. Donald Crowley (ed.), *Hawthorne: The Critical Heritage* (London: Routledge & Kegan Paul, 1970) pp. 111–34, 117.

16. Hawthorne, Preface to *Twice-Told Tales, Centenary Edition*, IX, p. 6.

17. Cooper, *The Notions of the Americans*, II, pp. 108–9.

18. Cooper, Preface to *The Red Rover*, (Philadelphia, 1828) quoted Arvid Shulenberger, *Cooper's Theory of Fiction* (1955; rpt. New York: Octagon Books, 1972) p. 31.

19. *Mohawk Edition*, p. 26.

20. Cooper's discourse of natural description is a variant of the factualist style: the perceiving eye tracks across a landscape and experiences conventional sentiments evoked by the sight. For all Cooper's apparent indebtedness to the European tradition of romantic landscape painting, he does not anthropomorphise nature but remains an alien observer who describes subjective responses to what is 'out there'. See Tony Tanner, 'Notes for a Comparison between American and European Romanticism', *JAS*, 2 (1968) pp. 83–103. Cf. Blake Nevius, *Cooper's Landscapes: An essay in the Picturesque Vision* (Berkeley: University of California Press, 1976) and Howard Mumford Jones, 'Prose and Pictures: James Fenimore Cooper', *Tulane Studies in English*, 3 (1952) pp. 133–54.

21. Perry Miller's essay 'An American Language', *Nature's Nation* (Cambridge, Mass.: The Belknap Press, 1967) pp. 208–40 supports the contention that the plain style persists as the valued United States discourse from Puritan times to the nineteenth century because it furnishes a language of practical utility. For analysis of the plain style's social functions see Robert Adolph, *The Rise of the Modern Prose Style* (Cambridge, Mass.: MIT Press, 1968).

22. Throughout his work Cooper was fascinated with the changes of the names of places and, correspondingly, with who had the power to name and with what was the 'right' name. See Chapter 4.2 below and Chapter 19 of *The Prairie* where Natty Bumppo argues his right to name buffaloes 'buffaloes' against Dr Obed Batt's scientifically approved 'bison'. In a sentence which provides a quite remarkable synthesis of Common Sense precepts about seeing, knowing, and naming, the trapper remarks, 'As if any man's eyes were not as good for names as the eyes of any other creatur'!' (p. 231). Natty further supports his rights as 'namer' by arguing that all men trace their origin to Adam and that God granted the right of naming to Adam in the Garden of Eden. Naming thus becomes, anarchically, a universal right. The whole chapter serves to exemplify the strain to which Common Sense linguistic precepts were subjected when democratic reforms and geographical expansion undermined the prerogatives of a small social group to decide what was within the bounds of sense, and what without. Compare note 26 below. On the connections between Natty's powers of seeing, killing and taking possession of the land, see John F. Lynen, *The Design of the Present: Essays on Time and Form in American Literature* (New Haven, Conn.: Yale University Press, 1969) p. 188.

23. Poe, *Complete Works*, III, pp. 148–9.

24. According to Jonathan Culler the resort to the stimulus-response model of subject-object relations is one of the easiest ways of resolving the fundamental semiological problem constituted by the absence of inherent correspondence between signifier and signified. See his 'Literary History, Allegory, and Semiology', *NLH*, 7 (1976) pp. 259–70, 265.

25. Characterisation and plausibility suffer the same limitations in England's masterpiece of the plain style: see Ian Watt's comments on *Moll Flanders*, *The Rise of the Novel: Studies in Defoe, Richardson and Fielding* (1957; rpt. Harmondsworth: Penguin, 1972) pp. 104–51.

26. Hawthorne, 'The Custom-House', *Centenary Edition*, I, p. 31. Cf. John T. Irwin's important article, 'The Symbol of the Hieroglyphics in the American Renaissance', *AQ*, 26 (1974) pp. 103–26, in which he connects Hawthorne's interest in the polysemantic and enigmatic sign to the contemporary interest in Egyptian hieroglyphics. Irwin's article is also relevant for its commentary on Hawthorne and Melville's shared interest in the difference between the interpretations of the same events experienced by a group of individuals. Notable examples are Ch. 12 of *The Scarlet Letter* in which the meteoric portent is variously interpreted, and the way in which the doubloon in Ch. 99 of *Moby-Dick* becomes the signifier of the desires of its perceiver. The recognition that the signified of the sign is interpellated rather than natural is thus located as a problem in Common Sense philosophy for it is dramatised in terms of the individual's perception of the material world.

27. Cf. Melville's letter of 8 January 1852 to Sophia Hawthorne (*Letters*, p. 146) in which Melville implies he was not aware of the meanings that she discovered in *Moby-Dick*. Every imaginative work contains significations not consciously intended by its author. The question is of extent and it is obvious that indeterminacy of signification constitutes a larger element in works of Melville than it does in socially mimetic works. In the climate of mystification in which these authors worked it is anyone's guess when they knew what they meant and when they did not. Cf. James Guetti's excellent commentary on Melville's

language, *The Limits of Metaphor* (New York: Cornell University Press, 1967) pp. 12–45.

28. Poe's arabesques and grotesques consistently feature a Common Sense narrator experiencing the return of what Common Sense has repressed. One can see in such tales a parodic portrait of contemporary thinking: gulled by the simplest tricks of factuality and logicality, its inability to deal with the ethical or metaphysical forces it to live constantly haunted by what it refuses to consider. Cf. Mark Twain's comments on Cooper's illogicality, note 60 to Chapter 4 below.

29. As Poe perceived in Hawthorne's 'The Minister's Black Veil', 'The *obvious* meaning will be found to smother its insinuated one. The *moral* put into the mouth of the dying minister will be supposed to convey the *true* import of the narrative; and that a crime of dark dye, (having reference to the "young lady") has been committed, is a point which only minds congenial to that of the author will perceive', *Graham's Magazine*, 20 (1842), pp. 298–300; rpt. Crowley, *Hawthorne: The Critical Heritage*, p. 88. On p. 117 of the same an anonymous reviewer in *Blackwood's Magazine*, 62 (1847), pp. 587–92, laments that Hawthorne's plots are implausible and that 'in Mr. Hawthorne's stories the human being himself is not probable, nor possible'. Thus Hawthorne is faulted on Common Sense grounds for failing to produce what Common Sense makes it almost impossible to produce.

30. Comparison with European realism is relevant here, for in realist discourse objects are represented as signs which signify their historical and social constitution. The signified is not denied but clamant. Although the act of authorial creation is effaced, the art of correctly deciphering the signified of the sign (by character and reader) is emphasised. This is not an act of *interpretation* in which the signs are taken as given and reliable (as the task for Dupin in 'The Murders of the Rue Morgue' is to construe enigmatic signs into a logical order which reveals their connections) it is more literally an act of *signification* where what one must do is learn to discriminate the socially correct signified from among the possible others: thus Waverley learns the true signified of 'chivalric', Julien Sorel the true signified of 'Jesuit', Marianne Dashwood the true signified of 'sense' etc.

3 THE AESTHETIC IDEOLOGY

1. Leon Howard, *Herman Melville: A Biography* (1950; rpt. Berkeley: University of California Press, 1967) pp. 89–101.

2. Charles Brockden Brown, 'The Difference Between History and Romance', *Monthly Magazine and American Review*, 2 (1800) pp. 251–3, 251. See also John C. Stubbs, 'Hawthorne's *The Scarlet Letter*: The Theory of Romance and the New England Situation', *PMLA*, 83 (1968) pp. 1439–47.

3. Brown, p. 252. According to Brown, Buffon, Linnaeus and Herschel possess the romancer's speculative capacity in addition to the historical and scientific spirit. Cooper provides an amusing parody of this extreme position in *The Deerslayer*, Ch. 25. Chingachgook plays the Scottish realist, asking Natty how white men know that the earth goes round the sun when what they see is a sun that rises and sets. Chingachgook says his eyes 'do not see the earth turn', to

which Natty replies 'that's what I call sense-obstinacy! Seeing is believing, they say; and what they can't see, some men won't in the least give credit to'. *Mohawk Edition*, p. 447.

4. Hawthorne, 'Sir William Phips', *Tales, Sketches, and Other Papers, The Complete Works of Nathaniel Hawthorne*, 12 vols (London: Kegan Paul, Trench, Trubner and Company, 1883) XII, pp. 227–34, 227. Compare the discussion of this passage by Nina Baym, *The Shape of Hawthorne's Career* (New York: Cornell University Press, 1976) pp. 35–6.

5. On the ideological function of historical works see Hayden White, 'What is a Historical System', in A. D. Breck (ed.), *Biology, History and Natural Philosophy* (New York: Plenum Press, 1972) pp. 233–42. For analysis of the congruence and divergence between romanticism and historicism see his 'Romanticism, Realism, and Historicism; Toward a Period Concept for Early Nineteenth Century Intellectual History', in Hayden V. White (ed.), *The Uses of History: Essays in Intellectual and Social History Presented to William J. Bossenbrook* (Detroit, Michigan: Wayne State University Press, 1968) pp. 45–58. See also David Levin, *In Defense of Historical Literature* (New York: Hill and Wang, 1967) pp. 1–33; Leszek Kolakowski, 'Historical Understanding and the Intelligibility of History', *Triquarterly*, 22 (1971) pp. 103–17; and Morse Peckham, 'Reflections on Historical Modes in the Nineteenth Century', in Malcolm Bradbury and David Palmer (eds), *Victorian Poetry: Stratford-upon-Avon Studies*, 15 (London: Edward Arnold, 1972) pp. 277–300.

6. Walter Scott, *Waverley, The Edinburgh Waverley*, I, pp. 13, 64; Dedicatory Epistle to *Ivanhoe*, *The Prefaces to the Waverley Novels*, ed. Mark A. Weinstein (Lincoln University of Nebraska Press, 1978) p. 34. The distinctiveness of the metahistorical position in nineteenth-century historiography has been explored in Hayden White's *Metahistory: The Historical Imagination in Nineteenth Century Europe* (Baltimore: Johns Hopkins Press, 1973). The ablest defence of historical understanding in recent philosophy is Lucien Goldmann's *The Human Sciences and Philosophy*, trans. Hayden V. White and Robert Anchor (London: Jonathan Cape, 1969). The idea of a constant human nature as providing epistemological access to history goes back to Montesquieu and Hume. See Karl Kroeber, 'Romantic Historicism: The Temporal Sublime', in K. Kroeber and William Welling (eds), *Images of Romanticism* (New Haven: Yale University Press, 1978) pp. 149–65. For an introduction to Scott's understanding of historical progress, and its origins in the Scottish enlightenment, see Avrom Fleishman, *The English Historical Novel: Walter Scott to Virginia Woolf* (Baltimore: Johns Hopkins Press, 1971) pp. 11–48. General accounts of the development of the historical world-view in late eighteenth- and early nineteenth-century European society can be found in Frank E. Manuel, *Shapes of Philosophical History* (London: Allen and Unwin, 1965) pp. 92–163; and John Passmore, *The Perfectibility of Man* (London: Duckworth, 1970) pp. 190–238.

7. Samuel Johnson, *The Rambler*, 4 (31 March 1750), quoted Ioan Williams, *Novel and Romance 1700–1800: A Documentary Record* (London: Routledge & Kegan Paul, 1970) pp. 142–6.

8. Scott, *The Quarterly Review*, 14 (1815) pp. 188–201, 192–93.

9. Scott, 'Essay on Romance' (1824), *The Miscellaneous Prose Works of Sir Walter Scott* (Edinburgh: Cadell, 1847) pp. 554–75, 554.

10. Webster's *An American Dictionary of the English Language* (New York: S.

Converse, 1828) defines romance as '1. A fabulous relation or story of adventures and incidents designed for the entertainment of readers; a tale of extraordinary adventures, fictitious and often extravagant, usually a tale of love or war, subjects interesting to the sensibilities of the heart or the passions of wonder and curiosity. *Romance* differs from the *novel*, as it treats of great actions and extraordinary adventures; that is, according to the Welsh signification, it vaults or soars beyond the limits of fact and real life, and often probability. 2. A fiction.' The verb 'to romance' is defined as 'to forge and tell fictitious stories; to deal in extravagant stories'. A romancer is 'one who invents fictitious stories'. A novel is 'a fictitious tale or narrative in prose, intended to exhibit the operation of the passions, and particularly of love'. The tendency to assume that all fiction is romance is apparent. For commentary on the European significations of the word see Ioan Williams's introduction to *Novel and Romance*, and Hans Eichner (ed.), *Romantic and its Cognates: The European History of a Word* (Manchester University Press, 1972).

11. William G. Simms, *Views and Reviews in American Literature and Fiction* (New York: Wiley and Putnam, 1845) p. 32.

12. Simms, p. 31.

13. Scott is explicit about this aspect of his work in the General Preface to the Waverley Novels where he admits an inspiration in Maria Edgeworth's novels which assisted the union between England and Ireland: 'she may be truly said to have done more towards completing the Union, than perhaps all the legislative enactments by which it has been followed up'. *The Edinburgh Waverley* 48 vols (Edinburgh: Constable, 1901) 1, p. xix. Martin Green provides a useful commentary on this aspect of Scott and Cooper in his 'Cooper, Nationalism and Imperialism', *JAS*, 12 (1978) pp. 161–9.

14. Simms, pp. 24–5.

15. Emerson, 'Self-Reliance', *Complete Works*, 1, p. 28.

16. The production of histories in the antebellum United States suffered similarly from the Common Sense separation of factual and romantic. Chronological accounts of local history and patriotic biographies flourished whilst great interpretative works were rarely produced, and were highly mythological when they were. The one great attempt at a national history was Bancroft's *History of the United States from the Discovery of the American Continent*, 10 vols (Boston: Little, Brown, 1834–74). Bancroft, as a good Jacksonian, represented the American people as inherently redeemed by nature and democracy and as reaching the end point of their history in Independence. On history writing at this time see Daniel Boorstin, *The Americans: The National Experience* (New York: Random House, 1965) pp. 362–73; David W. Noble, *Historians against History: The Frontier Thesis and the National Covenant in American Historical Writing Since 1830* (University of Minneapolis Press, 1965) pp. 3–36; David Levin, *History as Romantic Art: Bancroft, Prescott, Motley and Parkman* (Stanford University Press, 1959); Frederick Somkin, *Unquiet Eagle: Memory and Desire and the Idea of American Freedom, 1815–1860* (New York: Cornell University Press, 1967) pp. 175–206).

17. On Cooper's attitude to the romance, see George Dekker and J. P. McWilliams's introduction to their *Fenimore Cooper: The Critical Heritage* (London: Routledge & Kegan Paul, 1973).

18. *The Pioneers* (London: Richard Bentley, 1832) p. xi; *The Prairie*, 3 vols (London:

Henry Colburn, 1827) 1, p. v; *The Last of the Mohicans*, 3 vols (London: John Miller, 1826) 1, p. i.

19. Cooper, Preface to *The Pilot* (1823), quoted George Perkins (ed.), *The Theory of the American Novel* (New York: Holt, Rinehart & Winston, 1970) p. 19. For an interesting commentary on Cooper's metahistorical position see John F. Lynen, *The Design of the Present: Essays on Time and Form in American Literature* (New Haven, Conn.: Yale University Press, 1969).

20. Cooper, Preface to the Leatherstocking Tales, *The Deerslayer, Mohawk Edition*, pp. vi–vii. For further discussion see Chapters 4.2 and 4.3 below. Cooper may have in mind both Scott and the remarks of a reviewer who had written that for Heckewelder 'the Lenni Lenape constitute the very *beau idéal* of the perfect savage' and had gone on to accuse Cooper of idealising the Delaware. See the anonymous review of William Rawle's 'A Vindication of the Rev. Mr. Heckewelder's History of the Indian Nations', *NAR*, 26 (1828) pp. 366–403. Cooper would also have been familiar with '*le beau moral*' a key term in contemporary French conservative criticism which advocated that the moral lesson of the fiction was more important than correspondence with actual conditions. See Bernard Weinberg, *French Realism: the Critical Reaction, 1830–1870* (Oxford University Press, 1937) p. 37.

21. For a modern understanding of verisimilitude see Tzvetan Todorov, 'Introduction au Vraisemblable', *Poétique de la Prose* (Paris: De Seuil, 1971) pp. 92–9; Gerard Genette, 'Vraisemblable et Motivation', *Communications*, 11 (1968) pp. 5–21. In his introduction to *Novel and Romance* Ioan Williams reminds us that the seventeenth-century romance was considered verisimilar because it corresponded with aristocratic conventions of seemly behaviour. When reading American romance we should remember that some readers found the Leatherstocking Tales credible (Francis Parkman included) and should therefore question any easy assumptions about their relationship to social conditions. It is also important to note that the 'novel persuasion' was not without supporters in the United States. In 1849 Lewis Gaylord Clark asked why Americans did not write novels instead of romances and declared 'in no country, indeed, is there a broader field opened to the delineation of character and manners, than in our land'. See Perry Miller, *The Raven and the Whale: The War of Words and Wits in the Era of Poe and Melville* (New York: Harcourt, Brace and World, 1956) p. 259. The argument that the writing of romances receives its major impetus from a desire to escape from the criticism of Common Sense orthodoxy is supported by F. O. Mathiessen, *American Renaissance: Art and Expression in the Age of Emerson and Whitman* (1941; rpt. New York: Oxford University Press, 1970) pp. 266–8; by Henry Nash Smith, *Democracy and the Novel: Popular Resistance to Classic American Writers* (New York: Oxford University Press, 1978) pp. 16–34; and most recently by Michael Davitt Bell, *The Development of the American Romance: The Sacrifice of Relation* (Chicago University Press, 1981).

22. *The Deerslayer*, p. 1. The despair with history is yet more apparent in the opening words of *Satanstoe* (1845): 'It is easy to foresee that this country is destined to undergo great and rapid changes. Those that more properly belong to history, history will doubtless attempt to record, and probably with questionable veracity and prejudice that are apt to influence the labors of that particular muse.'

23. Mathiessen, *American Renaissance*, pp. 266–7.
24. *Centenary Edition*, II, pp. 1–3. In the final paragraph of the Preface Hawthorne is more explicit: 'The Reader may perhaps choose to assign an actual locality to the imaginary events of this narrative . . . the Author would very willingly have avoided anything of this nature. Not to speak of other objections, it exposes the Romance of an inflexible and exceedingly dangerous species of criticism, by bringing his fancy-pictures almost into contact with the realities of the moment . . . . He trusts not to be considered as unpardonably offending, by laying out a street that infringes upon nobody's private rights, and appropriating a lot of land which had no visible owner, and building a house, of materials long in use for constructing castles in the air', and more in the same vein. On the reception of 'The Custom-House' see Bertha Faust, *Hawthorne's Contemporaneous Reputation* (1939; rpt. New York: Octagon Books, 1968) pp. 68–84.
25. For Hawthorne's opinion on 'The Custom-House' see his letter of 4 February 1850 to Horatio Bridge in J. Donald Crowley (ed.), *Hawthorne: The Critical Heritage* (London: Routledge & Kegan Paul, 1970) p. 151. Hawthorne's description of his tales as 'not the talk of a secluded man with his own mind and heart . . . but his attempts, and very imperfectly successful ones, to open an intercourse with the world' is found in the 1851 Preface to *Twice-Told Tales*, *Centenary Edition*, IX, p. 6. In his 'Historical Commentary' to that edition Crowley points out that Hawthorne made careful word revisions when preparing the tales for volume publication so that the critic's prejudices would not be encountered (pp. 503–4). Longfellow had established the norm of Hawthorne criticism by declaring him 'a pleasant writer, with a pleasant style . . . a man who means no meanings' (p. 508). Hawthorne's tales were received as 'higher fiction – as personal spiritual autobiography addressed intimately to a large audience' (p. 513). For an especially fine example, see Andrew Preston Peabody's review in *The Christian Examiner*, 25 (1838) pp. 182–90, rpt. in *The Critical Heritage*, p. 64.
26. See Jesse Bier, 'Hawthorne on the Romance: his Prefaces related and examined', *MP*, 53 (1955) pp. 17–24. The distinction between the novel and the romance is made in precisely these terms by William Gilmore Simms in his Preface to *The Yemassee* (1835), a preface which shows that Simms experienced similarly hostile criticism to Cooper for his representation of the Indian.
27. Hawthorne, 'The Custom-House', *Centenary Edition*, I, pp. 35–6.
28. Hawthorne's belief in the power of the imagination may be usefully compared with Coleridge's praise of 'Tintern Abbey' *Biographia Literaria, or Biographical Sketches of my Literary Life and Opinions*, ed. George Watson (London: Dent, 1975) pp. 48–9. For Coleridge, the imagination modifies objects and refreshes them by spreading the atmosphere of the ideal, but it does not alter their materiality. In Hawthorne the sense of antithesis is acute and synthesis is evanescent.
29. Hawthorne's reading is described by Edward Wagenknecht, *Nathaniel Hawthorne: Man and Writer* (New York: Oxford University Press, 1961) pp. 29–39; Jane Lundblad, *Nathaniel Hawthorne and the European Literary Tradition* (1947; rpt. New York: Russell and Russell, 1965) pp. 33–47; and Marion Kesselring, *Hawthorne's Reading, 1828–1850: A Transcription and Identification of Titles Recorded in the Charge Books of the Salem Athenaeum* (1949; rpt. Folcroft, Pa.: Folcroft Press, 1969).

30. Hawthorne, 'The Custom-House', *Centenary Edition*, 1, p. 4. Hawthorne's metaphor of a 'neutral territory, somewhere between the real world and fairyland, where the Actual and the Imaginary may meet' (*Centenary Edition*, 1, p. 36) seems a reference to Scott's 'neutral ground'. For Hawthorne, like Cooper, the neutral ground is a zone in which ideological differences will be temporarily compromised. Cf. note 8 to Chapter 4 below.

31. Melville, 'Hawthorne and his Mosses', *Literary World*, 7 (1850) pp. 125–7, 145–7. Quoted G. Watson Branch, *Melville: The Critical Heritage* (London: Routledge & Kegan Paul, 1974) p. 123. J. Donald Crowley suggests Melville's comments were designed to reverse the idea that Hawthorne was a man 'who means no meanings'. *Centenary Edition*, IX, p. 508n. See also William Charvat, *The Profession of Authorship in America, 1800–1870: the papers of William Charvat*, ed. Matthew J. Bruccoli (Columbus: Ohio State University Press, 1968) p. 275.

32. Arthur Cleveland Coxe, 'The Writings of Hawthorne', *Church Review*, 3 (1851) pp. 489–511. Quoted Crowley, *Hawthorne: The Critical Heritage*, p. 183.

33. Hawthorne, Preface to *The Marble Faun*, *Centenary Edition*, IV, p. 3.

34. Cooper, *Notions of the Americans*, 2 vols (1828; rpt. New York: Frederick Ungar, 1963) II, pp. 108–12. In his 1832 Preface to *Lionel Lincoln* Cooper comes even closer to the sentiments of James and Hawthorne. 'Perhaps there is no other country, whose history is so little adapted to practical illustration as that of the United States of America. The art of printing has been in general use since the earliest settlement, and the policy of both the Provinces and the States has been to encourage the dissemination of accurate knowledge. There is consequently neither a dark, nor even an obscure, period in the American annals: all is not only known, but so well and generally known, that nothing is left for the imagination to embellish.' Quoted Arvid Shulenberger, *Cooper's Theory of Fiction* (1955; rpt. New York: Octagon Books, 1972) p. 26. Contemporary critics were not in unanimous agreement with Cooper. In a review entitled 'English Literature of the Nineteenth Century', *NAR*, 35 (1832) pp. 163–95, W. H. Prescott criticised Cooper's inability to represent social life and cited the *Notions of the Americans* passage as a fallacy. In *NAR*, 20 (1825) pp. 245–72, William Cullen Bryant had argued that there was an abundance of materials in America for the novelist. In *NAR*, 9 (1819) pp. 58–77, Edward Tyrell Channing had argued that the absence of clearly defined social classes allied to the 'strong, unpolished character' of the new nation offered the prose writer material for 'lively sketches of domestic manners' but little material for the longer tale. Channing's position seems typical of Common Sense.

35. Hawthorne, Preface to *The Marble Faun*, *Centenary Edition*, IV, p. 3.

36. James, *Hawthorne* (1878; rpt. London: Macmillan, 1967) p. 56.

37. Michel de Montaigne, '*Sur les Cannibales*', *Essais*, 3 vols (Paris: Gallimard, 1965) 1, pp. 263–4. (My translation.)

38. Melville, *Typee*, *Writings*, 1, p. 126. Jonathan Swift, *Gulliver's Travels* (Harmondsworth: Penguin, 1967) Ch. 10, p. 325; Henry Thoreau, *Walden* (London: Dent, 1968) p. 113.

39. James, *Hawthorne*, p. 31.

40. James, Preface to *The American*, *The Art of the Novel*, p. 33.

41. The word is Lionel Trilling's in 'Manners, Morals, and the Novel', *The Liberal Imagination* (Harmondsworth: Penguin, 1970) pp. 208–23, 214.

42. Frederic Jameson, *The Political Unconscious: Narrative as a Socially Symbolic Act* (London: Methuen, 1981).

4 JAMES FENIMORE COOPER

1. Sir Walter Scott, 'Essay on Romance' (1824), *The Miscellaneous Prose Works of Sir Walter Scott* (Edinburgh: Cadell, 1847) pp. 554–75, 555–6. Punctuation modernised.
2. See H. Daniel Peck, *A World By Itself: The Pastoral Moment in Cooper's Fiction* (New Haven, Conn.: Yale University Press, 1977); Leslie Fiedler, *Love and Death in the American Novel* (London: Paladin, 1974) p. 188; James Grossman, *James Fenimore Cooper* (New York: William Sloane, 1949) p. 45.
3. Albert T. Volwiler, *George Croghan and the Westward Movement, 1741–1782* (Cleveland, Ohio: Arthur H. Clark, 1926) p. 13. Edith M. Fox, *Land Speculation in the Mohawk Country* (New York: Cornell University Press, 1949) explains the procedures of land purchase in the eighteenth century.
4. William Cooper's relationship with Croghan is described in Volwiler, pp. 329–33, and defended by James Fenimore Cooper in *The Chronicle of Cooperstown*. Rev. edn., *A Condensed History of Cooperstown*, ed. Samuel T. Livermore (New York: J. Munsell, 1862) pp. 18–22. J. F. Cooper's defence is that Croghan had already profited handsomely from inflation in land values and that his heirs had little to complain about. For information on William Cooper's early life see George Dekker's *James Fenimore Cooper, the Novelist* (London: Routledge & Kegan Paul, 1967) pp. 1–19; David H. Ellis, 'The Coopers and the New York State Landholding System', *NYH*, 35 (1954) pp. 412–22; Lyman H. Butterfield, 'Judge William Cooper (1754–1809): A Sketch of his Character and Accomplishment', *NYH*, 30 (1949) pp. 385–408, and 'Cooper's Inheritance: The Otsego Country and its Founders', *NYH*, 35 (1954) pp. 374–411; Andrew Nelson, 'James Cooper and George Croghan', *PQ*, 20 (1941) pp. 69–74. Cf. Nicholas Wainwright, *George Croghan: Wilderness Diplomat* (Chapel Hill: University of North Carolina Press, 1959).
5. William Cooper, *A Guide in the Wilderness* (New York: George P. Humphrey, 1891) p. 31.
6. Cooper only adopted his mother's maiden name, Fenimore, in 1826. The move was officially prompted by his desire to perpetuate the family name but may well have been influenced by the established 'gentility' of the Fenimore family. See *Letters and Journals*, 1, p. 132. On Cooper and the De Lanceys see Dekker, pp. 15–19; J. P. McWilliams, *Political Justice in a Republic: James Fenimore Cooper's America* (Berkeley: University of California Press, 1972) pp. 32–5, and Stephen Railton, *Fenimore Cooper: A Study of his Life and Imagination* (Princeton University Press, 1978) pp. 39–42.
7. See Thomas Philbrick, 'Cooper's *The Pioneers*: Origins and Structure', *PMLA*, 79 (1964) pp. 579–93. Cooper's literary criticism in this period is reprinted as *Early Critical Essays, 1820–22*, ed. James F. Beard (Gainesville, Fla.: Scholars' Facsimiles and Reprints, 1959). On the influence of Scott on Cooper see Dekker, *James Fenimore Cooper*, pp. 20–63. *The Heart of Mid-Lothian* opens with an accident to a stagecoach, although other sources could be in Fielding and Smollett. The turkey shoot seems inspired by the archery contest in *Ivanhoe*; the

concealed will by the hidden letters in *Waverley*; and Effingham's hiding in a cave by Bradwardine's experience in the same novel. Dekker believes *The Bride of Lammermoor* to have been a significant inspiration for aspects of the Effingham plot.

8. It is important to note that Scott's 'neutral ground' is those aspects of human nature common to all ages whereas Cooper's is an area of freedom between two physical frontiers. Thus in Cooper, Scott's moral journey becomes an avoidance of decision, an escape from contradiction. It is in this space between alternatives that most of Cooper's novels are set. On the 'neutral ground' in Cooper see J. P. McWilliams, *Political Justice*, pp. 1–31.

9. The boundary between White and Indian lands leapt across the Otsego Lake in 1768 when by the first Treaty of Fort Stanwix the Iroquois ceded all lands south of the fort and east of the Unadilla River. See Butterfield, 'Cooper's Inheritance'. Between 1779 and 1780 the region was a battleground between Continental forces and the Iroquois. Any idea of there having been a discernible 'line of settlement' in New York State would fail before the fact that white settlement advanced along river valleys, effectively encircling Indian lands. This was evidently the experience on the Ohio, the Mississippi, and in the settlement of California. Each encirclement left a group of trapped Indians who then had to be 'removed'.

10. On the elevation of parents to higher social status, see Freud's 'Family Romance', *Standard Edition*, IX, pp. 235–41, and Marthe Robert's *Roman des origines et origines du roman* (Paris: Gallimard, 1972). Cooper acknowledged that Temple was modelled on his father in his Prefaces of 1830 and 1850, but he vigorously denied autobiographical intentions in 1842 when the Whigs suggested that the Effinghams were an attempt to represent himself as an aristocrat. See *Letters and Journals*, IV, pp. 232–46.

11. Unless otherwise specified, quotations from Cooper's works are from *The Mohawk Edition*. For bibliographical information see the Introduction to these notes.

12. Cooper was a considerable student of De Lancey history. See *Letters and Journals*, IV, pp. 492–5; V, pp. 274–7, 306, 410. Cooper's own great-great-grandfather settled at Trenton, New Jersey seventeen years later. On Cooper genealogy see James Fenimore Cooper (grandson of novelist), *The Legends and Traditions of a Northern County* (New York: G. P. Putnam, 1921) pp. 247–8.

13. Traces of Oliver's relationship to the Croghans can be seen at other places in the text: consider, for example, Temple to Oliver, 'Thy father retired with the troops to prosecute his claims on England. At all events, his losses must be great, for his real estates were sold, and I became the lawful purchaser. It was not unnatural to wish that he might have no bar to its just recovery'. 'There was none but the difficulty of providing for so many claimants, [Oliver replied]' (459). Oliver's remark makes no sense in the context but becomes explicable as a reference to the real events when one knows how many claimants there were on the Croghan estate. Similarly, when Temple remarks 'I really am inclining to the opinion of Richard, as to his origin; for it was no unusual thing for the Indian agents to rear their children in a laudable manner, and . . . ' (217). This is the first hint we have of Oliver being the son of an Indian agent (Croghan) and will remain an unexplained hint until the end of the narrative. Occurring as it does, without Richard Jones having made any such remark in

the narrative, it seems reasonable to assume that the real has slipped through the bar of censorship. The Effingham-Croghan association is confirmed by Andrew Nelson, 'James Cooper and George Croghan', pp. 69–73, and explored by Stephen Railton, *Fenimore Cooper*, pp. 104–6.

14. There are complexities concerning Indian John's claims to the land that become apparent only in *The Last of the Mohicans*. See below.

15. See Roy Harvey Pearce, *Savagism and Civilisation: A Study of the Indian and the American Mind* (1953); rpt. Baltimore: Johns Hopkins Press, 1967), and Albert K. Weinberg, *Manifest Destiny: A Study of Nationalist Expansionism in American History* (1935; rpt. Chicago: Quadrangle books, 1963).

16. In the early 1820s, financial difficulties forced Cooper to sell off some of the lands inherited from his father. This spur to his writing may have increased the need for an imaginary origin for his social position and increased his awareness of what the conquest had meant to its victims. *See Letters and Journals*, I, pp. 24, 83–5.

17. William Cooper, *A Guide in the Wilderness*, p. 8.

18. See above, Chapter 1, note 12.

19. Temple's discourse on the Otsego bass echoes a pamphlet by De Witt Clinton which extols the qualities of the fish. Taken together with Clinton's fostering of the Erie Canal this would seem to indicate deliberate modelling of Temple upon Clinton. See De Witt Clinton, *Account of the Salmo Otsego, or the Otsego Basse* (New York: Van Winkle, 1822). Cf. Chapter 1, note 9 above.

20. The nostalgia for a previous and more elemental way of life which animates the Leatherstocking novels is a *nostos algos*, a return to pain: the sentiment derives from a desire to renegotiate the problematic of a recollected past whilst denying the reality known to be there.

21. The absence of a verb in this sentence is significant. We recall Freud's belief that dreams occur in images before they occur in words and note that Cooper's narratives proceed by elaborating vivid tableaux which fuse the contradictions between reality and desire.

22. Paul Michael Rogin, *Fathers and Children: Andrew Jackson and the Subjugation of the American Indian* (New York: Alfred A. Knopf, 1975) provides a perceptive commentary on the importance of law and land-titles in this period.

23. The idea that Effingham had been accepted into the Mohegans is another displacement-condensation. The land was Mohawk. Croghan was Sir William Johnson's deputy and Sir William was an Indian agent with the Mohawk. When searching for his father Edwards went to the Mohawk to find him (p. 457), even though he was an adopted Mohegan (p. 460), a tribe which could expect no mercy from the Mohawks. See below.

24. James Fenimore Cooper, *Notions of the Americans*, 2 vols (1828; rpt. New York: Ungar, 1963) I, p. 282.

25. See *The Pioneers*, pp. 421, 432.

26. Gregory Lansing Paine, 'The Indians of the Leatherstocking Tales', *Studies in Philology*, 23 (1926) pp. 16–39; John G. Heckewelder, *History, Manners and Customs of the Indian Nations who once inhabited Pennsylvania and the Neighbouring States* (1819), rev. edn, ed. William C. Reichel, *Memoirs of the Historical Society of Pennsylvania*, 12 (Philadelphia, 1820); *A Narrative of the Mission of the United Brethren among the Delaware and Mohegan Indians* (Philadelphia, 1820). Heckewelder follows quite closely the account given by George Henry Loskiel

in his *History of the Mission of the United Brethren among the Indians of North America*, 3 vols (London, 1794), 1, pp. 123–9. Loskiel, however, contrasts Delaware with Iroquois accounts.

27. James Fenimore Cooper, *The Last of the Mohicans*, 3 vols (London: John Miller, 1826), 1, pp. ix–x. All subsequent references to the 1826 Preface will be given as *LOM* (1826). The history of the tribes given in the 1826 Preface is a slight revision of that given in *The Pioneers*, pp. 75–6.

28. Accounts published before 1825 include Captain Jonathan Carver, *Three Years Travels through the Interior Parts of North America* (Philadelphia: Key and Simpson, 1796); Rev. P. F. X. de Charlevoix, *Journal of a Voyage to North America* (London, 1761); Cadwallader Colden, *History of the Five Indian Nations* (New York, 1727; London, 1747, 1750–55), subsequent references to 1750 edn; John Long, *Voyages and Travels of an Indian Interpreter and Trader* (London, 1791); Pehr Kalm, *Travels into North America*, 3 vols (Warrington: Wm. Eyres, 1770–71); William Smith, *The History of the Province of New York*, 2 vols (1757), improved edn (Albany, 1814); Henry R. Schoolcraft, *Narrative Journal of Travels* (Albany, 1821). Of these Susan Cooper tells us that her father had studied Colden, Smith, Heckewelder and Lang (sic); Susan Cooper, *The Cooper Gallery: Pages and Pictures from the Writings of James Fenimore Cooper* (New York: James Miller, 1865) p. 129. Her remarks may, however, be more conventional than accurate. Accounts published after 1826 include Lewis Henry Morgan, *The League of the Ho-de-sau-nee, or Iroquois* (New York: Sage and Brother, 1851); Henry R. Schoolcraft, *Historical and Statistical Information Respecting the History, Conditions, and Prospects of the Indian Tribes of the United States*, 6 vols (Philadelphia: Lippincott, Grambo and Company, 1851–7), v, vi; Francis Parkman, *Montcalm and Wolfe* (1884), 2 vols (London: Macmillan, 1888). The best modern accounts are found in Douglas E. Leach, *Arms for Empire: A Military History of the British Colonies In North America, 1603–1763* (West Drayton: Collier Macmillan, 1973) and Anthony F. C. Wallace, *The Death and Rebirth of the Seneca* (New York: Random House, 1972). On the Delawares see Anthony F. C. Wallace, *King of the Delawares: Teedyuscung 1700–1763* (Philadelphia: University of Pennsylvania Press, 1949); Clinton A. Weslager, *The Delaware Indians: A History* (New Brunswick, NJ: Rutgers University Press, 1972).

29. Paine notes the major distortions of Indian history that are to be explored in the present analysis but his general thesis is that Cooper 'was following . . . the most reliable authority known at that time' (p. 39) and that having adopted Heckewelder's views in the early Leatherstocking novels 'he was forced to keep to these views in the later' (p. 30). A similar thesis is assumed by Paul A. Wallace, 'Cooper's Indians', *NYH*, 35 (1954) pp. 423–46.

30. The critical controversy surrounding Heckewelder's *History* is discussed by Gregory Lansing Paine, and by Marcel Clavel, *Fenimore Cooper: sa vie et son oeuvre* (Aix-en-Provence: Imprimerie Universitaire de Provence, 1938) pp. 567–87. In distinction to Paine, Calvel makes the important observation that the detailed knowledge of Indian customs in Cooper's work indicates extensive reading in available accounts. Heckewelder cannot have been Cooper's only source (p. 571). A review in *NAR*, 9 (1819) pp. 155–78, was favourable to Heckewelder but noted that his account of the Iroquois was 'entirely different' from the established view. Lewis Cass attacked Heckewelder and Cooper, *NAR*, 22 (1826) pp. 53–119. The quoted remark is from p. 66. W. H. Gardner

followed suit in *NAR*, 23 (1826) pp. 150–97. The *United States Review and Literary Gazette*, 2 (1827) pp. 40–53, repeated the accusations against Heckewelder and Cooper. William Rawle published 'A Vindication of the Rev. Mr. Heckewelder's History of the Indian Nations', *Memoirs of the Historical Society of Pennsylvania* (Philadelphia, 1826) 1, Pt 2, pp. 268–84. Cass replied to Rawle in *NAR*, 26 (1828) pp. 357–403. These criticisms of Heckewelder put in question Pearce's belief that Cooper had 'an essential "authority" in [his] Indian materials', *Savagism and Civilisation*, p. 201.

31. Clinton's relationship with Cooper is mentioned in Henry W. Boynton, *James Fenimore Cooper* (New York: Ungar, 1966) p. 142; and Thomas R. Lounsbury, *James Fenimore Cooper* (Boston: Houghton Mifflin, 1892) p. 127. See also *Letters and Journals*, 1, pp. 24, 129–30; *The Correspondence of James Fenimore Cooper*, ed. J. F. Cooper (Freeport: Books for Libraries Press, 1971) pp. 97–8; James Fenimore Cooper, *Notions of the Americans*, 1, pp. 262–3. De Witt Clinton's 'Address before the New York Historical Society on the Iroquois or Six Nations' was delivered on 6 Dec. 1811 and published in the *New York Historical Society Collections*, 2 (1814). It is reprinted in *The Life and Writings of De Witt Clinton*, ed. William W. Campbell (New York: Bakers and Scribners, 1849) pp. 205–64. Selections from Clinton and Heckewelder were reprinted in James Buchanan, *Sketches of the History, Manners and Customs of the North American Indians* (London, 1824), a work favourably reviewed in *NAR*, 19 (1824) pp. 463–5. Clinton's 'Address' was favourably noticed in Cass's attack on Heckewelder, *NAR*, 22 (1826) pp. 53–119, 60.

32. In his Preface to *The Pilot* (1823), Cooper writes that the romancer 'is permitted to garnish a probable fiction, while he is sternly prohibited from dwelling on improbable truths'. It is the duty of the historian 'to record facts as they have occurred, without reference to the consequences, resting his reputation on a firm foundation of realities, and vindicating his integrity by his authorities'. Quoted George Perkins, *The Theory of the American Novel* (New York: Holt, Rinehart & Winston, 1970) p. 19.

33. *LOM* (1826) p. iii.

34. The episode may be a transformation of an incident described by Long, pp. 164–6. In *Wyandotté* a Tuscarora has suffered the same treatment.

35. David P. French, 'James Fenimore Cooper and Fort William Henry', *AL*, 32 (1960) pp. 28–38. French observes that Cooper's claim to historical veracity is more emphatic in *The Last of the Mohicans* than for any of the other Leatherstocking novels. He suggests that Cooper made use of private papers to which he had access through his wife's relations in the De Lancey and Munro families. It is interesting to note that James De Lancey was Acting Governor at the time of the battle, and, according to Smith's *History of the Province of New York*, pp. 216–17, was blamed by some for Webb's failure to relieve Munro. Thomas Philbrick, in 'The Sources of Cooper's Knowledge of Fort William Henry', *AL*, 36 (1964) pp. 209–14, suggests that Cooper's research was more superficial than French believed. Cooper's sources were Carver's *Travels*, pp. 204–12; David P. Humphreys' *An Essay on the Life of Major-General Israel Putnam* (Hartford, Conn., 1788) pp. 39–43. More recent accounts are found in Parkman, *Montcalm and Wolfe*, 1, pp. 509–10; Leach, pp. 351–414. Cooper's use of the captivity theme may well have been directly inspired by James E. Seaver, *A Narrative of the Life of Mrs. Mary Jemison who was taken by the Indians in the year*

1755 (New York, 1824). The tracking episode in Chapter Twenty-Three of the novel seems to follow Chapter One of Seaver's narrative.

36. Recent scholarship recognises that the Seneca, being at the western end of the Confederacy and far from the influence of the British, did on occasion take the French side. There was also, from 1688 onwards, a small band of Iroquois at Caughnawaga, Montreal. Converted by the Jesuits, they aided the French. However, these are exceptions to the general pattern and have at no time warranted the representation of the Iroquois as 'French' Indians. See Wallace *Death and Rebirth*, p. 112; Leach, pp. 55, 315–17, *et passim*. Colden, p. 34; Clinton, pp. 208, 212–13, 232; Kalm, p. 268; Heckewelder, *History*, pp. xxxii–iii, 68; Schoolcraft, *Historical and Statistical*, vi, pp. 49, 188.

37. Heckewelder, *History*, pp. xxxvii–iii, pp. 62–4; *Narrative*, p. 49. For modern accounts see Weslager, pp. 221–260; Wallace, *King of the Delawares*, pp. 67–160.

38. Leslie Fiedler remarks 'the novel is so all of a piece that reality does not intrude'. *Love and Death*, p. 189. As will be seen, reality not only intrudes, it is radically transformed by the novel. For Barthes on myth, see *Mythologies*, trans. Annette Lavers (London: Jonathan Cape, 1972) pp. 109–59.

39. *LOM* (1826) p. v. In 1831 Cooper revised this to read 'the Whites have assisted greatly in rendering the traditions of the Aborigines more obscure by their own manner of corrupting names' (London: Colbourn and Bentley, 1831) p. vii.

40. The one confusion in Cooper's sources is the assumption that the Mahiccani were the same tribe as the Mohegans or Mohicans. Modern historians recognise that the Mahiccani lived in Maine, the Mohegans between the Hudson and Thames River in Connecticut. However, this confusion is consistent throughout the sources and has no effect upon the narrative. See Heckewelder, *History*, p. 98; Clinton, p. 210; Colden, p. xv; Long, pp. 8–27. Where Cooper is more significantly astray is in his amalgamation of the Delawares and Mohegans, on which see Paine, pp. 34–5.

41. Sigmund Freud, *The Interpretation of Dreams, Standard Edition*, vi, p. 327. At the centre of Cooper's dream was 'a clear and vivid picture of the struggle between Magua and Chingachgook' which occurs in Chapter Twelve. See Susan Cooper, *The Cooper Gallery*, p. 129. Fenimore Cooper mentions this illness, *Letters and Journals*, i, p. 120. For another theory of the importance of this scene see Railton, *Fenimore Cooper*, pp. 34–7. A contemporary reviewer also remarked that 'on the first reading . . . we are carried onward, as through the visions of a long and feverish dream'. Unsigned review, *New York Review and Atheneum*, 2 (1826) pp. 285–92; quoted George Dekker and John P. McWilliams (eds), *Fenimore Cooper: The Critical Heritage* (London: Routledge & Kegan Paul, 1973) p. 90. The two most detailed commentaries in recent years tend to the same conclusion. In '*The Last of the Mohicans* and the Sounds of Discord', *AL*, 43 (1971–2), Thomas Philbrick describes the shrieks and cries which constantly erupt into moments of pastoral calm. He also notes the obsessive frequency with which the words 'blood' and 'bloody' occur. Peck, in his *A World By Itself*, describes the first narrative as 'a landscape of difficulty' for the barriers which constantly prevent progress. When one understands the role of the Iroquois in history it is only necessary to read the first paragraph of the novel to know why: 'It was a feature peculiar to the colonial wars of North America, that the toils and dangers of the wilderness were to be encountered before the adverse hosts could meet in murderous contact. A wide, and apparently impervious

boundary of forests, severed the possessions of the hostile provinces of France and England' (1). This 'impervious boundary' was the Iroquois; with their permission one moved through it with ease.

42. For general accounts of the richness of Iroquois agriculture see Wallace, *Death and Rebirth*, pp. 141–3 *et passim*; and Thomas R. Wessel, 'Agriculture and Iroquois Hegemony in New York, 1610–1779', *The Maryland Historian*, 1 (1970) pp. 93–104. On Mohawk remains at Cooperstown, see Livermore (ed.), *A Condensed History of Cooperstown*, p. 11; Birdsall, pp. 1–15; Adrian A. Pierson, 'The Prehistoric Indian in Otsego and his Immediate Successor', *Proceedings of the New York State Historical Association*, 14 (1917) pp. 103–19; James Fenimore Cooper (grandson of novelist), *Legends and Traditions*, pp. 10, 13, 28, 89, 90.

43. In a list of the Iroquois tribes, *LOM* (1826), I, p. vii; and in this sentence: 'If Webb wants faith and honesty in an Indian, let him bring out the Delawares, and send these greedy and lying Mohawks and Oneidas, with their six nations of varlets, where in nature they belong, among the outlandish Frenchmen!' (p. 51). In 1831 Cooper deleted the prefatorial list of Iroquois tribes but still felt it necessary to record that 'Oneida is the name of a particular and powerful tribe in the confederation'. In 1850 this line was also deleted.

44. The admission that the Delawares were with the French in 1757 enables the second narrative of the novel in which the Hurons and Delawares live as good neighbours in the hills of the Iroquois. With some difficulty the condensation of Iroquois and Hurons is continued, and, stretching plausibility to the limit, the famous seventeenth-century Chief Tammenund is brought on to lead the Delawares. On the history of the Delawares at this time, see Wallace, *King of the Delawares*, pp. 138–46.

45. On the theory of the 'irruption of the real', see Pierre Macherey, *A Theory of Literary Production*, trans. Geoffrey Wall (London: Routledge & Kegan Paul, 1978) p. 39.

46. On the expropriation of the Oneidas Cooper could have referred to Clinton, pp. 236, 240–1. For later accounts see Schoolcraft, *Historical and Statistical*, v, p. 49; Morgan, *League*, p. 30, offers a more ambivalent comment. The official historian was Franklin B. Hough, *Proceedings of the Commissioners of Indian Affairs* (New York: Joel Munsell, 1861) p. vi, pp. 119–27. Cf. Barbara Graymont, *The Iroquois in the American Revolution* (Syracuse University Press, 1972) pp. 34–9, p. 297; and Wallace, *Death and Rebirth*, pp. 323–4. Susan Cooper's remark is from *The Cooper Gallery*, p. 130. It is confirmed in *The Pioneers* where Natty remarks 'it raises mournful thoughts to think that not a redskin is left of them all; unless it be a drunkard vagabond from the Oneidas, or them Yankee Indians. . . .' (p. 473).

47. For the sake of clarity I have avoided mentioning that the Mingoes were in fact a separate Iroquoian group living on the Ohio and not properly part of the Six Nations. For most of the eighteenth century they were allied with the Delaware. Whether Cooper was aware of this it has not been possible to establish. On the Mingoes see Leach, p. 318; Wallace, *Death and Rebirth*, p. 113; Clark Wissler, *The Indians of the United States* (New York: Doubleday, 1966) p. 134; Francis Jennings, 'The Indian's Revolution', in Alfred F. Young (ed.), *The American Revolution: Explorations in the History of American Radicalism*, (Dekalb: Northern Illinois University Press, 1976) pp. 324–5.

48. On the Mohegans see Heckewelder, *History*, pp. 23, 53, 93; Clinton, p. 209;

Wallace (1972), p. 132; Hough, pp. 85–116; Francis Jennings, *The Invasion of America: Indians, Colonialism, and the Cant of Conquest* (Chapel Hill: University of North Carolina Press, 1975) pp. 179, 218, 299–300. At least by 1829 Cooper was aware of the value of the Mohicans to the whites. In *The Wept of Wish-ton-Wish* the Mohicans, whose chief is another Uncas, join with the Pequots to pursue the Narragansetts in King Philip's War. We may deduce from *The Pioneers* that Cooper thoroughly understood the post-war fusion of Algonkin and Iroquois. He tells us that 'as the original distinctions between these nations were marked by a difference in language, as well as by repeated and bloody wars, they were never known to amalgamate, until after the power and inroads of the whites had reduced some of the tribes to a state of dependence . . .' *Mohawk Edition*, p. 75. In the early nineteenth century the Oneida and Mohican reservations were at Augusta and Stockbridge to the south of Utica, New York. Accounts of these reservations which may have been available to Cooper were Jeremy Belknap and Jedediah Morse, *Report on the Oneida, Stockbridge and Brotherton Indians* (1798; rpt. New York: Hay Foundation, Museum of the American Indian, 1955); and Rev. Jedediah Morse, D. D., *A Report to the Secretary of War of The United States on Indian Affairs Comprising A Narrative of a Tour Performed in the Summer of 1820* (New Haven: S. Converse, 1822). In this latter report Morse notes that 'the Tuscaroras, . . . the Moheakunnuck or New Stockbridge, the Moheagans and Narragansetts, or Brotherton Indians, have been adopted into the Confederacy of the Six Nations, and by invitation, are settled in the vicinity of each other, on lands originally belonging to the Oneidas, and near their village'. Appendix, p. 76.

49. Sigmund Freud, 'Creative Writers and Day-Dreaming', *Standard Edition*, IX, pp. 141–54, 152.

50. *Letters and Journals*, I, p. 140. The 'expiatory offering' was the projected *History of the United States Navy*.

51. Barthes, *Mythologies*, pp. 125–31. For a complementary understanding of the relationship of romance to myth, see Frederic Jameson, 'Magical Narratives: Romance as Genre', *NLH*, 7 (1975) pp. 135–63.

52. Quoted by Michael Paul Rogin, *Fathers and Children*, p. 210.

53. *Standard Edition*, p. 148.

54. *The Deerslayer*, pp. vi–vii. Pearce points out that Cooper is replying to Cass's criticism of 1826 and 1828. One would assume that these criticisms had struck a sore spot since Cooper still felt piqued by them thirteen years later. See *Savagism and Civilisation*, p. 211.

55. On Cooper's income from writing at this time see William Charvat, 'Cooper as Professional Author', *The Profession of Authorship in America, 1800–1870: the Papers of William Charvat*, ed. Mathew J. Bruccoli (Columbus: Ohio State University Press, 1968) pp. 68–83. Cooper's volume sales had increased but reduction in price and in royalty resulted in a much lower income. On Cooper's struggle with the Whig press see Dorothy Waples, *The Whig Myth of James Fenimore Cooper* (New Haven, Conn.: Yale University Press, 1938), and James F. Beard's Commentary to *Letters and Journals*, IV. On land re-purchase see *Letters and Journals*, IV, p. 112.

56. See Railton, *Fenimore Cooper*, p. 207.

57. See *The Deerslayer*, p. 2. France actually declared war on Britain 4 March 1744. See Leach, *Arms for Empire*, p. 224. Delaware-Iroquois relationships at this time

are explained in Wallace, *King of the Delawares*, pp. 31–39. The historical basis of *The Deerslayer* does not even agree with the chronology established by the other Leatherstocking novels. In *The Pioneers* Natty says he met Chingachgook 'some thirty years agone, in the old war, when I was out under Sir William' (pp. 13–14), a statement which roughly corresponds with *Mohicans* (1757) and *The Pathfinder* (1756) but contradicts *The Deerslayer* where they are already old friends in 1740–45. In *The Deerslayer* Cooper also seems in some measure embarrassed by the fact that in *The Last of the Mohicans* he has Chief Tammenund, already old when he signed treaties with William Penn in the late seventeenth century, still alive in 1757, and talking to Uncas, the famous seventeenth-century Mohican chief. (See notes 44 and 48 above.) In *The Deerslayer* Cooper takes some pains to establish a genealogy for Uncas and Tammenund that will make their appearance in *Mohicans* more plausible. See *The Deerslayer*, pp. 154, 174, 473. In the last chapter of *The Deerslayer*, however, secondary revision of the dream-history of the *Mohicans* comes to nought: Deerslayer, Chingachgook and Uncas (son of Chingachgook) return to the Otsego Lake 'fifteen years later', i.e. between 1755 and 1760. Uncas would then be fourteen years old and either too young to play the manly young warrior of *Last of the Mohicans* or dead as a result of it. One further point of historical record is that the first Moravian mission to the Delawares was established in 1741 so Natty is too old to have been brought up, as he claims he was, by the Moravians. See Leach, *King of the Delawares*, p. 32. These points are pedantic and superfluous except in so far as they reveal Natty's mythic nature: called by different names and styled by different roles (hunter, trapper, scout) he is never materially the same but always essentially the same. But his essence is his nature in his materiality. Hence he is always materially the same. The circularity of the logic is perfectly mythic because one is never there to be found yet always there to be seen.

58. The idea of the Iroquois living in kennels needs to be corrected by Thomas R. Wessel's research, which reports the Iroquois living in wooden houses with stone chimneys and glass windows before General Clinton destroyed their townships in 1779.

59. The skill of this particular reference is that it could be taken as true if 'frontier' meant the northern boundary of the Iroquois lands. The context implies the southern boundary, which is a falsehood so that we are confronted with a true sign pointing in the wrong direction. The poetics of this misdirection merit special analysis.

60. Mark Twain, 'Fenimore Cooper's Literary Offenses', *NAR*, 161 (1895) pp. 1–12; rpt. in Dekker and McWilliams, *Cooper: The Critical Heritage*, pp. 276–87. Balzac also commented upon Cooper's illogicality: 'Cooper is illogical; he proceeds by sentences which, taken one by one, are confused, the succeeding phrase not allied to the preceding, though the whole presents an imposing substance'. *Paris Review*, 25 (July 1840), quoted Dekker and McWilliams, p. 200.

61. A nice example being Chingachgook's reluctance to dress in white man's clothes when asked to disguise himself from the Iroquois (a fair improbability in itself) and his eagerness not ten pages later to dress in the clothes that Judith takes out of the chest. (Ch. 12, pp. 199–213.)

62. Dekker and McWilliams, pp. 277–8.

63. Railton, *Fenimore Cooper*, pp. 3–32, provides an interesting commentary on Cooper's method of literary production.

64. On thing-representations see Freud, 'A Metapsychological Supplement to the Theory of Dreams', *Standard Edition*, XIV, pp. 222–36.

65. McWilliams, *Political Justice in a Republic*, pp. 276–91.

66. On the Cherokee see Rogin, p. 168; and Gordon Brotherston, *Image of the New World: the American Continent portrayed in native texts* (London: Thames & Hudson, 1979) p. 253. If Cooper read Heckewelder with care he would have come across an account of Delaware hieroglyphic writing. See *History, Manners and Customs*, pp. 117–19. In 1826 Cooper may have known that the Delaware had a written epic of their history, the *Walum Olum*, first published in Constantine Samuel Rafinesque, *The American Nations or, outlines of their general history, ancient and modern*, 2 vols (Philadelphia, 1836). The *Walum Olum* furnished the structure of Book 14 of Longfellow's *Hiawatha*.

67. There is a significant absence of reference in the author's letters to Indians. Only two refer to Indians dealt with here, one to Cooper's having spoken to a Brotherton (a Christianised Delaware or Mohican) who lived at Cooperstown in the 1840s, and one to the Mohawk in a letter in which Cooper denies all knowledge of Indian history. See *Letters and Journals*, IV, p. 25; V, p. 401. The evidence of Cooper's novels belies this completely. On Iroquois torture rituals see Cornelius J. Jaenen, *Friend and Foe: Aspects of French-Amerindian Cultural Contact in the Sixteenth and Seventeenth Centuries* (New York: Columbia University Press, 1976) pp. 139–41.

68. Cooper has come a long way since he had Natty remark in *The Pioneers*, 'There's Mr. Oliver, as bad as the rest of them, firing into the flocks, as if he was shooting down nothing but Mingo warriors' (p. 251). The idea of innate 'white' and 'red' gifts derives directly from the belief of Scottish Common Sense philosophers in an innate moral sense shaped by the stage of social organisation. See Pearce, *Savagism and Civilisation*, p. 95, on the adoption of the idea by Jefferson from Kames' *Principles of Morality and Natural Religion* (1751). For specimen exchanges on the concept of 'white' gifts in *The Deerslayer*, see pp. 36, 46, 75. As a good mythologist Natty has at least two meanings of the word 'gifts', one which acknowledges that customs are the product of socialisation (p. 455), and another which asserts them as innate racial characteristics. The latter use is the more frequent. See note 73 below.

69. Pearce provides a valuable commentary on these anthropologists in his *Savagism and Civilisation*, pp. 105–34.

70. See Mark Lane, *Conversations with Americans* (New York: Simon and Schuster, 1967) for evidence of the continuity of white savagery.

71. On the Gnadenhutten massacre see Heckewelder, *History, Manners and Customs*, p. 81. For another account see Schoolcraft, *Historial and Statistical Information*, VI, pp. 317–18. In his *Narrative of the Mission*, Heckewelder relates that Governor Morris of Philadelphia issued scalp bounties for the Delaware who had joined the French in 1755 (p. 49). Lovell's fight was the source for Hawthorne's story 'Roger Malvin's Burial'. For a useful and intelligent commentary on the Lovell story's popularity in the 1840s, and on Hawthorne's use of it, see Robert J. Daly, 'History of Chivalric Myth in "Roger Malvin's Burial"', *Essex Institute Historical Collections*, 109 (1973) pp. 99–115. On Hannah Dustin, and for one of the most penetrating analyses of Cooper's work, see

Richard Slotkin, *Regeneration Through Violence: The Mythology of the American Frontier, 1600–1860* (Middletown, Conn.: Wesleyan University Press, 1973) pp. 94–115, 466–516.

72. See Dekker, *James Fenimore Cooper*, pp. 170–91, esp. p. 176. McWilliams, *Political Justice in a Republic*, p. 289, and Mike Ewart, 'Cooper and the American Revolution: the Non-Fiction', *JAS*, 11 (1971) pp. 61–79, for a commentary on the changes in Cooper's political sentiments.

73. On treachery see *The Deerslayer*, pp. 61, 115–18; on revenge see p. 79; on scalping see pp. 36, 74. Marius Bewley's commentary on *The Deerslayer* is found in *The Eccentric Design: Form in the Classic American Novel* (New York: Columbia University Press, 1963) pp. 73–100, 90.

74. On the instability of Natty's opinions see Robert H. Zoellner, 'Conceptual Ambivalence in Cooper's Leatherstocking', *AL*, 31 (1960) pp. 397–420.

75. It would be a premise of the present argument that Cooper was an intentionally honest man. It is not my intention to question the eulogy pronounced by Fitz-Greene Halleck, 'He was a remarkable model of Sincerity. His regard for truth in the most minute things as in the most important, excelled that of any man I have ever known, and his life, in its controversies with those he deemed in the wrong, was a long martyrdom to his principles'. *Letters and Journals*, IV, pp. 4–5. It is precisely in such high principles that his writings originate.

5 NATHANIEL HAWTHORNE

1. Page references given in brackets refer to *The Centenary Edition of the Works of Nathaniel Hawthorne*. Where reference is to volume 1, *The Scarlet Letter*, no volume number appears. In references to other volumes, the volume number in roman numerals precedes the page number in arabic numerals.

2. For biography of Hawthorne in these years see Hubert Hoeltje, *Inward Sky: The Mind and Heart of Nathaniel Hawthorne* (Durham, NC: Duke University Press, 1962) pp. 256–96; Randall Stewart, *Nathaniel Hawthorne: A Biography* (New Haven, Conn.: Yale University Press, 1948) pp. 75–100; Arlin Turner, *Nathaniel Hawthorne: A Biography* (New York: Oxford University Press, 1980) pp. 108–207. On Hawthorne's interest in myth see Hugo MacPherson, *Hawthorne as Myth-Maker* (University of Toronto Press, 1969); and Robert D. Richardson, Jr., *Myth and Literature in the American Renaissance* (Bloomington: Indiana University Press, 1978) pp. 165–94).

3. Larzer Ziff, 'The Ethical Dimension of "The Custom-House" ', in *Hawthorne: A Collection of Critical Essays*, ed. A. N. Kaul (Englewood Cliffs, NJ: Prentice-Hall, 1966) pp. 123–28.

4. The contemporaneous story 'The Great Stone Face' experiments with a similar trinitarian allegory; Gathergold, the businessman; Old Blood-and-Thunder, the militarist; Old Stony Phiz, the Presidential candidate. As in *The Scarlet Letter* the trinity becomes quadrate with the appearance of a fourth character, the poet.

5. See Ray Allen Billington, *The Protestant Crusade, 1800–1860: A Study of the Origins of American Nativism* (1938; rpt. Gloucester, Mass.: Peter Smith, 1963) pp. 53–84; and Theodore M. Hammett, 'Two Mobs of Jacksonian Boston: Ideology and Interest', *JAH*, 62 (1975) pp. 845–68.

6. On Hawthorne's plan to have Dimmesdale confess see *The American Notebooks, Centenary Edition*, VIII, p. 611. On Emerson's sympathy with Catholicism, see Richard D. Birdsall, 'Emerson and the Church of Rome', *American Literature*, 31 (1959) pp. 257-72.

7. It is usual to cite Augustine's *Confessions* as influential on Hawthorne and Melville but the arguments of the *City of God* seem so parallel as to imply direct influence. On Ahab and Ishmael see Book XV, Chs. 1–3. On the interpretation of the paradise of Eden, see Book XII, Ch. 22. On symbolic narratives and three-fold interpretations, see Book XVI, Ch. 2; Book XVII, Ch. 3. On the relationship between sensory evidence and speculative knowledge see Book XI, Ch. 3. On the innocence of nature, Book XI, Ch. 17. On the Trinity in human nature see Book XI, Chs. 26–8. On sexual intercourse in paradise see Book XIV, Chs. 18–23, and below, note 11.

8. A full description of medieval hermeneutics can be found in William G. Madsen, *From Shadowy Types to Truth: Studies in Milton's Symbolism* (New Haven, Conn.: Yale University Press, 1968) pp. 18–53. Cf. Paul E. Beichner, 'The Allegorical Interpretation of Medieval Literature', *PMLA*, 82 (1964) pp. 33–8. Typology in the American Puritan tradition is discussed by Ursula Brumm, *American Thought and Religious Typology* (New Brunswick, NJ: Rutgers University Press, 1970).

9. The interpretative scheme suggested here benefits from and adapts many commentaries on Hawthorne, notably Gabriel Josipovici, 'Hawthorne: Allegory and Compulsion', in his *The World and the Book* (London: Macmillan 1971) pp. 155–78; Rudolph von Abele, *The Death of the Artist: A Study of Hawthorne's Disintegration* (The Hague: Martinus Nijhof, 1955) pp. 45–58; Edward H. Davidson, 'Dimmesdale's Fall', *NEQ*, 36 (1963) pp. 358–70; Marvin Laser, ' "Head," "Heart," and "Will" in Hawthorne's Psychology', *NCF*, 10 (1955) pp. 130–40; Donald A. Ringe, 'Hawthorne's Psychology of the Head and Heart', *PMLA*, 65 (1950) pp. 120–32; Robert Shulman, 'Hawthorne's Quiet Conflict', *PQ*, 47 (1968) pp. 216–36.

10. Jacques Lacan suggests that the very form of metonymy signifies its production as a way of bypassing censorship. See his 'The Insistence of the Letter in the Unconscious', trans. Jan Miel, in Jacques Ehrmann (ed.), *Structuralism* (Garden City: Anchor, 1970) pp. 101–37, 117. On over-interpretation see Freud, *The Interpretation of Dreams*, Standard Edition, IV, p. 214; V, p. 525. On Hawthorne's interest in dreams see Rita K. Gollin, *Nathaniel Hawthorne and the Truth of Dreams* (Baton Rouge: Louisiana State University Press, 1979).

11. Saint Augustine, *Concerning the City of God Among the Pagans*, trans. Henry Bettenson (Harmondsworth: Penguin, 1972), XIV, Ch. 23, p. 585.

12. J. Donald Crowley cites the delicious example of Hawthorne's changing 'female' to 'woman' when revising his tales for *Twice-Told Tales*. See 'The Artist as Mediator: the Rationale of Hawthorne's Large-Scale Revisions in his Collected Tales and Sketches', in Howard P. Vincent (ed.), *Melville and Hawthorne in the Berkshires: A Symposium* (Ohio: Kent State University Press, 1968) pp. 79–88.

13. In 'Tale-Writing: Nathaniel Hawthorne', *Godey's Lady's Book*, 35 (1847) pp. 252–5; rpt. *Hawthorne: The Critical Heritage*, ed. J. Donald Crowley (London: Routledge & Kegan Paul, 1970) pp. 141–50.

14. 'Intercourse' was first used to denote sexual relationships in Malthus's *Essay on the Principle of Population* (1796; rpt. London: Macmillan, 1966). The *Essay* is a critique of Godwin's belief in human perfectibility which one would expect Hawthorne to have read. Whether from direct influence or similarity of religious training there are many interesting parallels between the *Essay* and *The Scarlet Letter*. There is Godwin's version of 'Earth's Holocaust': 'And thus it appears, that in a society constituted according to the most beautiful form that imagination can conceive, with benevolence for its moving principle . . . and with every evil disposition . . . corrected by reason and not force, would, from the inevitable laws of nature, and not from any original depravity of man, degenerate into a society, constructed upon a plan not essentially different from that which prevails in every known state at present' (p. 207). There is also a commentary on 'the very natural origin of the superior disgrace which attends a breach of chastity in the woman, than in the man', (pp. 200–201) and on 'the passion of love' by which 'men have been driven into acts highly prejudicial to the general interests of society' (p. 215).

15. Whilst Hawthorne wrote *The Scarlet Letter* his wife Sophia decorated lampshades and screens to support the family, working within a putting-out economy which was then in the last stages of decline. (See Turner, *Hawthorne*, p. 190.) Hawthorne's association of art with outmoded artisanship is more explicit in 'The Artist of the Beautiful', as is the genteel dread of exposure to market forces that he expresses when Hepzibah, too old to live as a sempstress, opens her cent shop. (See *Centenary Edition*, II, pp. 40–44.) Economic change is the warp in the weave of Hawthorne's symbols. For a general history of these changes see Richard D. Brown, *Massachusetts: A Bicentennial History* (New York: W. W. Norton, 1978) pp. 129–56. The change from putting-out to factory is described in Rolla M. Tryon, *Household Manufactures in the United States* (1917; rpt. New York: Johnson Reprint, 1966); the decline of the carrying trade in Samuel E. Morison, *The Maritime History of Massachusetts, 1783–1860* (1921; rpt. Boston: Houghton Mifflin, 1961).

16. Karl Marx, *The German Ideology*, ed. C. J. Arthur (London: Lawrence and Wishart, 1977) pp. 39–48. Marx and Hawthorne have comparable awareness of the alienation of head from heart, and of the interdependence of material and spiritual forms of intercourse.

17. Hester's decision to stay, learn and morally grow, rather than flee westward, may be a sign of this new ethos.

18. Eric Foner, *Politics and Ideology in the Age of the Civil War* (New York: Oxford University Press, 1980); Frederick J. Blue, *The Free Soilers: Third Party Politics, 1848–54* (Urbana: University of Illinois Press, 1973).

19. See Turner, *Hawthorne*, p. 252. A valuable commentary on Hawthorne's politics is found in Larzer Ziff's *Literary Democracy: The Declaration of Cultural Independence in America* (New York: Viking, 1981) pp. 108–45.

20. I owe this insight to Alan Heimert's important study, '*Moby-Dick* and American Political Symbolism', *AQ*, 15 (1963) pp. 498–534, which discusses Melville's handling of the Ahab parable.

21. Turner's suggestion (*Hawthorne*, pp. 64–5) that these words echo the curse of Sarah Good on Colonel John Hawthorne, should not necessarily be seen as competitive.

22. For example, Melville: 'be not too grasping nearer home. It is not freedom to filch. Expand not your area too widely, now . . . . Neighbouring nations may be free, without coming under your banner'. *Mardi, Writings,* III, pp. 529–30.

6 HERMAN MELVILLE

1. It is hardly possible to give full credit to the achievement of Melville scholars, but here one should mention H. Bruce Franklin, *The Wake of the Gods* (Stanford University Press, 1963); T. Walter Herbert Jr., *'Moby-Dick' and Calvinism: A World Dismantled* (New Brunswick, NJ: Rutgers University Press, 1976); Charles Olson, *Call Me Ishmael: A Study of Melville* (1947; rpt. London: Jonathan Cape, 1967); Henry F. Pommer, *Milton and Melville* (1950; rpt. New York: Cooper Square Publishers, 1970); Gerard M. Sweeney, *Melville's Use of Classical Mythology, Melville Studies in American Culture,* 5 (Amsterdam: Rodopi, 1975); Lawrence Thompson, *Melville's Quarrel with God* (Princeton University Press, 1952); Thomas Woodson, 'Ahab's Greatness: Prometheus as Narcissus', *ELH,* 33 (1966) pp. 351–69; Thomas Vargish, 'Gnostic Mythos in Moby-Dick', *PMLA,* 81 (1960) pp. 272–7; Howard Vincent, *The Trying-Out of Moby-Dick* (Carbondale: Southern Illinois University Press, 1965); Nathalia Wright, *Melville's Use of the Bible* (Durham NC: Duke University Press, 1949); Robert Zoellner, *The Salt-Sea Mastodon: A Reading of 'Moby-Dick'* (Berkeley: University of California Press, 1973).
2. See Nina Baym, 'Melville's Quarrel with Fiction', *PMLA,* 94 (1979) pp. 909–21, 917. Melville's reviews are summarised in Hugh W. Hetherington, *Melville's Reviewers: British and American, 1846–1891* (Chapel Hill: University of North Carolina Press, 1961). For a collection of the most important see Watson G. Branch, *Melville: The Critical Heritage* (London: Routledge & Kegan Paul, 1974) pp. 251–91.
3. James Guetti, *The Limits of Metaphor: Melville, Conrad and Faulkner* (New York: Cornell University Press, 1967).
4. M. M. Bakhtine, *Esthétique et théorie du roman,* trans. Darìa Oliver (Paris: Gallimard, 1978) pp. 83–234.
5. On the writing of *Typee* see Leon Howard's 'Historical Note' to *The Writings of Herman Melville,* I, pp. 277–302, and his *Herman Melville: A Biography* (1950; rpt. Berkeley: University of California Press, 1967) pp. 89–101.
6. Charles R. Anderson, *Melville in the South Seas* (1939; rpt. New York: Dover, 1960) pp. 117–78. For critical comment on *Typee* see Faith Pullin, 'Melville's *Typee*: The Failure of Eden', in Faith Pullin and Hershel Parker (eds), *New Perspectives on Melville* (Edinburgh University Press, 1978) pp. 1–28; Richard Ruland, 'Melville and the Fortunate Fall: *Typee* as Eden', *NCF,* 23 (1968–69) pp. 312–23; Robert Stanton, '*Typee* and Milton: Paradise Well Lost', *MLN,* 74 (1959) pp. 407–11.
7. On the stone constructions of the Typees compare Anderson, p. 156, with *Typee,* Ch. 21, p. 155. On agriculture compare Anderson, p. 144 with *Typee,* Ch. 14, p. 112; Ch. 23, p. 165: 'not a single atom of the soil was under any other cultivation than that of shower and sunshine'. See also Greg Dening's introduction to *The Marquesan Journal of Edward Robarts* (Honolulu: University of Hawaii Press, 1974). Dening points out that crime, genocide, famine, and

social classes were as much part of Marquesan experience as of any other. See also Robert C. Suggs, *The Hidden Worlds of Polynesia* (London: Cresset Press, 1962) on agricultural production.

8. This anecdote is reported by Lewis Hanke, *Aristotle and the American Indians: A Study of Race Prejudice in the Modern World* (1959; rpt. Bloomington: Indiana University Press, 1970) p. 8.

9. Nina Baym makes the important point that in his theory of language Emerson naturalises the sign as a message from God to man inscribed in the material world. Meaning, therefore, cannot be arbitrary, conventional, or fanciful. See her 'Melville's Quarrel with Fiction', note 2 above. Many of Webster's dictionary entries seem inspired by a parallel belief that words originate from a primal expression of natural qualities. The idea still seems active in Ezra Pound's thoughts on Chinese calligraphy.

10. The evolution of Melville's concern with mythology from *Mardi* through to *Moby-Dick* and beyond has been studied by H. Bruce Franklin, *The Wake of the Gods*, and by Robert D. Richardson, Jr., *Myth and Literature in the American Renaissance* (Bloomington: Indiana University Press, 1978) pp. 195–233. See also Merrell R. Davis, *Melville's Mardi: A Chartless Voyage* (1952; rpt. Hamden, Conn.: Shoe String Press, 1967). Much of Melville's concern in *Mardi*, especially in the Vivenza and Yillah episodes, might be better understood as a relatively naive interest in the processes of mystification similar to that shown in Ch. 102 of *Moby-Dick*, 'A Bower in the Arsacides'. It is not until the representation of Ahab that Melville entertains the full psychological complexity of mythological consciousness.

11. Guetti, *The Limits of Metaphor*, p. 21.

12. Guetti, p. 30.

13. Guetti, p. 45.

14. On the genesis of *Moby-Dick* see Charles Olson, *Call Me Ishmael*, p. 35; Leon Howard, *Herman Melville: A Biography*, pp. 150–79; Howard Vincent, *The Trying-Out of 'Moby-Dick'*, pp. 35–52; George R. Stewart, 'The Two *Moby-Dicks*', *AL*, 25 (1954) pp. 418–48; Harrison Hayford, 'Unnecessary Duplicates: A Key to the Writing of *Moby-Dick*', in Faith Pullin and Hershel Parker (eds), *New Perspectives on Melville*, pp. 128–61. When considering the two *Moby-Dicks* it is worth bearing in mind that the desire to break out of the 'true-life' convention was apparent before August 1850. On the 14 December 1849 Melville had written Evert Duyckinck and lamented his 'beggarly' *Redburn*. 'When [an author] attempts anything higher – God help him and save him! . . . What a madness and anguish it is, that an author can never – under no conceivable circumstances – be at all frank with his readers.' On 1 May 1850 he had written Richard Henry Dana that his text was already a little 'ungainly': 'It will be a strange sort of book, tho', I fear, blubber is blubber you know; tho' you may get oil out of it, the poetry runs as hard as sap from a frozen maple tree; – and to cook the thing up, one must needs throw in a little fancy, which from the nature of the thing, must be ungainly, as the gambols of the whales themselves. Yet I mean to give the truth of the thing, spite of this.' *Letters*, pp. 95, 108.

15. For the impact of Hawthorne on Melville see Leon Howard, *Herman Melville*, pp. 158–69; Randall Steward, 'Melville and Hawthorne', in Tyrus Hillway and Luther S. Manfield (eds), '*Moby-Dick': Centennial Essays* (Dallas: Southern Methodist University Press, 1953) pp. 153–65; Nathalia Wright, '*Mosses from*

an Old Manse and *Moby-Dick*: The Shock of Discovery', *MLN*, 67 (1952) pp. 387–92. Melville's review is reprinted in J. Donald Crowley (ed.), *Hawthorne: The Critical Heritage* (London: Routledge & Kegan Paul, 1970) pp. 111–25.

16. Alan Heimert, '*Moby-Dick* and American Political Symbolism', *AQ*, 15 (1963) pp. 498–534. A previous account, Charles H. Foster, 'Something in Emblems: A Reinterpretation of *Moby-Dick*', *NEQ*, 34 (1961) pp. 3–35, suggested that Ahab was modelled upon Daniel Webster, the Whig exponent of industrial development. Heimert argues that Ahab is modelled on Calhoun and that the whale is an emblem of Webster, a strained interpretation which is needless if one allows that Ahab stands for both agrarian Democratic expansionism and for Whig industrialism, a condensation already implicit in 'The Pequod' itself.

17. H. Bruce Franklin, *The Wake of the Gods*, p. 10.

18. The relationship of whaling to the national economy is described by Charles Olson, *Call Me Ishmael*, pp. 15–28. Further information on the growth of the whaling industry can be found in Richard D. Brown, *Massachusetts: A Bicentennial History* (New York: W. W. Norton, 1978); Foster R. Dulles, *America in the Pacific* (1932; rpt. New York: Da Capo, 1969); Elmo P. Hohman, *The American Whaleman: A Study of Life and Labor in the Whaling Industry* (1928: rpt. Clifton, NJ: Augustus M. Kelley, 1972); Samuel E. Morison, *The Maritime History of Massachusetts, 1783–1860* (1921; rpt. Boston: Houghton Mifflin, 1961); Geoffrey Sutton Smith, 'The Navy Before Darwinism: Science, Exploration and Diplomacy in Antebellum America', *AQ*, 28 (1976) pp. 41–55.

19. Howard P. Vincent, *The Trying-Out of Moby-Dick*.

20. Cf. the letter to Richard Henry Dana, quoted in note 14 above.

21. Melville's use of Bayle has been discussed by Millicent Bell, 'Pierre Bayle and *Moby-Dick*', *PMLA*, 66 (1951) pp. 626–48.

22. A contemporary reviewer experienced the same need for unity: 'he has resorted to the original authorities – a difficult and tedious task, as every one who has sought out the sources of statements set forth without reference in Cyclopaedias knows too well. For our own part, we believe that there must have been some old original Cyclopaedia, long since lost or destroyed, out of which all others have been compiled'. The book of God perhaps? *Literary Gazette*, 6 December, 1851, pp. 841–2; rpt. Branch, *Melville: The Critical Heritage*, p. 276.

23. See Melville's letter to Hawthorne, 1 June 1850: 'the silent grass-growing mood in which a man *ought* always to compose, – that, I fear, can seldom be mine. Dollars damn me; . . .' *Letters*, p. 128.

Index